Building Websites with Joomla!

A step by step tutorial to getting your Joomla! CMS website up fast

Hagen Graf

BIRMINGHAM - MUMBAI

Building Websites with Joomla!

A step by step tutorial to getting your Joomla! CMS website up fast

First published: February 2006

Production Reference: 4050307

Published by Packt Publishing Ltd.
32 Lincoln Road
Olton
Birmingham, B27 6PA, UK.

ISBN 1-904811-94-9

www.packtpub.com

Cover Design by www.visionwt.com

Copyright © 2005 by Pearson Education Deutschland GmbH, München.

First published in the German language under the title "Joomla!" by Addison-Wesley, an imprint of Pearson Education Deutschland GmbH, München.

Credits

Authors
Hagen Graf

Technical Editor
Nanda Padmanabhan

Editorial Manager
Dipali Chittar

Indexer
Abhishek Shirodkar

Proofreader
Chris Smith

Production Coordinator
Manjiri Nadkarni

Cover Designer
Helen Wood

About the Authors

Hagen Graf was born in July 1964. Born and raised in Lower Saxony, Germany, his first contact with a computer was in the late seventies with a Radioshack TRS 80. As a salesperson, he organized his customers' data by programming suitable applications. This gave him a big advantage over other salesmen. With the intention of honing his skills, he joined evening courses in programming and became a programmer. Nowadays he works in his wife's consulting company as a trainer, consultant, and programmer (http://alternative-unternehmensberatung.de).

Hagen Graf has published three other books in German, about the Apache web server, about security problems in Windows XP, and about Mambo. Since 2001, he has been engaged in a nonprofit e-learning community called "machm-it.org e.V.", as well as in several national and international projects. All the projects are related to content management, community building, and harnessing the power of social software like wikis and weblogs. He chose Mambo CMS, from which Joomla! has forked, because of its simplicity and easy-to-use administration. You can access and comment on his blog (http://hagen.take-part.org).

This is the second time, a book of mine has been translated from German to English. It isn't easy to organize the translation in another language in a reasonable way, especially on a topic on Open Source Software. One point is that most of the software is developed in international communities basically in English language. Another point is the speed of the development. Release fast, release often! Today we have Joomla 1.0.7 and the development is going on.

It is now time for thanks...

I wish to thank the Joomla community who made this wonderful world wide project possible.

I also wish to thank the Packt Publishing team, especially Louay, Nanda, Dipali, Abhishek, Chris, Manjiri, and Helen (for the dynamic cover picture). I also wish to thank Alex Kempkens, core member of the Joomla! devteam and Angie Radtke who is very much engaged in improving the accessibility of Joomla! websites.

They all have done an excellent job!

Table of Contents

Preface

This book is being written in a small village in Sachsen-Anhalt in Germany, among other places. I live in this village. There is no access to DSL here; there are no public WLAN hotspots, no UMTS, no large companies and no city noise.

My work consists of activities like lecturing, advising, listening, testing and trying, programming, learning how to understand structures, trying to get to the bottom of things, and constantly testing again. This means customers in different countries, with different languages and cultures. A lot of these activities can be done online. But I am often on the road for weeks on end. Long car, bus or train trips; short to extremely short response times for email customer inquiries.

This type of work has ramifications on what we used to call an office.

Five years ago, it was normal to store e-mails on your home or office computer. Today, various service providers are offering almost inexhaustible disk space for these purposes. In larger companies, terminal servers are becoming more and more influential. The bandwidth of Internet connections is increasing; maybe in my village soon as well!

The terminal with which you and I access our information becomes ever less important. What you really need is a stable, affordable Internet connection over WLAN, UMTS, telephone, or satellite, a browser, a screen that can display the information, and a keyboard that is as ergonomic as possible and, of course, electricity. You can access your pool of e-mails, pictures, and documents from anywhere in the world.

In this world, a company, an institution, an association, an organization needs an Internet presence that is also user-friendly and flexible. One that is in tune with the times, one that can be easily modified from a browser, and that replaces your briefcase and your address directory, that can communicate with all kinds of systems, and that is easily expanded.

This website is the place where you can explain to others what you do, and/or what your company does. It is the place that is available 24 hours a day, 7 days a week to maintain your customer relations. Until recently, the production of such a homepage was a difficult thing. You didn't have to be a designated specialist, but a certain perseverance combined with an interest in the topic was necessary to produce an appealing result. You had to create static HTML pages with an HTML editor and subsequently load them onto a server via File Transfer Protocol. To provide even the simplest interactivity like a guest book or a forum, you had to learn a programming language. Many people, for understandable reasons, were reluctant to take on this hardship and therefore either handed the production of their homepage to a web agency or decided to not even start such a project.

But rescue is near, because what you now have in your hand, this book, is the travel guide to Joomla!, one of the smartest website administration system of the world.

The word Joomla! is derived from Jumla from Swahili and means "all together".

Joomla! is the software result of a serious disagreement between the Mambo Foundation founded in August 2005, and its development team.

Joomla! is the continued development of the successful Mambo system and, like Mambo, is a piece of software that enables simple administration of websites from a web browser.

Joomla!, according to its own description, is a "Cutting Edge Content Management System" and one of the most powerful Open Source Content Management systems in the world. It is used world-wide for anything from simple homepages to complicated corporate websites. It is easy to install, easy to manage, and very reliable.

What This Book Covers

Joomla! is a full-featured content management system that can be used for everything from simple websites to complex corporate applications. This book begins by introducing the basic principles that underlie the operation of Joomla!.

Chapter 1 explains the difficulty of defining a term such as 'content management'. It explores the structure of a CMS and lists the various features of Joomla!. To get an overview of the areas of application for Joomla!, a few Mambo-based websites are used as examples.

Chapter 2 guides us through the process of installing Joomla! in an appropriate server environment. It lists the prerequisites for Windows and Linux, and cites the need for selecting a directory for installation. *Chapter 3* guides us through a tour of the created homepage.

Chapter 4, *Chapter 5*, and *Chapter 6* deal with the customization of Joomla!, according to the users' needs. It shows you how to install a local language file for different users. It also explains the configuration of Joomla! administration and shows you how to install new mambots.

Chapter 7, *Chapter 8*, and *Chapter 9* deal with the creation of extensions. These chapters discuss how to extend the functional range of Joomla! with new components, modules, and mambots.

Chapter 10 explains the corporate identity of an enterprise. It studies the Internet technologies that Joomla! works with, HTML/XHTML, CSS, and XML. It also shows you how to create your own template packages. Few content management systems provide web accessibility for users with disabilities but Joomla! is one of them. The Joomla! project tries to make Joomla! web pages usable by people with disabilities.

Chapter 11 discusses creating your own program extensions for Joomla!. It discusses how to extend the functional range of Joomla! with new components, modules, and mambots.

Appendix A provides a list of necessary software packages. It also guides you about what to do if you forget your admin password.

What You Need for This Book

The prerequisite for this book is a working installation of Joomla!. To run Joomla!, the typical environment consists of PHP/Apache/MySQL.

As a beginner, you will be able to administer your own website from a browser.

Familiarity with HTML, CSS, and editing of images on a computer will be required to create your own templates for your website.

A basic understanding of the PHP programming language is necessary to be able to create components, modules, and mambots.

Conventions

In this book, you will find a number of styles of text that distinguish between different kinds of information. Here are some examples of these styles, and an explanation of their meaning.

There are three styles for code. Code words in text are shown as follows: "We can include other contexts through the use of the `include` directive."

A block of code will be set as follows:

```
<tr>
    <!-- Area 4 -->
    <td width="197" height="233" bgcolor="#F5EE28">   </td>
    <!-- Area 5 -->
    <td width="389" height="233"> </td>
    <!-- Area 6 -->
    <td width="178" height="233" bgcolor="#FFFF33">   </td>
</tr>
```

When we wish to draw your attention to a particular part of a code block, the relevant lines or items will be made bold:

```
<tr>
    <!-- Area 4 -->
    <td width="197" height="233" bgcolor="#F5EE28">   </td>
    <!-- Area 5 -->
    <td width="389" height="233"> </td>
    <!-- Area 6 -->
    <td width="178" height="233" bgcolor="#FFFF33">   </td>
</tr>
```

New terms and **important words** are introduced in a bold-type font. Words that you see on the screen, in menus or dialog boxes for example, appear in our text like this: "clicking the Next button moves you to the next screen".

> Warnings or important notes appear in a box like this.

Reader Feedback

Feedback from our readers is always welcome. Let us know what you think about this book, what you liked or may have disliked. Reader feedback is important for us to develop titles that you really get the most out of.

To send us general feedback, simply drop an email to feedback@packtpub.com, making sure to mention the book title in the subject of your message.

If there is a book that you need and would like to see us publish, please send us a note in the SUGGEST A TITLE form on www.packtpub.com or email suggest@packtpub.com.

If there is a topic that you have expertise in and you are interested in either writing or contributing to a book, see our author guide on www.packtpub.com/authors.

Customer Support

Now that you are the proud owner of a Packt book, we have a number of things to help you to get the most from your purchase.

Downloading the Example Code for the Book

Visit http://www.packtpub.com/support, and select this book from the list of titles to download any example code or extra resources for this book. The files available for download will then be displayed.

> The downloadable files contain instructions on how to use them.

Errata

Although we have taken every care to ensure the accuracy of our contents, mistakes do happen. If you find a mistake in one of our books—maybe a mistake in text or code—we would be grateful if you would report this to us. By doing this you can save other readers from frustration, and help to improve subsequent versions of this book. If you find any errata, report them by visiting http://www.packtpub.com/support, selecting your book, clicking on the Submit Errata link, and entering the details of your errata. Once your errata have been verified, your submission will be accepted and the errata added to the list of existing errata. The existing errata can be viewed by selecting your title from http://www.packtpub.com/support.

Questions

You can contact us at questions@packtpub.com if you are having a problem with some aspect of the book, and we will do our best to address it.

1

Terms and Concepts

Before you can understand how to operate Joomla!, allow me to explain the basic principles that underlie the Joomla! Content Management System. **Content Management System (CMS)** contains the terms *content* and *management* (administration) that imprecisely refer only to a system that administers content. Such a system could be a board and a piece of chalk (menu or school chalkboard), or it could be something like Wikipedia (the free online encyclopedia at http://www.wikipedia.org), or an online auction house such as eBay (http://www.ebay.com/). In all these cases, content is administered; at times even for a large number of participants as in the case of the last two examples. These participants play a major role with the CMS, on one hand as the administrators, and on the other hand as users.

In general, the term *content management* is used in connection with web pages that can be maintained by a browser. This doesn't necessarily make the definition any easier. Apart from CMSs there are **Enterprise Resource Planning Systems (ERP**, administration of corporate data), **Customer Relationship Management Systems (CRM**, care of customer contacts), **Document Management Systems (DMS**, administration of documents), **Human Resource Management Systems (HRM**, administration of staffing), and many others. An operating system such as Windows or Linux also administers content.

Joomla! belongs to the category of **Web Content Management Systems (WCMS)**, since it exclusively administers content on a web server.

It is difficult to define the term CMS because of its encompassing nature and variety of functions. Lately **ECMS** has established itself as the nickname for **Enterprise Content Management Systems**. The other systems listed above are subsets of ECMS.

Since these terms are still relatively new in the enterprise world, these systems will surely be developed even further. In principle, however, there will always be an integration system that tries to interconnect all these systems.

A Quick Glance into History

While Sun Microsystems maintained in the nineties that "the Network is the computer", Microsoft was not going to rest until a Windows computer sat on every desk.

The computer that Microsoft was concerned with was a mixture of data files and binary executable files. Files with executable binary contents are called **programs** and were bought and installed by customers to manipulate data. Microsoft Office was the winner in most of the offices around the world. The computer that Sun was working with was a cheap, dumb terminal with a screen, a keyboard, a mouse, and access to the Internet. The programs and data were not stored on this computer, but somewhere on the net.

The *mine* philosophy governed Microsoft's practices whereas the *our* philosophy was adopted by Sun. The motivation for these philosophies was not for pure humanitarian reasons, but for economic interest. Primarily, Microsoft sold software for PCs to the consumer market; Sun, on the other hand, sold server hardware and programs to the enterprise market.

The Internet, invented in the sixties, spread like an explosion in the mid-nineties. Among other things, **HyperText Markup Language** (**HTML**)—the language used to write web pages—and the development of web servers and web clients (browsers) helped its expansion. The Internet itself was a set of rules that could be understood by different devices and was developed so skillfully that it covered the entire planet in almost no time.

An individual without an e-mail address could no longer be reached and a company without a website was not only old-fashioned, but didn't exist in the eyes of many customers. The whole world swarmed to the Internet within a short time to become a part of it. Movies like *The Matrix* (http://whatisthematrix.warnerbros.com/) became huge hits and *1984* (http://en.wikipedia.org/wiki/1984), a book by George Orwell, was forgotten.

New net citizens came from the *mine* world on one hand and from the *our* world on the other hand. Those who were used to buying programs bought HTML editors and created Internet pages with them. The others preferred to write their own HTML code with any text editor they had on hand. And the web agency, where one could order a homepage, was born.

Both groups faced the problem that HTML pages were static. To change the contents of the page, it first had to be modified on a PC and then copied to the server. This was not only awkward and expensive, but also made web presences like eBay or Amazon (http://amazon.com/) impossible. Both groups found more or less good solutions for this problem.

The *mine* faction developed fast binary programs with which one could produce HTML pages and load them via automated procedures onto the server. Interactive elements such as visitor counters, among others, were built into such pages.

The *our* faction discovered Java applets, and with them, the capability of writing a program that resided centrally on a server, which was operated via a browser. Entire business ideas were based on this solution—like online booking and flight reservation concepts. Both groups tried to develop market share in different ways.

The result was quite a stable market for both, in which passionate battles over the correct operating system (Windows, Linux, or Mac OS X) constantly drove the version numbers higher and higher. Customers got used to the fact that the whole thing wasn't that easy.

There is always a third option in these situations. As in our case, it was the emergence of open-source scripting languages like PHP (http://www.php.net/). Rasmus Lerdorf had the goal of offering interactive elements on his homepage, and with that a new programming language was born. From the outset, PHP was optimized in a perfect cooperation with the MySQL database, which also worked on the GNU/GPL platform (http://www.gnu.org/licenses/gpl.html).

Fortunately, on the server there was a Linux operating system and an Apache web server that offered the necessary infrastructure. Display medium at the client side was the browser, which was certainly available. Soon **LAMP** (Linux, Apache, MySQL, and PHP) became synonymous with database-supported, interactive presence on the Internet.

The most diverse systems like forums, communities, online shops, voting pages, and similar things that made it possible to organize contents with the help of a browser were developed in an enthusiastic creative rush.

After 'difficult' things such as Linux and Apache, 'soft' products were developed. The nineties were nearing their end; the Internet share bubble burst and suddenly the trend was to build unmitigated classical business models with unmitigated classical methods.

Whenever the economy isn't doing well, costs are scrutinized and the possibility of lowering costs is contemplated. There are now, as there were earlier, numerous possibilities. PHP applications always had distribution numbers in the millions. Only the **phpBB** (http://www.phpbb.com/) and **phpMyAdmin** (http://www.phpmyadmin.net) projects are mentioned here as examples. One was developed into the quasi-standard for forum software, the other one into the standard for manipulating MySQL databases via web interfaces. The source code of the PHP language and that of applications were improved because they had an enormous number of users and developers.

The more open a project was, the more successful it became. Individual gurus were able to save enterprises immense costs in the shortest time. Static HTML pages were considered old and expensive and were overhauled. They had to be dynamic! Developers have been working in this environment for a few years now. Linux, Apache, MySQL, and PHP are readily accepted in industry. The search for professionally usable PHP applications had begun.

With this search, one looks for:

- A simple installation process
- Easy serviceability of the source code
- Security of the source code
- User-friendliness
- Easy expandability

The special advantage of PHP applications is the independence from hardware and operating system. LAMP also exists as WAMP (Windows, Apache, MySQL, and PHP) for Windows, MAMP (Mac, Apache, MySQL, and PHP) for Apple, and for numerous other platforms. And now finally Joomla! comes into the fray.

Joomla!—How was it Developed?

An Australian company, Miro (`http://www.miro.com.au/`), developed a CMS named **Mambo** in the year 2001. It made this system available as open-source software to test it and to make sure of a wider distribution. In the year 2002, the company split its product Mambo into a commercial and an open-source version. The commercial variant was called **Mambo CMS**, the open-source version **Mambo Open Source (MOS)**. In the meantime, all parties involved agreed that MOS can officially be called **Mambo** and together a successful future for the fastest developing CMS of the moment was secured.

The advantages of the commercial version for companies are primarily in increased security and the fact that they have the company Miro, which also supports further development, as a partner. The advantage the open-source version offers is that it is free and that an enormous community of users and developers alike provide continuous enhancements. In addition, it is possible for enterprises to take Mambo as a base and to build their own solutions on top of it.

In order to secure the existence and the continued development of Mambo, there were deliberations on all sides in the course of the year 2005 to establish a foundation for the open-source version of Mambo.

On August 10, 2005 it finally happened: The Mambo Foundation was announced on the Mambo project page. After the positive reactions in the first few hours, it quickly became obvious that Miro in Australia established the foundation and that the developer team had not been included into the incorporation modalities. Heated discussions erupted in the forums of the community and the developer team wrapped itself in silence for a few long days.

On the August 17, 2005 a statement was finally published by OpenSourceMatters, announcing that it would be advised by the neutral Software Freedom Law Center and was planning the continued development of Mambo.

Discord quickly developed between the Miro Mambo Foundation that was all of a sudden without a development team and an inflamed international community of hundreds of thousands of users. The parties sometimes called each other names in blogs, forums, and the respective project pages.

Meanwhile, development of both projects continued. The Mambo Foundation released a beta version of Mambo 4.5.3 on the August 26, 2005, which was not well received in the relevant forums.

The development team itself, of course, needed a new name for the split entity. On September 1, 2005, the name for the split entity was announced—**Joomla!**. This time the developer team secured itself the rights for the use of a name and also gave the community the option of changing their existing Mambo domains over to the new name before it was announced publicly. In no time at all, 8,000 users registered with the new forum.

The new project needed a logo and thus, on the September 7, 2005, a competition was announced to the community. A number of logo suggestions were published on September 14, 2005 and the new (old) community was asked to agree on the new Joomla! logo. The suggestions and results can, of course, be found online.

Gradually many of the third-party developers—developers who program their own extensions, for example, a forum or a picture gallery on a foundation of Joomla! or other systems—also switched from Mambo to Joomla!. VA software, the company that, among other things, operates the SourceForge.net developer page, decided to sponsor the Joomla! project's server infrastructure.

As interim high point Joomla! won two prizes at Linuxworld in London in October. One was for the best Linux or Open Source project in the year 2005 and the other was the prize received by core member Brian Teeman for his support of Open Source projects (UK Individual Contribution to Open Source).

You can find a detailed summary of the events in English on the Internet at http://www.devshed.com /c/a/BrainDump/Joomla is the new Mambo/.

Structure of a CMS

This section explains the basic structure of Joomla!. The different functionalities offered by a CMS can be split up into a number of categories. These categories together form the structure of a CMS.

Front End and Back End

A CMS consists of a front end and a back end. The **front end** is the website—what the visitors and the logged-on users see.

The **back end**, on the other hand, contains the administration layer of the website for the administrator. Configuration, maintenance, cleaning, creation of statistics, and new content creation are all done in the back end. The back end is at a different **Uniform Resource Locator (URL)** than the website.

Configuration Settings

Settings that apply to the entire website are specified using the **configuration settings**. These include the title text in the browser window, passwords for search engines, switches that permit or forbid logging on to the site, switches that switch the entire page offline or online, and many other functions.

Access Rights

Whenever we talk of management, we talk of the clever administration of existing resources. In a CMS, usernames are assigned to people involved and these are provided with different **access rights**. This ranges from a simple registered user through an 'author' and 'editor' up to the 'super-administrator', who has full control over the domain. Based on the rights, the website then displays different content, or the user works in administrative areas apart from the website.

Content

Joomla! handles all kinds of **content**; in the simplest case, it is text. But content can also be a picture, a link, a piece of music, or a combination of everything. To keep an overview of the content, one embeds it in structures, for example, texts of different categories. The categories, of course, are also content that needs to be administered.

Templates

A **template** is a kind of visual edit format that is placed on top of content. A template defines the colors, character fonts, character sizes, background pictures, spacing, and partitioning of the page—in other words, everything that has to do with the appearance of the page.

Extensions (Components)

Every system has to be expandable and be able to grow with the requirements. Functionalities that belong to one context are also covered by the term **components**. For example, typical components are an online shop, a user manager, a newsletter maintenance system, or a forum. Components contain the business logic of their page.

Modules within the components are used to integrate content in the desired form into templates. For example, a `recent news` module supplies the headings of the five most recent pieces of news to the template. Another module delivers the number of users that are online at the time, or the meteorological data for your current town or city.

Workflow

By **workflow** one understands a work routine. The bureaucratic set of three (mark, punch, and file) is an example of a workflow. A recipe for baking a cake is a workflow. Since several people usually work with CMS content, well-organized workflows are a genuine help. In this connection, one sometimes speaks of work supplies that a certain user has. For example, the editor sees a list of posted pieces of news that he or she has to examine for correctness. After examining, the editor marks the pieces of news as correct and they appear in the work supply of the publisher. The publisher then decides whether to publish the piece on the front page.

Joomla! as Real Estate

Joomla! is a kind of construction kit that lets you create and maintain your website once it is installed on the server. Joomla! is like a house that you build on a property of your choice and that you can furnish gradually. Thus, to a certain extent, it is real estate.

Stop! I was talking about mobility all the time and now I'm asking you to build real estate? Have no fear, the real estate you build is physically at one place (your server), but is accessible from every place. To make a piece of real estate habitable, you need necessary services such as heating, electricity, and water supply. That is the reason your Joomla! is deposited at a server that is as safe as possible and where, hopefully, the electricity will never be cut. Think of the abbreviation 24/7.

Just like your house, you also have a certain room layout in Joomla!. You have a room for presentations, for cooking and talking, for working, and a completely private one that you only show to good friends. Perhaps you also have a large room that integrates all areas.

It doesn't matter which room layout you decide on. You have to furnish your house, lay a beautiful floor, paper the walls, hang a few pictures, and of course, clean it regularly. The numerous guests leave traces that are not always desirable. To find your house the visitors need an address. This address has to be familiar to as many people as possible. Since there is no residents' registration office on the Internet, you have to be the one that takes care of the topic, "*How can I be found?*"

Perhaps you also have a garden that surrounds your house and has different entry gates. There is an official entrance portal, a back door, and perhaps another small, weathered garden gate for good friends.

And perhaps you don't like such houses and would rather use trailers, tents, mobile homes, hotels, or maybe prefer community living and are glad to pay rent and don't want to think about all the details.

If you apply the last few ideas to your website, then you are already noticing how important it is to know what you want, who you are, and how you want to look at your community. One cannot *not* communicate! One can, however, be quickly misunderstood.

So plan your website on the Internet properly. Put thought into the texts, into possible interactive elements like a calendar or a forum, and of course, areas that only registered users are allowed to see.

Think about what prompts that move and don't patronize users. Take a look at how others do it. Talk with the people you want to address through your website and invest your heart and soul into those things that are absolutely crucial for the success of your entry.

Joomla! Versions

As with all software, there are different development versions with Joomla!. The Joomla! team published a roadmap on September 1, 2005 and started with the Joomla! version 1.0, which is also with what this book concerns itself.

The first Joomla! version received the number 1.0, in order to not be confused with existing Mambo versions. Version 1.0 is a revised version of the last Mambo version, 4.5.2.3. The revisions relate to the changed name, known errors, and security patches.

Numbering System of Joomla! Versions

Joomla! Versions abide by the X.Y.Z system.

- x = **major release number**: It is incremented whenever profound changes are made at the source-code level. The version with the higher number sometimes is not compatible with earlier versions.
- y = **the minor release number**: It is incremented whenever significant changes to functionality are made. The higher version number is usually compatible (with minor customizing) with earlier versions.
- z = **the maintenance release number**: It is incremented whenever errors are repaired and safety gaps are plugged. An increase of this number indicates only minor changes and very minor new features. These versions are fully compatible with the versions of the same x and y number.
- **Full release**: This is a change in the x and y numbers. With these, alpha and beta test periods are given. The length of the test periods is not fixed and is at the discretion of the development team. Beta versions should be available for testing for at least three weeks in order to give component developers the chance to customize their components.
- **Maintenance release**: This can be used immediately.

Roadmap

This roadmap can, of course, change at any time. It does, however, represent a good framework for orientation.

Version	Date of Release	Comments
Mambo 4.5.2	17 Feb, 2005	Last stable version of Mambo
Joomla 1.0.x	From Sep. 2005	Transfer of Mambo version 4.5.2.3 corrections of bugs and security patches
Joomla 1.1	Q4 2005 / Q1 2006	Enhancements to the user interface Administration interface capability for every language New functions
Joomla 1.2	No date	Currently planned enhancements: Rights enhancements—Part 1 WCAG priority 1-compatibility (only front end) Google summer of code—enhancements
Joomla 1.3	No date	Currently planned enhancements: Rights enhancements—Part 2 Google summer of code—enhancements
Joomla! 2.0	2006	New CMS-structure on the foundation of PHP 5 language version

Table 1.1: Joomla! roadmap—status as of September 2005

- **Rights enhancements—part 1**: The option of adding and of modifying user groups is to be added. The administrator will have the capability of assigning individual authorizations to every group. Thus for example, group A may change the template of a page, group B, however, may not.

- **Rights enhancements—part 2**: Access rights on an object level are to be made possible. Thus, for example, a category may only be viewed by group A, but may be modified by group B.

- **WCAG priority 1-compatibility**: Barrier freedom is an important topic. The W3C has set up standards for this that have to be observed starting with Joomla! version 1.2 (see also Chapter 6). These standards are to be attained by the complete separation of the HTML code from the business logic in the underlying programs.

- **Google Summer of Code Projects**: In 2005 Google supported talented students and their ideas with certain Open Source projects with $4,500 each. The results of these projects will be gradually integrated into Joomla!.

    These projects include, among others:

    o Access to Joomla!'s file system by means of a defined interface from other programs
    o A system to pick up and install updates
    o Content version control, in order to be able to backtrack the modifications in business applications
    o Speed optimization of Joomla!

Joomla! Features

The following lists a few Joomla! features:

- Free source code
- Simple workflow system
- Caching mechanism to secure fast page creation with favorite pages
- Wastepaper basket
- Banner management
- Data manager for uploading and administering data
- Publication system for content
- Content summaries in RSS format
- Search-engine-friendly URLs
- Multilingual front end
- Macro language for data content (Mambots)
- Administration interface that is separated from the homepage
- Simple, expandable template, and component system
- Simple, but powerful template system (HTML, CSS, PHP) without a complicated template language
- Hierarchical user groups
- Simple visitor statistics
- WYSIWYG editor for content
- Simple polling
- System of evaluation for contents
- Free extensions at http://www.mamboforge.net
- After the split, a large and eager community of users and developers was quickly established

Examples of Joomla! Pages

In order to get a feeling of how Joomla! pages look and whether "the" Joomla! page even exists, just have a look at a few. Because of the project history, these pages are still based mostly on the Mambo CMS. The Joomla! development team has developed Mambo for years, so these can definitely be consulted as references.

Joomla.org

In the ongoing development of Joomla! an emphasis is put on barrier freedom, among other things. At `joomla.org` you can, for example, change the font size of the text with a simple mouse click.

Figure 1.1: http://www.joomla.org/

Porsche, Brazil

You're probably familiar with Porsche, the manufacturer of sports cars from Germany.

Figure 1.2: http://www.porsche.com/latin-america-en/

PC Praxis, Germany

A computer magazine from Germany:

Figure 1.3: http://www.pc-praxis.de/

BSI DANS, Norway

My knowledge of Norwegian is unfortunately not very advanced, but I really like the design.

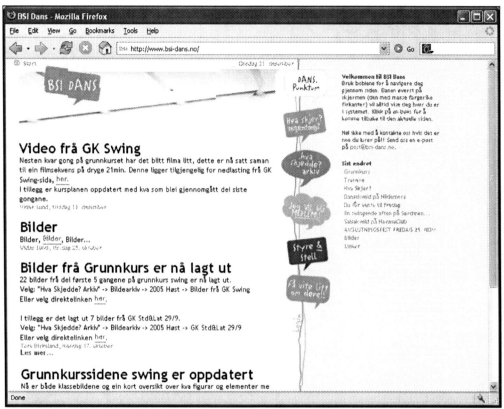

Figure 1.4: http://www.bsi-dans.no/

Team Lesotho, Lesotho

The page of the development support team of Aaron & Debbie Smart:

Figure 1.5: http://www.teamlesotho.com/

You can find a list of Joomla! websites at http://www.joomlapowered.com/.

Summary

In this chapter we briefly discussed the history of content management systems and introduced Joomla! as the CMS of our choice. We familiarized ourselves with the Joomla! versions and features and even saw a few Joomla!-powered pages. We are now ready to move to the next chapter where we discuss the Joomla! Installation process.

2
Installation

The installation of Joomla! is a matter of two minutes. To install Joomla!, it would be best to have the dream team mentioned in Chapter 1—Apache, MySQL, and PHP—installed as the development environment. Of course, Joomla! does not make any special demands on Apache or MySQL. So you can also use any other web server that works with PHP.

PHP has to be of version 4.1.2 or higher and it should be compiled with support for MySQL and Zlib. **Zlib** is a library that makes it possible for PHP to read file packages that are compressed with the ZIP procedure.

The installation has to be done on a server that can be accessed over the Internet, usually located at the Internet Service Provider. But before we venture into the wilderness of the Internet, we should first practice on our local computer. This is an advantage as there are no connection fees, it is very fast, and we can practice at a leisurely pace. We can even have a small local network at home where we can install Joomla! on one computer and access it from another.

All the necessary downloads discussed in this book can be downloaded from `http://www.alternative-unternehmensberatung.de/component/option,com_weblinks/ catid,2/Itemid,40/lang,en/`. A list of file packages can be found in the Appendix. These files are suitable for local installation, since the examples in this book can be reconstructed that way.

Remember, however, that there are more current versions on the respective project sites on the Internet. If you install Joomla! on a server on the Internet, you should always use the latest stable version.

Setting Up the Local Server Environment

To install Joomla! locally, we have to set up the appropriate server environment.

Windows

Due to its user-friendliness, majority of computers work with Windows as operating system. Unfortunately, Apache web server, MySQL database, and PHP are not included with Windows. A practical approach would be to install each of these programs separately, or grab a preconfigured package.

Log on to the system in administrator mode. To check your account type, click Start | Control Panel | User Accounts and change it to Computer administrator if required:

Figure 2.1: User Accounts

XAMPP for Windows

XAMPP is a project of Kai 'Oswald' Seidler and Kay Vogelgesang. These two have been creating a complete development environment with the ingredients Apache, MySQL, PHP, Perl, and various extensions for several years.

XAMPP can be downloaded from http://www.apachefriends.org/en/xampp.html as zip archives for various operating systems. This is an immense advantage for people like you and me, who are primarily interested in Joomla! and not so much in how all of it works. Also, the entire installation can be removed from the computer with one mouse-click without leaving a trace. To download and install XAMPP:

1. Download the `xampplite-win32-1.4.14.zip` file from `http://www.apachefriends` `.org/en/xampp-windows.html#641` and extract it on the local drive:

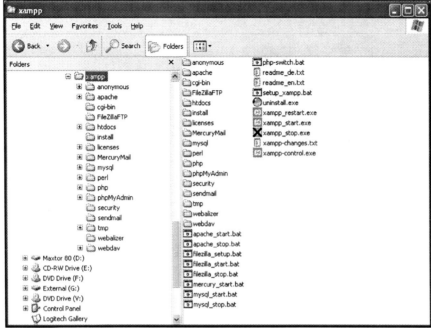

Figure 2.2: XAMPP Lite Directory

2. Open the `setup_xampp.bat` file from the `xampplite` folder. XAMPP makes no entries in the Windows Registry and sets no system variables:

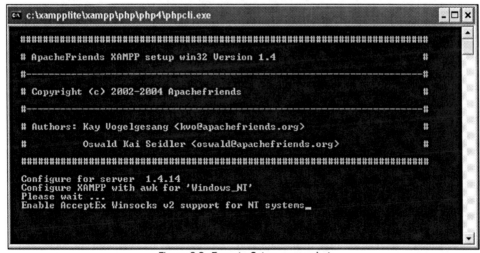

Figure 2.3: Execute Setup_xampp.bat

3. PHP starts automatically as a module. To start Apache, open the `apache_start.bat` file from the `xampplite` folder. A command prompt window opens, which indicates that Apache has started:

Figure 2.4: Start Apache Web Server

> The command window can be minimized, but closing it will terminate the Apache web server.

4. Start MySQL by opening the `mysql_start.bat` file. As opposed to Apache, MySQL has a separate script to terminate itself. To accomplish this, open the `mysql_stop.bat` file.

Figure 2.5: Start MySQL

5. Open the `http://127.0.0.1/` or `http://localhost/` page to check if XAMPP is correctly installed. On the XAMPP start page, click on the English link and the start page shows up (Figure 2.6).

The document directory of your website is `htdocs` in the `xampplite` folder. This directory contains all the pages that are accessible by a remote computer on the Internet. More information on usernames and passwords can be found in the `readme_en.txt` file. To uninstall the package, close all current servers and delete the `xampplite` directory.

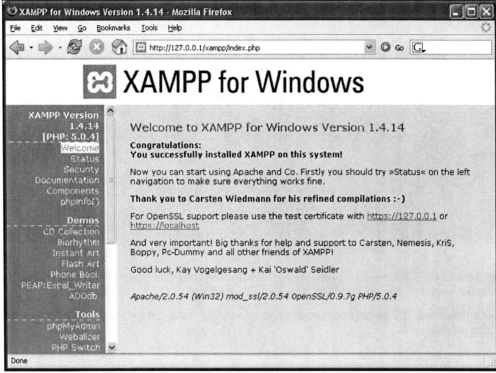

Figure 2.6: XAMPP Start Page

Linux

With Linux everything is usually simple. Different distributions with different standard configurations are available. Usually our dream team is pre-installed and just needs to be started. An XAMPP version can also be installed for Linux. My opinion, however, is that it makes more sense to grab the original programs. The installation is done by a package manager and is very simple.

SUSE (10.x) OpenSUSE

You can check whether Apache, MySQL, and PHP are already installed with the help of the YaST configuration program. If that is not the case, select the appropriate packages for installation and let YaST install them. These are the packages in detail:

- `apache2`
- `apache2-level`
- `apache2-mod_php4`
- `mysql`
- `php4-mysql`

You can find these packages via the YaST interface on your SUSE distribution media or on the Internet:

Figure 2.7: YaST Accessed from a Windows PC in a Shell

Start the Apache web server with the /etc/init.d/apache2ctl start command and the MySQL database server with the /etc/init.d/mysql start command.

You can stop both the servers with the stop command. By typing help, you get an overview of all parameters.

Debian/Ubuntu

With Debian and with Ubuntu, apt is the agent of choice. You can install Apache, MySQL, and PHP with the apt program.

```
apt-get install [packetname]
```

The following are the packages in detail:

- apache-common: Support files for all Apache web servers
- php4: Server-side HTML-embedded scripting language
- mysql-common: MySQL database common files (for example, /etc/mysql/my.cnf)
- mysql-server: MySQL database server binaries

You can find these packages automatically over the Internet or on the Debian CD/DVD by using apt.

Now start Apache with the /etc/init.d/apachectl start command and MySQL with the /etc/init.d/mysql start command.

Your Own Server at a Provider

If you have rented a complete server from a provider, then you usually have a shell entrance and free choice of the Linux distribution that you want to use. In addition, the system is preconfigured and contains all necessary file packages and configurations. Usually special administration interfaces, such as Confixx (http://www.sw-soft.com/en/products/confixx/) or Visas, are used for configuring these servers. You can comfortably start, stop, and configure your server and the Apache and MySQL services from a browser interface with this tool.

On a Virtual Server in the Net

This topic is very complex, since there is an unmanageable number of providers and an even more unmanageable combination of installed Apache, PHP, and MySQL versions and Webspace administration tools such as Confixx and Visas.

These are the sticking points:

- A PHP safe mode, possibly activated in the php.ini
- Prohibited conversion of URLs with Apache because of the non-activation of the *rewrite engine*
- Directory rights in Linux set differently than in Windows

In principle the simplest approach that actually always works is the following:

1. Load the Joomla_1.0.0-stable.tar.gz file onto your local PC and unpack it in a temporary directory.
2. Load the just unpacked files by means of FTP onto your rented server. The files must be installed in the publicly accessible directory. These directories are usually named htdocs, public_html, or simply html. You can specify a subdirectory within the directory into which you install your Joomla!. Many web hosts allow you to link your rented domain name to a directory. This name is necessary to call your website from a browser.
3. You have to find out what your database is called. Usually one or several databases are included in your web-hosting package. Sometimes the user name, database name, and password are fixed; sometimes you have to set them up. There is usually a browser-based configuration interface at your disposal. You can see an example of such an interface in Figure 2.8. You will need these data for Joomla!'s web installer.

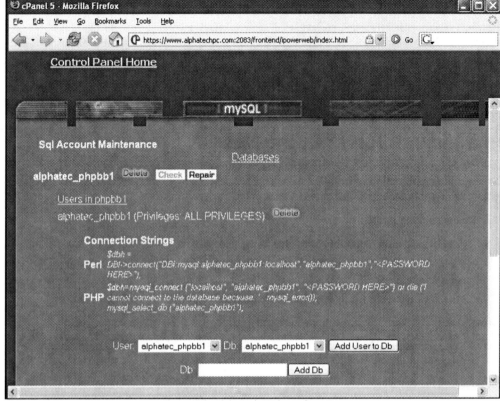

Figure 2.8: Alphatech Web configurator

Installing Joomla!

To install Joomla! You need the source code. Download the Joomla_1.0.0-Stable.tar.gz and save it on your system. (The latest version of Joomla! is 1.5 Beta. If you are using this version, you can refer to the book *Building Websites with Joomla! 1.5 Beta 1* from Packt Publishing.)

Selecting a Directory for Installation

You need to decide whether Joomla! needs to be installed directly into a document directory or a subdirectory. This is important, since many users prefer a short URL to their homepage.

An Example

If Joomla! is unzipped directly in /htdocs, the web page starts when the domain name http://www.myhomepage.com is accessed from its local computer as http://localhost/ or from the server on the Internet. If subdirectories are created under /htdocs/, for example, /htdocs/ Joomla100/ and we unzip the package there, we have to enter http://localhost/Joomla100/ in the browser. This isn't a problem locally, but doesn't look good on a production Internet page.

Some HTML files and subdirectories, however, are already in /htdocs in the local XAMPP Lite environment under Windows, which, for example, displays the greetings page of XAMPP Lite (as shown in Figure 2.6). In a local Linux environment, a starting page dependent on the distribution and the web server settings is also displayed.

Local Installation of Joomla!

Let us now go ahead with the actual installation of Joomla! on our PC and begin exploring our new CMS.

Directory

In Windows, create a subdirectory named Joomla100 under the document directory by using Windows Explorer. With Linux, use the Shell, KDE Konqueror, or Midnight Commander.

[Document home]**/htdocs/Joomla100/**

The directory tree in Windows Explorer should look like this:

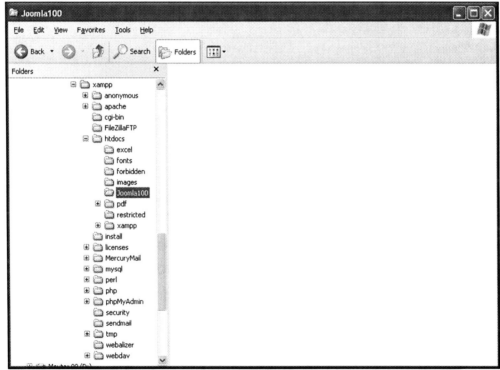

Figure 2.9: Joomla! Directory

An empty index appears in the XAMPP Lite version when the http://localhost/Joomla100 URL is entered in the browser:

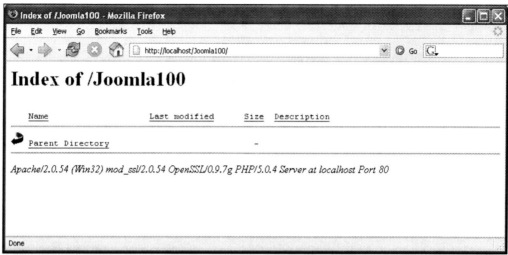

Figure 2.10: Apache Directory Display

With Linux or with another configuration it can happen that you don't get a message and therefore you don't have access to this directory. This depends on the configuration of the web server. For security reasons, the automatic directory display is often deactivated. A potential hacker could draw many interesting conclusions about the directory structure and the files on your homepage. From this information the hacker could target your computer for hacking.

For security reasons, you are usually not allowed to access the appropriate configuration file of the Apache web server. Should you be able to, you should leave the content directories deactivated because of this.

Unpacking

In Windows XP, the Joomla_1.0.0-Stable.tar.gz file can be directly unpacked from Windows Explorer. In all other versions of Windows a separate unpacking program is required, for example, the shareware program Filzip that can be downloaded from http://www.filzip.com/en/index.html.

In Linux, type the following command to unpack the file package, called a **compressed tarball**, in the prepared directory:

```
$ tar -zxvf Joomla_1.0.0-Stable.tar.gz
```

After unpacking, the following directories and files can be seen in Windows Explorer:

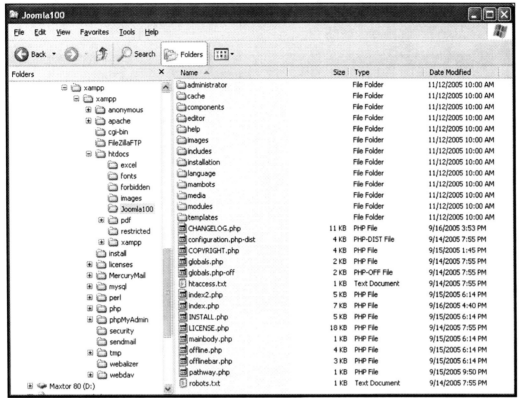

Figure 2.11: Joomla! Source Code Files

This structure is the same on all operating systems—only the presentation differs. The following figure shows a presentation in an FTP client where the local PC is in the left window and the remote web server in the right:

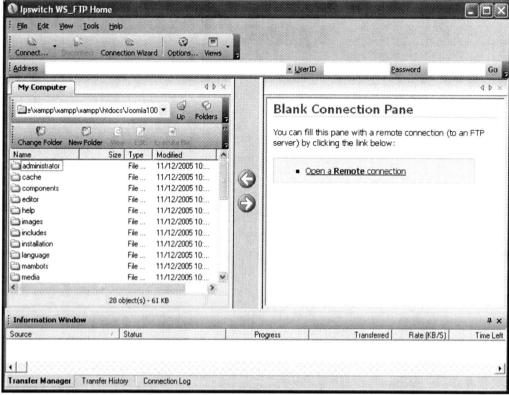

Figure 2.12: Joomla! Files in FTP Client WS_FTP

Joomla! Web Installer

From now on, everything is going to go lightning fast because the Joomla! web installer will be taking over command. Go to the `http://localhost/Joomla100/` page where the web installer announces itself with a pre-installation check. This check determines whether your environment is suitable for installing Joomla!. If there are many green test results, then it is already a good sign. Depending on your configuration there can be differences here.

The web installer takes the configuration settings of Apache, PHP, and the operating system into consideration. On Linux-based systems, attention should be given to writing rights. If you are working with the XAMPP Lite solution under Windows, the web installer should look as shown in the following figure:

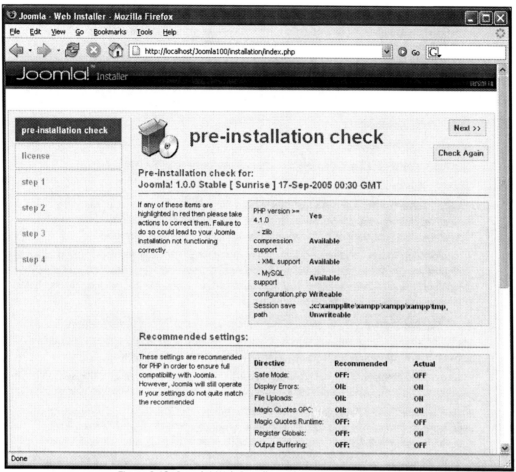

Figure 2.13: Joomla! Web Installer with Pre-Installation Check

Click on Next to get the announcement of the GNU/GPL license. The installation with the web installer takes place in the following four steps:

Step 1

Database parameters are queried in a questionnaire. You can set up as many databases as required in the XAMPP Lite server environment. As there is a MySQL user set up with the name `root` without a password, enter the name of a database that doesn't exist yet in the installer. Users usually have the rights to access databases in a working environment.

Enter the following parameters in a local XAMPP Lite installation:

- Host Name: localhost
- MySQL User Name: root
- MySQL Password: (leave this empty—but be aware of the security risk!)
- MySQL Database Name: joomla100
- MySQL Table Prefix: The web installer writes the text that is entered in the field before producing each table. By default, the web installer suggests jos _, because sometimes you get only one MySQL database from an Internet provider.

  If you needed to operate two Joomla! pages, there would be a problem, since you cannot differentiate one table from the other. By means of Table Name Prefix, it is possible to keep apart the tables of different Joomla! installations (`jos_smith_` or `jos_jones_`). At this time you should accept the default jos_.

- Drop Existing Tables: If you are dealing with a 'new' installation into an empty database, do not check this checkbox. If there is an old version of Joomla! in your database, you can overwrite the old files by checking this checkbox.
- Backup Old Tables: With Joomla!, data security (backups) can be set up. The backups are stored in special backup tables. To replace old backup tables, check this checkbox.
- Install Sample Data: By default, this checkbox is checked. This fills your homepage with sample data so that you get a conception of its appearance down the road. Fill your installation with these sample data; we will work with them later on in the book.

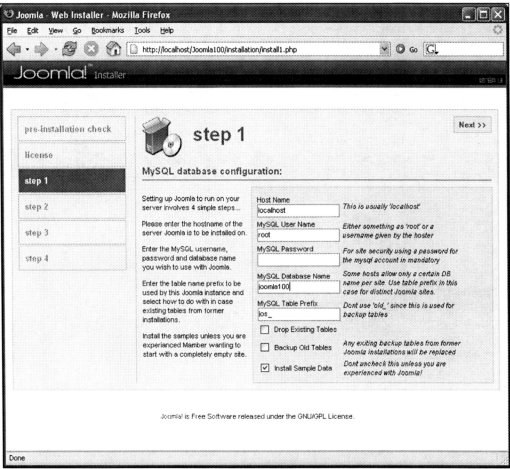

Figure 2.14: Web Installer, Step 1

Click on the Next button. After a security question, asking whether the installation should indeed go ahead, the web installer creates the database and the appropriate tables.

Step 2

In step 2, you set the name of your website. This name shows up in the header of the browser window when someone accesses your website. This name is also used in other places, for example, with confirmation e-mails to registered users. Select a meaningful name. For our example page, we have chosen the name Joomla100. Click on Next to set the name.

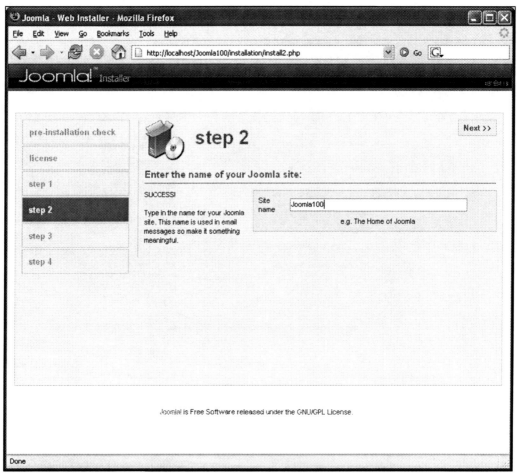

Figure 2.15: Web Installer, Step 2

Step 3

In step 3 you must confirm a few basic settings. These settings are important as they permit the Joomla! system navigation on your server.

- URL: This is the URL of your homepage.

- Path: This is the file path on your server that leads to your homepage. In our case it is in the Windows environment.

- Your E-Mail: Enter your e-mail address. As a Super Administrator you will receive e-mail from your homepage.

- Admin password: Joomla! suggests a password. You can accept it or create a similarly complicated password. A simple one would be sufficient for a local installation.

Accept the default options in the File Permissions and Directory Permissions dialog. During installation, Joomla! automatically sets access rights to those parts of the system where files are uploaded or programs are installed.

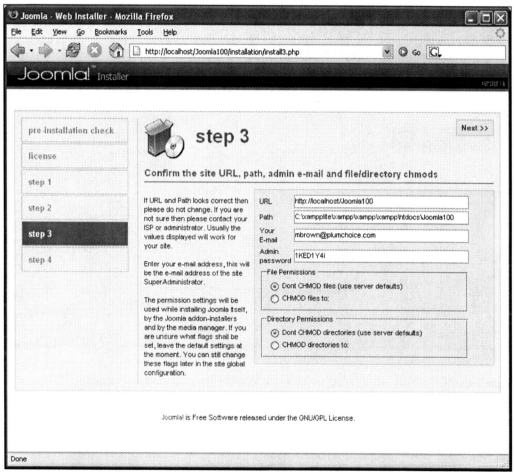

Figure 2.16: Web Installer, Step 3

Step 4

The fourth and final step congratulates you on a successful installation.

Figure 2.17: Web Installer, Step 4

There is a notice in bold, red text that prompts you to delete the installation directory. Take good heed of this notice, because your Joomla! website will not run if you don't delete the directory.

In addition, your Administration Login Details are indicated. Note down the username and password.

> Joomla! assigns a new password when you go backwards from step 4, for instance, if you want to change your settings or if the installation wasn't quite successful. If you have forgotten or mislaid the administrator password, there is a solution in the Appendix.

The installation is now complete. You have a choice between View Site (to start your homepage) and Administration (administration interface). To take a look at your newly created homepage, click on View Site. If you haven't deleted the installation directory as of yet, you will get a friendly reminder to delete it and to check out your page after you've done that.

Figure 2.18: Homepage after Installation

Summary

The result is very impressive. Look it over at your own pace, click on a few options, and try to orient yourself. Lots of Joomla!'s functionalities are used on this homepage, which is loaded with example data. We will take a good look at these in the further chapters.

3

A Tour of Your New Homepage

Now that you have installed your homepage and carefully explored it, we can take a look at the result together. At first glance, these pages look a bit confusing. In principle, they are divided into a **front end** and a **back end**. Customers and web surfers see the front end; the back end is only accessible by coworkers or administrators.

Front End

After spending some time on the homepage, you will realize that many different functions are integrated into the page. In order to get a better overview, I have marked and labeled the different areas of the page, illustrated in Figure 3.1 overleaf:

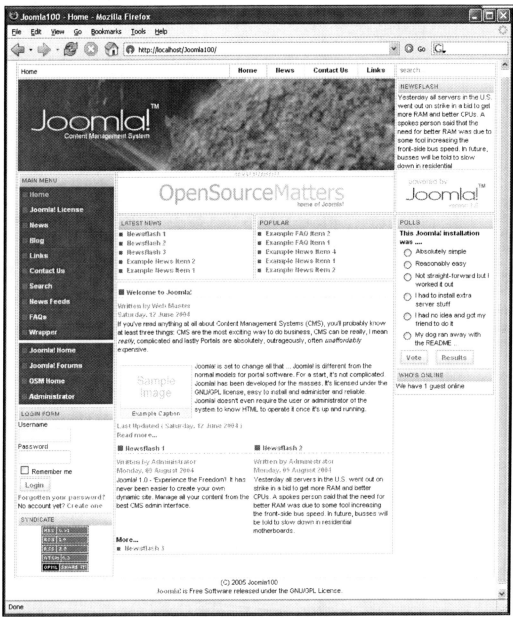

Figure 3.1: Structure of the Sample Website

The art of web designing now consists of recognizing the elements that are important for your homepage, omitting the unimportant ones, and presenting them to the user in a logical, easy-to-understand, and attractive format. The result is always a compromise between functionality and organization.

From the configuration, this structure reminds one of a daily newspaper or a portal like Yahoo! or Freenet. On the left and right there are boxes with clearly defined contents. In the centre are announcements.

A **Template** determines the layout of the page. Templates are exchangeable and modifiable, meaning that the same content can be displayed in different layouts. Every daily newspaper would envy you for this functionality. Let's go over the example layout a bit more closely.

There are five different categories of areas on the page:

- Menus
- Content
- Advertising
- Functions
- Decorative Elements

Menus

Menus are there to make navigation on the page as easy as possible for the user. There are different menus for different tasks. Joomla! has four kinds of menus in the example data. You can add as many additional menus as you want. The fourth menu, by the way, is not shown in our example. The registered user sees the **user menu** after he or she has logged on.

Top Menu

The **top menu** is as high up on the page as possible. It gives the user quick access to the most important content of the page. Such a menu often displays products, contacts, and company information:

Home		Home	News	Contact Us	Links

Figure 3.2: Top Menu

Main Menu

The **main menu** is the central navigation area of the page. There should always be a link to return to the first page. This menu should appear in exactly the same position on every page of the website. The main menu is an important orientation place for the user:

Figure 3.3: Main Menu

Other Menu

An additional menu, the **other menu** can pop up in all kinds of places (module positions, refer Chapter 4 for more information). Depending on the content and context of the page it can make sense to offer additional menu options:

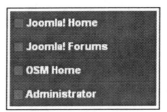

Figure 3.4: Other Menu

Content

Finally the content that we want to manage is here!

What is Content?

Content can be a message, an editorial article, or a static page with explanations. Content can also be a dynamic link directory (http://www.google.com/), a shop (http://dell.com/), or a flea market (http://www.ebay.com/).

Content can also be something completely dynamic and open to everybody. The free encyclopedia Wikipedia (http://www.wikipedia.org/), for example, uses a content administration system that allows everyone to change the content. This special form of content administration is called a **wiki** (http://en.wikipedia.org/wiki/Wiki). Everyone can change and even delete content. So far it is working amazingly well.

The opposite of a wiki is static content, which once written is valid for a long time. For example, take this book. It will become outdated regarding the version numbers of the software discussed, although it has the advantage of explaining and illuminating the topic comprehensively in that connection, at present. I produce content in a certain format and therefore operate a type of content management.

Folders, flyers, stickers, business reports, and manuals are also usually of static nature. Created for a certain event, after some time they become outdated or simply wrong.

Many older web pages consist exclusively of static elements. On the Internet, however, the clock ticks a little faster. That which is complaisantly tolerated with books, folders, and other printed materials (after all, I can also read the book at the beach and in the subway), is regarded to be a serious shortcoming by visitors to your website. Nothing is worse for the image of your company than a four-year old static website with a button announcing Powered by... that refers to hopelessly outdated software.

The presentational possibilities of content are inexhaustible. They depend on the available terminal, bandwidth, and many other things that are in turn dependent on the user. The user of the message plays an increasingly important role. Who actually form your target group?

A platitude says, "Content is king!"

It depends on the content. Every web agency would now probably crack a smile and get on with the daily job of creating the next website. Millions of dollars in advertising budgets for products such as frozen spinach or beer are proof of the fact that successful communication also works without unique content. The statement that content is crucial, is, however, fundamentally correct. If you have nothing to say or nothing to offer, nobody will listen to you of his or her own free will. Since you probably don't have a million-dollar advertising budget, you also can't force people to do it. No matter how beautiful websites without content may look, or how many terminals may display them, nobody will voluntarily visit them.

First Page/Front Page

Content is announced on the first page of the website, as illustrated in Figure 3.5. Content has an author, a date of preparation, a heading, a hook, and perhaps a picture. The hook is to make the visitor curious and to get him or her to click on a Read more link in order to read the entire message:

Figure 3.5: Front Page

The Latest Messages/The Most Often Read Messages

The message can be displayed in different formats. People are usually interested in the *newest* and in what *others* are reading as illustrated in Figure 3.6:

LATEST NEWS	POPULAR
■ Newsflash 1	■ Example FAQ Item 2
■ Newsflash 2	■ Example FAQ Item 1
■ Newsflash 3	■ Example News Item 4
■ Example News Item 2	■ Example News Item 1
■ Example News Item 1	■ Example News Item 2

Figure 3.6: The Latest Messages/The Most Often Read Messages

Because of that, our example layout has an appropriate area within which the last five messages are always displayed, and another area where the most read messages are announced. The second area is possible because Joomla! logs each hit on a message in the database and tracks the number of times it has been accessed.

Plan the content of your site carefully! Everyone in the world can read it and use it against you in cases of doubt. You could become the victim of a litigation lawyer, disappointed colleagues, or other unpleasantries.

On the other hand this has an unbeatable advantage: Everyone in the world can read your content, add his or her opinion to it, and contact you. What an opportunity!

You should be aware of both of these directions when you conceptualize content.

Advertising

When your site becomes popular, and if the content is right, you can sell advertising space. Advertising space usually means banner links.

Banners are small graphics (in `.gif`, `.jpg`, `.png`, or `.swf` format) that induce the visitor to leave your website via a single click on the banner. If you really want that, look for a space in your layout and consider using it for advertising.

Banner Area

The size of the banner area is determined by the current banners. In our case this is 468 x 60 pixels as illustrated in Figure 3.7:

Figure 3.7: Banner Area

Functions

Functions are elements needed to make interactivity possible. In Joomla! these functions are called **modules**. A module is something that takes up space on the web page and fulfils a certain function.

Login Area

A **login module** is important if you want to separate your website into a public and a protected area. The visitor then has to have a way of registering and of logging on. Perhaps he or she even occasionally forgets his or her password. The login module should be able to take all situations into consideration as illustrated in Figure 3.8:

Figure 3.8: Login Module

Polling

Since our content is designed for certain target groups, we should now and then ask the group that actually surfs our site for their opinion. This is the simplest way of getting utilizable opinions about your site.

Joomla! has integrated a survey component, whose display module is on the example page as illustrated in Figure 3.9:

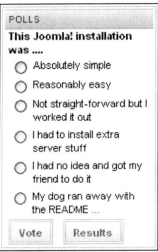

Figure 3.9: Survey Module

Who is Online?

This module is about communication and community. After the user has been able to see which messages are recent and particularly popular, naturally he or she would like to know who is navigating the site right now. In this case a distinction is made between guests and logged on users as illustrated in Figure 3.10:

Figure 3.10: Who is Online

Feeds

News feeds are becoming more and more popular. These are standardized collections of content, which can be processed further—the content of your site, without the dead weight of the rest of the website. The syndication module (Figure 3.11) offers the most diverse feeds:

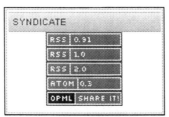
Figure 3.11: Syndication Module

You will learn more about this technology in Chapter 6.

> Deliberate carefully whether you want to offer such features on your website. If you claim in your content that you are the largest website in U.S. and only one guest cavorts on your site, it will hurt your credibility. But if you do indeed constantly have 10-20 visitors and logged on users, then this is a good way to demonstrate dynamics.

Back

Back is a small word of great importance and forms a giant portion of user friendliness. After one has pressed on a link, sometimes it is not at all easy to return exactly to the spot where one was just before. The Back button tries to make that possible:

Figure 3.12: Back

Search Field

Similar to the Back button, the Search field also contributes greatly to the user friendliness of a website. Many pages have search fields. Often, however, the programs behind the Search field don't scan the entire content of the page. With Joomla, however, all pages are definitely scanned:

Figure 3.13: Search Field

You can type a search term and press *Enter* on the keyboard. The result is a hit list, with the desired term visually emphasized.

Decorative Elements

After so many functions, modules, and contents, the issue of design, corporate identity, and the *look* and *feel* of the website pops up.

A **template** represents the layout of the page and is laid on top of the content like a screen. Since it is hard to argue either about taste or beauty, you have the option of providing different templates for the same content. For example, the look of your website in winter could be different than that in summer, or it could have a baseball look during the World Series.

In principle, a template consists of one or more logos, a certain color combination, selected character fonts and sizes, and as clever an arrangement of the available content as possible. There are two logos (Figures 3.14 and 3.15) and a footer line (Figure 3.16) in the example template:

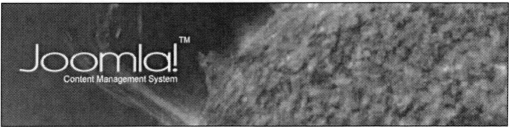

Figure 3.14: Logo 1

Figure 3.15: Logo 2

(C) 2005 Joomla100
Joomla! is Free Software released under the GNU/GPL License.

Figure 3.16: Footer

Prospects

After this tour and from your own experience, I am sure you can understand that the administration of contents can be a very demanding task. Above all, it is important not to lose sight of the overview.

Back End

The administration of the website takes place in the back end with the name Joomla! Administration. You can reach the Joomla! Administration in the [Domain name]/administrator/ page.

If you are working with a local installation, the URL will be http://localhost/joomla100/ administrator/.

Log on with your admin ID. You have specified the user data yourself in the web installer during installation.

Figure 3.17: Joomla! Administration—Login

You will see an interface with menus, icons, and tabs, identical to the graphic interface of your operating system, as illustrated in Figure 3.18:

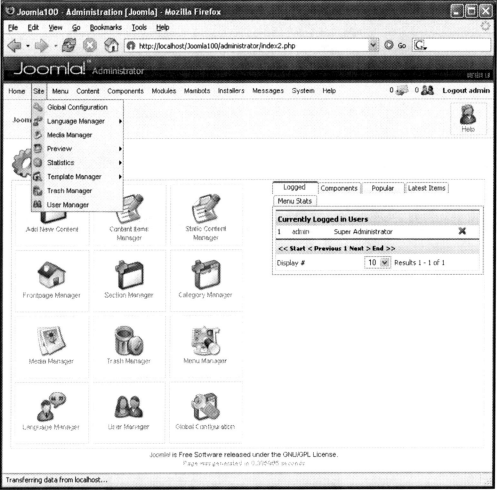

Figure 3.18: Joomla! Administration

In a working environment you should, for security purposes, protect the [pathtoJoomla!]/administrator/ directory with a .htaccess file. Because of the widespread use of Joomla!, the first successful hacker attempt at the administration is expected. You can find a useful tutorial (in German) for creating such a file at http://de.selfhtml.org/servercgi/server/htaccess.htm.

Summary

We had our first taste of the Joomla! interface in this chapter. We familiarized ourselves with the Joomla! front end and back end. We are all set to begin configuration of our website from the next chapter onwards.

4

Customizing Joomla!

Customizing means adaptating a standard program to the needs of the user. In our case, you are the user and the standard program is Joomla!, or more exactly the front end of your Joomla! installation.

In the Joomla! administration (referred to in Chapter 3), you can customize your site, make changes, and fill it with content.

Typically, the first thing that the owners of a site want to do is to change the colors and layouts. So, we will first discuss this first.

A Different Look and Feel

Now that everything looks a bit more familiar, you may want your site to have a completely different design. You can do this by renaming your menus and changing the template.

Modifying the Menu Name

In order to rename the Main Menu to, say, Check this Out, open the Module Manager by clicking Modules | Site Modules (Figure 4.1).

Figure 4.1: Module Manager

Click on the Main Menu link to edit it. Change the text in the Title field to Check this Out and the Main Menu becomes Check this Out.

Changing the Template

In order to see what is included in Joomla! as standard, switch to Site | Template Manager | Site Templates in the Template Manager. "Site" means your website, that is, the front end. As you can see, there are administrator templates as well.

Two finished templates are included with Joomla!. The currently active template is marked with a green checkmark. If you slide your mouse cursor over the name of the template, a small thumbnail view appears, as shown in Figure 4.2. The Solarflare template was taken from the last Mambo version and adapted to Joomla!. Marc Hinse's madeyourweb template is new. You can find out more about his templates and get tips and tricks for Joomla! in his blog.

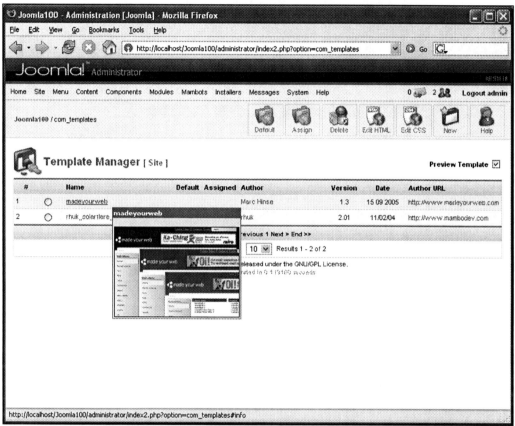

Figure 4.2: Preview

To assign this template to your site, select the radio button before the name of the desired template and click Default in the menu bar. Switch to your site and click the Update button in the browser:

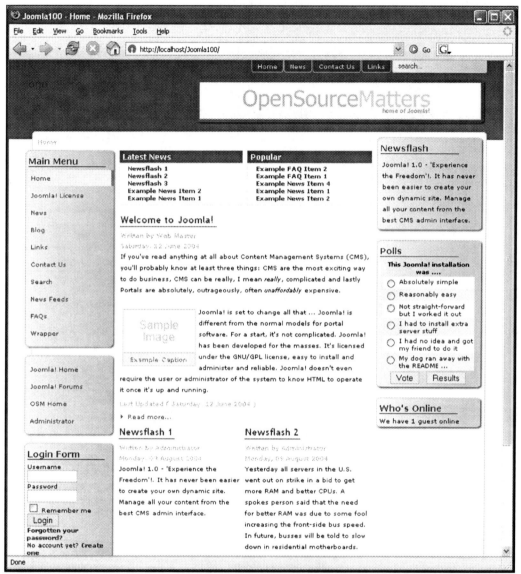

Figure 4.3: A Different Template

You have a different layout and a completely new appearance. After this first round of satisfying our urge to play, we now get to some more elaborate customization.

Configuration of Joomla! Administration

Joomla! offers nearly the same comfort level as any program with a graphical user interface, such as Windows, KDE, Gnome, or Aqua (Mac OS X). This is not self-evident for web pages and is made possible by the generous use of JavaScript. JavaScript is executed locally on your computer and can be deactivated in the browser. If this is done, you can no longer work with Joomla! administration. Browsers, however, have been able to deal with JavaScript quite well for several years now and there aren't any serious security concerns any more. For this reason, you should enable JavaScript. In this context, I would highly recommend the open source Mozilla Firefox browser (http://www.mozilla.org). It is more secure and easier to use than Internet Explorer.

The Joomla! administration, just like your site, consists of different elements:

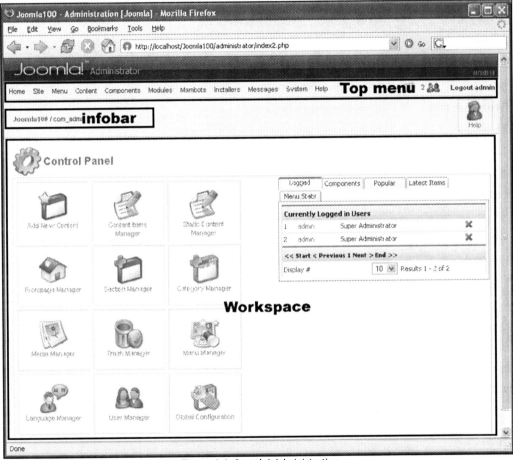

Figure 4.4: Joomla! Administration

In the **top menu** bar are the menus and on the right side are two notifications about whether you have received messages and how many users are logged on right now.

Below that is a field with a link (**infobar**) that has information about which components are applicable to the currently shown manager (in this case, Joomla100 / com_admin). On the extreme right is the toolbar with various dimmed icons (in this case, the Help icon) for the most important Joomla tasks. The tasks are organized in **managers** and the icons that are displayed depend on the manager. If you slide your mouse cursor over one of these icons, it lights up. You can click the icon and implement the appropriate function. The following table lists the common Joomla! icons and their functions:

Toolbar element	Relevance
Publish	The chosen element is published.
Unpublish	The chosen element is hidden from view.
Archive	The chosen element is moved to the archive.
New/New Item	The creation of a new element (link, contact, or message) is started.
Edit	The chosen element is loaded into the edit module.
Delete/Remove	The chosen element is deleted.
Trash	The chosen element is put in the trash container.
Restore/Untrash	The chosen element is retrieved from the trash container.
Move	The chosen element is moved to another section or category.
Copy	The chosen element is copied to another section or category.
Save	The chosen element is saved and the dialog is closed.
Apply	The changes are saved and the dialog remains open.
Cancel	The function being worked on is ended without any changes being saved.
Preview	The chosen element is shown in a preview window.
Upload	The chosen file is uploaded to the server.
Create	A subdirectory is created on the server.
Help	Mambo online help function is available.
Default	The chosen element becomes the default.
Assign	The chosen element is assigned to another element.

Table 4.1: Toolbar Elements

Under the toolbar is the **workspace** of the current manager. As shown in Figure 4.4, this is the Control Panel. It is displayed after logging in and offers quick access to the most important elements. If you do not see the Control Panel, simply click Home at the top left corner in the menu bar.

On the left, there are icons that refer to various managers. On the right, you find five tabs that give you an overview of the current status of your site. In the lower area you see a navigation bar that extends right across Joomla!. Here you can set the number of lines displayed and navigate through the table if say 600 users are online at the same time. This number is quite realistic with well-frequented Joomla! sites. Changing the number of lines displayed is possible with all table displays.

- Logged: This tab gives an overview of the currently logged in users. As the administrator, you can log the user out by clicking on the red cross (x) next to the user name.

- Components: This tab shows the currently installed software components. If these have several options (for example, Web Links), then this component is represented as a heading with subpoints.

- Popular: This tab tells you about the most surfed pages of your site. By clicking the page name, you switch to the Content Manager and see the respective page in editing mode. If you are in Edit mode, you have to terminate the function with Cancel or Save and subsequently click Home to get back to the Control Panel.

- Latest Items: This tab is similar to Popular. Here the content is shown in reverse chronological order. Clicking on the name also switches you to the Content Manager.

- Menu Stats: This tab displays the number of menu elements in each menu.

The menu bar consists of nine options. On the far left is the Home link that sends you back to the Control Panel. On the far right you can see the Help link.

You can configure the Control Panel by clicking Modules | Administrator Modules.

Help Menu

The Joomla! Help work area is divided into three sections. On the top there is a search field and a bar with links as shown in Figure 4.5. On the left is an index of the available help texts and on the right is the main display area. By default, anything new about your version of Joomla! is displayed in this space.

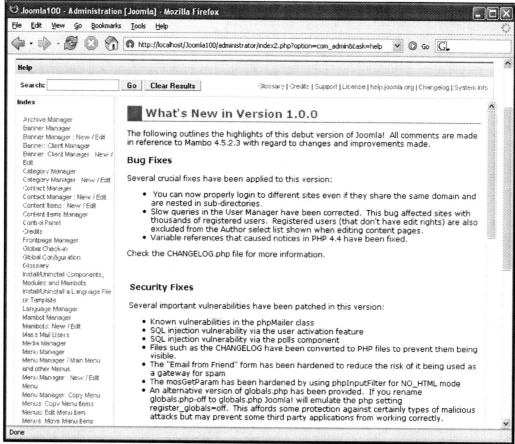

Figure 4.5: Joomla! Online Help

All but three links refer to the Joomla! server at `http://help.joomla.org/`. In order to use this search, you have to be connected to the Internet. You *have* to do this unless you are working with a local version. The other links refer to the text of the GNU Public License, to system information about your server as illustrated in Figure 4.6, and the change log, which documents the modifications of the individual developers. For instance, you can find out that Alex Kempkens added the `madeyourday` template on the September 16 and that Rey Gigataras installed a new version of the WYSIWYG editor on the September 14.

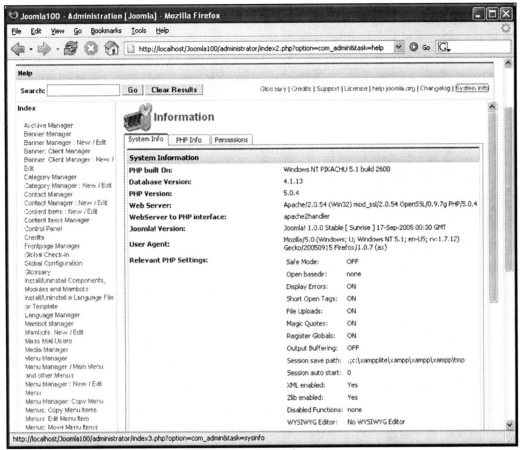

Figure 4.6: System Information

The system information is divided into three tabs.

- **System Info**: This tab displays a summary of the most important data. Right now I am working locally with Windows and the xampplite environment (refer to Chapter 2 for the installation procedure). Therefore I'm running very up-to-date software versions (Apache 2.0.53 and PHP 5.03) compared to the servers rented on the Internet.

- **PHP Info**: This tab displays all information from the phpinfo() function. This is the complete configuration of the PHP interpreter.

- **Permissions**: This tab displays the rights of your subdirectories. All directories must be writable for Joomla! to run error-free.

Site Menu

There are settings that apply to all individual pages and to your server. All of these settings are summarized in the Site menu.

Figure 4.7: Site Menu

Global Configuration

The Global Configuration workspace administers changes in the `configuration.php` file. It contains vitally important pieces of information like the access details for the database server. This workspace is divided into ten tabs:

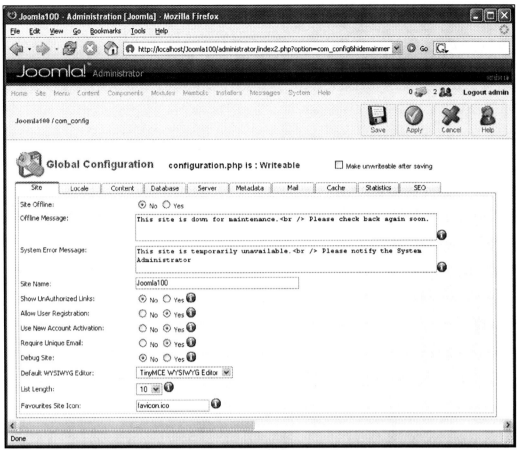

Figure 4.8: Site

Site

The Site tab contains parameter switches related to various settings concerning your entire website:

- **Site Offline**: This gives you the option of turning off your site while, for instance, you are carrying out changes to your site and you don't want visitors to track your development progress.

- **Offline Message**: The text entered here is displayed on your site when it is switched off. If you want to use another logo, you can save one with the name of [joomla]/images/logo.png. Otherwise, you have to customize the path accordingly.

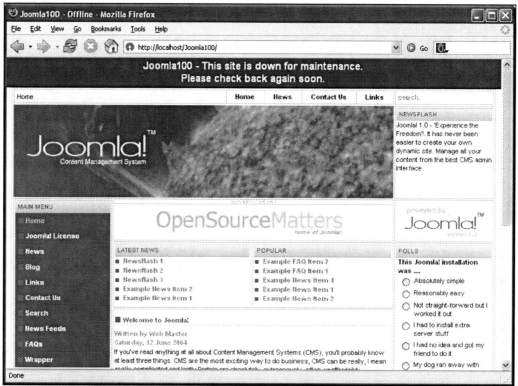

Figure 4.9: Display notice when
the site is switched off

- **System Error Message:** Here you can type in a message that is displayed if no connection can be established with the database server.

- **Site Name:** This is the name of the site that you entered during the installation.

- **Show UnAuthorized Links:** You have the ability to display individual pages only to registered users. It is possible that these pages get linked from a public connection. If you choose Yes, these links are displayed. When a visitor clicks on such a link without logging on, a message appears announcing that this is a protected area that requires registration.

- **Allow User Registration:** This allows you to select whether you want to permit users to do their own registration or not. If you operate a company site, you could set up user accounts for your coworkers, but forbid them to create their own account. On the other hand, with a community site, it is desirable for users to log themselves on.

- **Use New Account Activation:** In order to protect yourself from automated programs that can create 20,000 user accounts on your site, you can ask for separate activation. The user gets an automatic email sent to the address given by him or her. There is a link in this email that activates the account. After activation he or she can log on normally.

- **Require Unique Email:** Choose whether each email address is to be used for one account only.

- **Debug Site:** Here you can switch the site into debug mode. After activating this function, the database queries of the site are displayed. In order to generate a single Joomla! page, 83 database queries are required, as shown in Figure 4.10:

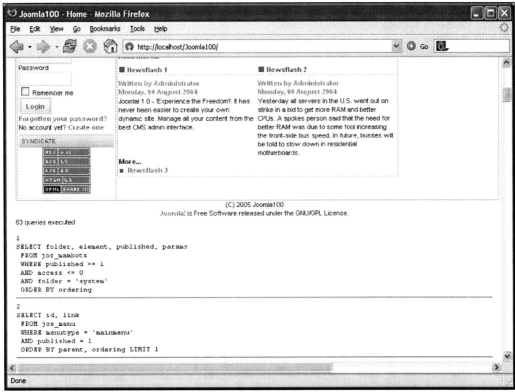

Figure 4.10: Debug Mode with Database Queries

- **Default WYSIWYG Editor: WYSIWYG** is the abbreviation for **"What You See Is What You Get"**. The term originated at the beginning of graphic user interfaces, when it first became possible to see how the printed document would look as you typed the text into your word processor.

On the Internet, you normally fill out forms with no formatting ability. Formatting is done by HTML tags or program-specific mnemonics. A WYSIWYG editor is user-friendly, since you have to click an appropriate icon, just as when formatting text. This editor is automatically invoked for the text fields that require formatting as illustrated in Figure 4.11. It works with all the usual browsers:

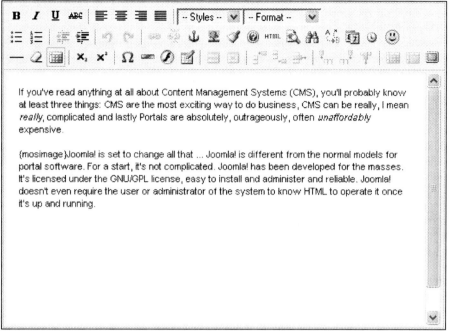

Figure 4.11: WYSIWYG Editor

Joomla! also offers the ability to integrate other HTML editors. The default editor, **TinyMCE**, is used at this time. You can find out more about it from `http://tinymce.moxiecode.com/`.

- **List Length**: Lists, like news and links, will crop up every now and then on your site. With this, you can set the default number of entries that such a list can have.

- **Favorites Site Icon**: Every site can offer the surfer a **favorite-site icon (favicon)**. This small picture is displayed to the left of the URL, as well as in the bookmarks of the browser. This works really well in most browsers:

Figure 4.12: Favicon in Firefox

In Internet Explorer, however, this works only under certain conditions (see Figure 4.13):

Figure 4.13: No Favicon in Internet Explorer (Version 6.0.29)

The icons have to be available in a specific format. You can specify the name for the icon. You will find the file in the main directory of Joomla!. You can create icons using an icon editor such as **SnIco Edit** (`http://www.snidesoft.com/staticpages/index.php?page=20050504142037205`).

Locale

With this tab, you can localize your page as illustrated in Figure 4.14. Localization means adaptation to country-specific conventions. The options available are:

- Language: Here you specify the language of the site. All available languages are indicated in the option drop-down menu. The *Language Manager* subsection discusses the installation of new language packs.

- Time Offset: This setting can be used to display the correct time; for example, if the server that Joomla! runs on is located in the USA, but the site is meant for visitors in Germany.

- Country Locale: Every country has certain conventions for the display of numbers and dates (`http://en.wikipedia.org/wiki/Locale`). This option lets you specify the format. PHP offers the ability to implement different functions depending on the mnemonic entered as `locale`. The approach is sound; however, this does not always work when creating a template.

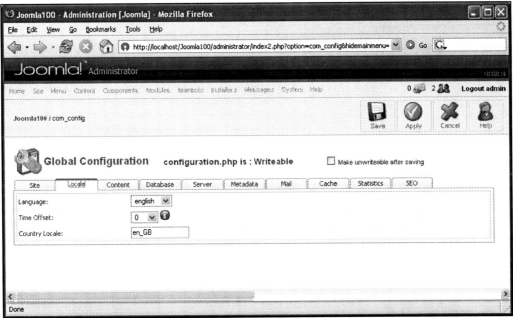

Figure 4.14: Locale

Content

The settings for the content display of the entire site are set here. You may set your preferred settings in the following options:

- Linked Titles: Here you can set the title of a content element to be shown as a link. This link then refers to the same target as the Read More link.

- Read More Link: A lot of content consists of a *hook* (intro text) and the actual text. Here you decide whether you want to have a Read More link under the hook, which refers to the complete text:

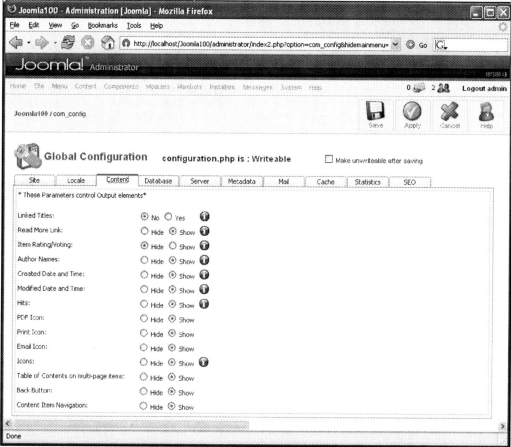

Figure 4.15: Content

- Item Rating/Voting: This lets your visitors evaluate the contents of the site. If you click Show, an evaluation component is displayed above the item (see Figure 4.16).

- Author Names: This setting allows you to display the name of the author of the content. If you select Show, then the name of the author appears above the article as shown in Figure 4.16:

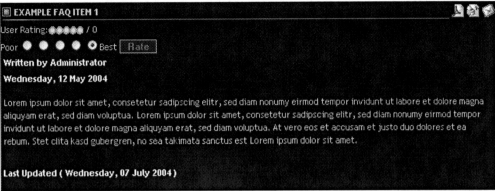

Figure 4.16: Sample Content

- Created Date and Time: This setting allows you to display the date and time of creation of content. If you select Show, text such as **Wednesday, 12 May 2004** is written above the article as shown in Figure 4.16.

- Modified Date and Time: This setting allows you to display the date and time when the content was modified last. If you select Show, text such as **Last Updated** (Wednesday, 07 July 2004) is displayed under the text, as illustrated in Figure 4.16.

- Hits: Here you decide whether to display the number of hits on a content item:

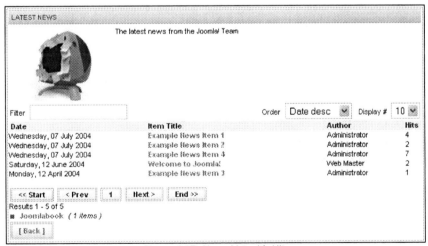

Figure 4.17: News List with Hits

- PDF Icon: Here you can assign a PDF icon to be displayed above the content (see Figure 4.16). After clicking this icon, your content is prepared as a PDF file! In order to view the PDF file, you need the free Acrobat Reader (`http://www.adobe.com/products/acrobat/`).

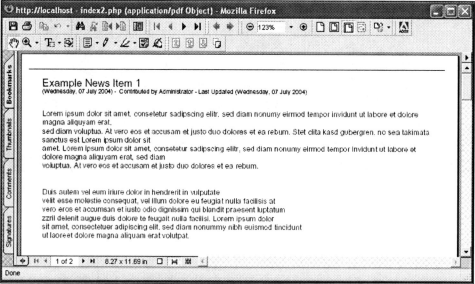

Figure 4.18: Release of Content in PDF

- Print Icon: Here you can determine whether a print icon is to be displayed above the content (see Figure 4.16). After clicking this icon, the content is prepared for printing.

- Email Icon: Should an email icon be displayed above the content? After clicking this icon, a form is displayed that allows you to send a reference about this content to somebody else, as illustrated in Figure 4.19:

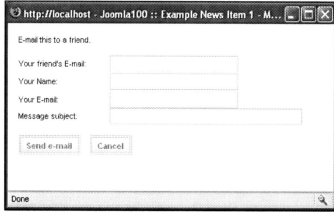

Figure 4.19: Email Referral

- Icons: Here you decide whether to show PDF, Print, and Email as icons or as links.

- Table of Contents on multi-page items: It is possible to write content that covers several pages. For that, a Mambot is contained in the text. We will discuss this Mambot in greater detail in Chapter 6. If you select Show, a table of contents is automatically produced for this piece of content.

- Back Button: This setting allows you to have a Back button on every page.

- Content Item Navigation: If you select Show here, a bar with Next and Previous buttons that you can use to navigate through items is placed under the content.

Database

This tab shows you the access information for your MySQL server:

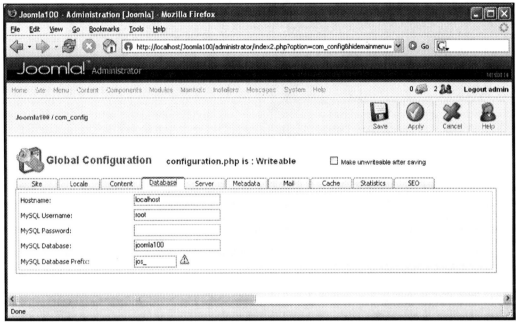

Figure 4.20: Database

Server

In the server section you'll find more information about settings that you can change:

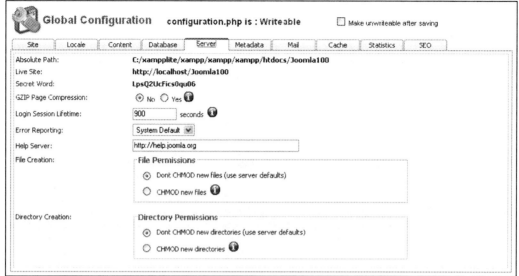

Figure 4.21: Server

- **Absolute Path**: The absolute path on your server is the path from the root directory of the server to your Joomla! installation. For example, on a local machine running under Windows, it will be C:/xampplite/xampp/htdocs/Joomla!; on a Linux server, however, it is something like /is/htdocs/wp1007226_40G0RIWV3E/www.

- **Live Site**: The Live Site is the URL by which the site is accessible on the Internet.

- **Secret Word**: This is the encoded administrator password. Refer to the Appendix to find out what to do if you forget your admin password.

- **GZIP Page Compression**: This enables you to compress pages. If the browser and web server support this function, the pages are delivered in ZIP format and unpacked by the client browser. This can substantially increase the speed of page download, especially with slow Internet connections.

- **Login Session Lifetime**: If you log on as a user, you produce a session. Even if you do not log yourself out, this session is deleted after the number of seconds that you set here.

- **Error Reporting**: With these switches, PHP's own error reporting mechanism is activated.

    o **System Default**: Here the settings from the php.ini configuration file are used.
    o **None**: Errors are not logged.
    o **Simple**: Errors and warnings are logged. This setting corresponds to the error_reporting (E_ERROR|E_WARNING|E_PARSE) parameter.

- o Maximum: Errors, warnings, and references are logged. This setting corresponds to the error_reporting (E_ALL) parameter.

- **Help Server:** Here you can register another URL for the Joomla! help server.

- **File Creation:** If files on the server are created by Joomla!, the standard rights set up on the server are applied to these files. These settings are usually sufficient. If you have problems with uploads, select the second CHMOD new files option and overwrite the server settings.

- **Directory Creation:** The setup options described for files (refer to the above point) also apply to directories.

Metadata

Metadata is data about data, for example a description of your site. Metadata plays a role with search engines. How large this role is, however, is disputed. Nevertheless, metadata represents a good way to describe your site in short and concise words. If you look at the HTML source code of a Joomla! page, you can see the following meta tags in the upper area:

```
<meta name="description" content="Joomla - the dynamic portal engine and
content management system" />
<meta name="keywords" content="Joomla, joomla" />
```

Here you can set default values as shown below:

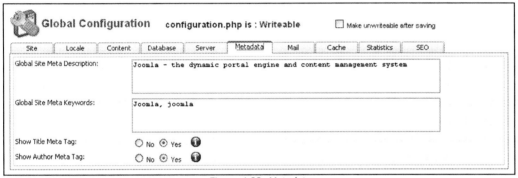

Figure 4.22: Metadata

- **Global Site Meta Description:** This description of site content is often displayed as the result by search engines. One should therefore pay special attention to this tag, because it is on the basis of this information that the surfer decides whether to visit your site or not.

- **Global Site Meta Keywords:** Keywords are the most important words in a document. They should describe the main purpose of your site. Some search engines particularly favor the keywords. Individual words are separated by commas and several words can be included between two commas with normal blanks.

The keywords should be limited to a maximum of 1,000, as more than that are not selected. Note that the use of fewer key words helps each individual word get a higher priority in the search engine. Deliberate about which the most often used keywords are and which are likely to be searched for most.

- Show Title Meta Tag: With individual content pages, the content title is blended in as a meta tag.

- Show Author Meta Tag: With individual content pages, the author's name is blended in as a meta tag.

Mail

Under this tab, you can decide the methods for sending Joomla! mail, as shown below:

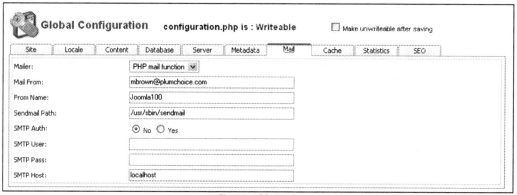

Figure 4.23: Mail

- Mailer: Here you can select whether you want to use the PHP mail function, Sendmail, or another email account, for example, Yahoo! or GMX.

- Mail From: For mail generated by Joomla!, this email address is automatically displayed as the sender.

- From Name: This name is automatically displayed as the sender for mail generated by Joomla!.

- Sendmail Path: If, instead of the PHP mail function, you want to use the Sendmail program that is presumably available to all Linux servers, you have to enter the path to the program in this textbox.

- SMTP Auth: Chose whether you want to use an external mail server.

- SMTP User: This is your user name for this email provider.

- SMTP Pass: This is your password for this email provider.

- SMTP Host: This is the SMTP server of this email provider.

Cache

A cache is a temporary storage facility. Your browser, for example, has a picture cache, which makes pictures already downloaded available faster:

Figure 4.24: Cache

Joomla! uses a similar mechanism on the server to cache pages generated by PHP. This option can drastically reduce response time with frequently visited pages.

Statistics

Here, you can enable or disable the statistics functions for your site:

Figure 4.25: Statistics

- Statistics: Here you determine whether or not to generate statistics.

- Log Content Hits by Date: Here you enable daily updated content statistics. Not just the complete page accesses, but hits on individual elements of an HTML page are also tracked here. Unfortunately, there is still no analysis program for this data at this time. By the way, very large data sets are produced within a very short time.

- Log Search Strings: This switch can give very interesting results. It collects words that visitors to your site enter into the search field.

SEO (Search Engine Optimization)

This subject is about search engine-friendly URLs. Normally a URL of a content management system looks something like http://localhost/Joomla!/index.php?option=com_contact&Itemid=3. Such URLs are not normally stored by search engines, since the search engine assumes that the content is constructed dynamically and will probably change soon.

Figure 4.26: SEO

- Search Engine Friendly URLs: With this switch you can make a search engine-friendly URL from a dynamic URL. If you set the switch to Yes, links look something like this: `http://localhost/component/option,com_contact/Itemid,47/`.

  The principle is based on a feature of the Apache web server. With its rewrite engine it can manipulate URLs at will. Besides the switch, you also have to rename the file `htaccess.txt` in the Joomla! directory to `.htaccess`. With Windows, such a renaming is only possible with certain programs, for example, the Ultraedit editor. With Linux, the renaming function is problem-free; the file, however, is subsequently no longer displayed in its FTP client (depending on the server configuration). In addition, the provider may not permit `.htaccess` files, since they represent a security risk for the web server.

- Dynamic Page Titles: No matter what, you should switch this to Yes. The title of your content is then displayed with the page name in the title bar of the browser window for each and every page access:

Figure 4.27: Dynamic Page Title

Language Manager

The Language Manager allows you to select the language for the site; it also allows you to install new language files here. This can be accomplished by uploading the language file. Joomla!, however, also allows you to load files onto the server via FTP and then to install them from the file system. The advantage with this is that you can install several language files in one processing step:

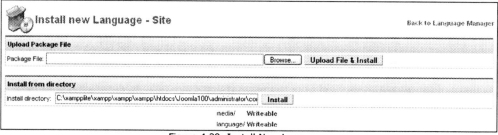

Figure 4.28: Install New Language

Media Manager

You can think of the media manager as a file explorer or an FTP program in your operating system. With it, you can upload files with the .gif, .png, .jpg, .bmp, .pdf, .swf, .doc, .xls, or .ppt extensions into different directories and administer them.

This manager is extremely convenient, especially if you have administration rights but no FTP access:

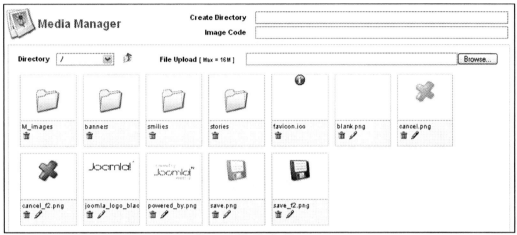

Figure 4.29: Media Manager

- **Create Directory**: You can enter a name for a new subdirectory in this field. After clicking the Create icon in the toolbar, the subdirectory is created and can be selected from the options list in the top area (directory).

- **Directory**: Select the desired directory, whose content is to be displayed.

- **File Upload**: Click Browse and select the desired file from your local hard drive. Subsequently, click the upload icon in the toolbar. The file is uploaded and displayed. Joomla! uses media as it is. Remember that it is not a good idea to put a 3 MB picture from a digital camera on your web page in that size. On the Internet, pictures should be no larger than 50 KB. There are people who still do not have high-speed access to the Internet!

You should have the following times in the back of your mind as a ground rule for the download time for 100 KB (about the size of a portal web page with pictures):

Connection type	100 Kilobyte download
DSL	Depending on the configuration, less than a second!
ISDN	About 15 seconds.
Modem (56 kbps)	About 25 seconds.

Table 4.2: Time taken to download a 100 KB file

> The maximum upload size per file depends on the PHP configuration of your provider. In my case it is 16 MB. Larger files would have to be uploaded via FTP.

- Media Bar: This bar lists the files (media). Depending on the type of file, you will find more information about each below. A stylus icon and a trash can icon are displayed. With a click on the stylus you can create a complete HTML link, which you can then copy and paste into your content. If you click on the stylus of the Joomla! logo, for instance, the Code field displays the following:

```
<img src="http://localhost/Joomla100/images/stories/asterisk.png"
align="left" hspace="6"
alt="asterisk.png" />
```

That is the HTML code to display a picture left justified with a border of 6 pixels.

Preview

Here you get a preview of your site:

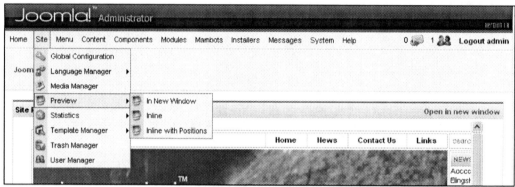

Figure 4.30: Preview

You have three options:

- In New Window: The preview is displayed in a new browser window.
- Inline: The preview is shown in the workspace, with scroll bars on the sides, if the page is too large to fit on the monitor.
- Inline with Positions: The preview is shown in the workspace, with markings for the individual module positions.

Statistics

Here you can evaluate the statistical data that was collected by enabling the feature in the Statistics tab in Global Configuration (refer the *Global Configuration* subsection) as shown in Figure 4.31:

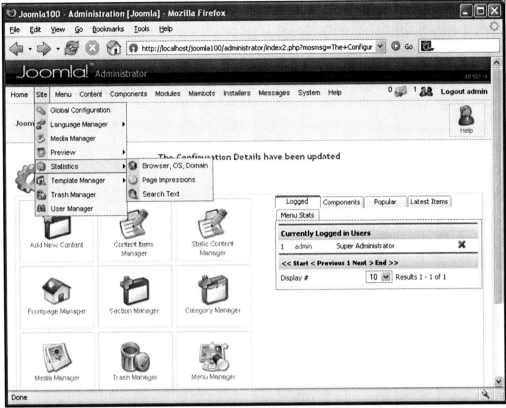

Figure 4.31: Statistics

- Browser, OS, Domain: In this area you get three tabs with information as to which browser, operating system, and domain has visited your site. This is based on the data that a browser supplies automatically to the web server. However, if any spider—for example, Google—visits your site with a program to incorporate your pages in its index, no information is retained.

- Page Impressions: Here you can see the individual pages, their creation date, and the number of hits.

- Search Text: The search words entered by your visitors are tracked here.

Template Manager

You are already familiar with the Template Manager from where we installed another template for the site in the *Changing the Template* subsection:

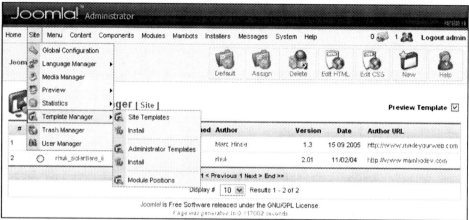

Figure 4.32: Template Manager

Site Templates

Here you can set up the templates for your site.

- Default: Pick a template and click the Default icon to use it as the default template for your site.

- Assign: Select a template and click on assign to apply it to individual pages:

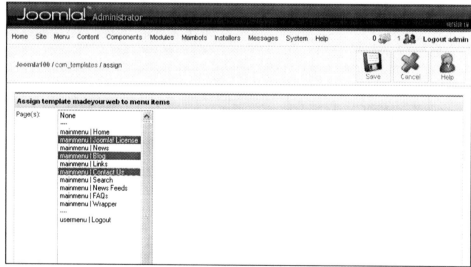

Figure 4.33: Assign

- The existing menu elements are indicated to you. Mark the appropriate elements that you want to which to apply the template. You can choose more than one by holding down the *Control* key while clicking on all desired elements one after the other.

- New: You install a new template here. There is a large selection of existing templates (http://www.mambohut.com/), which you can install either by means of an upload or via installation from a directory.

- Edit HTML/Edit CSS: Here you can work directly on the HTML or CSS source code of the selected template (as shown in Figure 4.34). I'm sure that seeing how a template is developed is interesting even for the beginner. Templates always consist of an HTML and a CSS file:

Figure 4.34: HTML Editor

> If you get involved in this, you have to know what you are doing. Knowledge of HTML and CSS is essential.

- Delete: Here you can completely delete an installed template.

Install

This is the installation mask for site templates. You wind up here if you click New in site templates or if you come directly from the Site | Templates Manager | Install menu. You can install new template file packages by uploading or by doing a directory installation.

Administrator Templates

What applies to your site, naturally also applies to the administration interface. You can assign other templates and install new ones, just as with the site templates of your non-administration interface. Currently Joomla! has only one administrator template that you can use.

Install

Just as with the site templates, you can also install administrator templates. You wind up here if you click New in administrator templates or if you come directly from the Site | Templates | Install menu. New template file packages can be installed by uploading or by a directory installation.

Module Positions

Here the display positions of the modules of a template are administered. You can define up to 56 different positions. You can display module content in these positions (also refer the *Module Menu* section in Chapter 6).

Trash Manager

The Trash Manager contains your garbage bin. It collects content and menu elements that you have disposed of by clicking on the trash icon, and files it under two tabs, Content Items and Menu Items. You can retrieve items from the trash by selecting the element and clicking Restore; if you click Delete, it is irretrievably deleted.

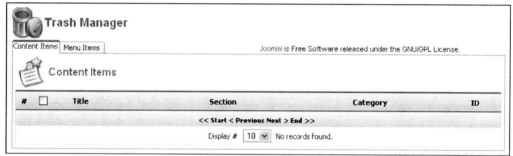

Figure 4.35: Trash Manager

User Manager

Users play a very special role on your Joomla! site. At the moment, you are the only user (*admin*) that the Joomla! administration knows. If you allow user registration on your site (see the *Global Configuration* section), there will be a lot more very shortly.

In the User Manager (illustrated in Figure 4.36), you can change, delete, block, and assign different rights to users.

In the overview list you can see the real name of the user, if the user is logged in at the moment—symbolized by a green check mark (Logged In), if the user is activated (Enabled), the UserID, the Group, his or her email address, and the date of his or her last access to your site. This refers to their last login to your *site*, not login to Joomla! administration.

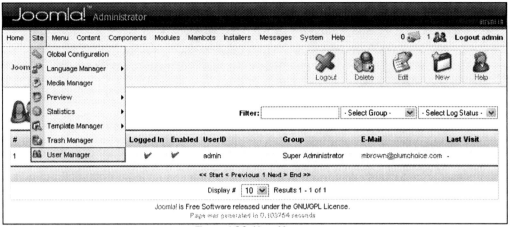

Figure 4.36: User Manager

New

With New you can create a new user. By clicking on New you get an appropriate form (Figure 4.37). The following options are available for you:

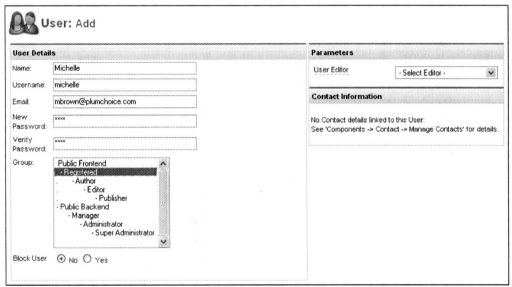

Figure 4.37: New

- Name: The real name of the user.
- Username: The user ID.
- Email: The email address. Depending on the settings in the Site | Global Configuration menu, an email address can be used just once or several times (see the *Global Configuration* section).

- Password: The password has to be entered twice for verification.
- Group: The group affiliation is divided into two large areas:
  - Users that are only allowed to visit your Public Frontend (Table 4.4)
  - Users that are allowed in the Joomla! administration (Public Backend) (Table 4.5).

All content in Joomla! can be allotted to these groups.

The front-end user group consists of the Registered used, Author, Editor, and Publisher:

Group	Rights
Registered	A registered user can log in and see some parts of the site that the visitor cannot see.
Author	The author can see everything that a registered user can. An author can write and modify his or her information. There is generally a link from the user menu for this.
Editor	The editor can do everything that an author can. An editor can write and change any information that appears in the front end.
Publisher	The publisher can do everything that an editor can. A publisher can write and change any information that appears in the front end. In addition, a publisher can decide whether information is published or not.

Table 4.4: Front-end User Groups

The back-end user group consists of the Manager, Administrator, and Super Administrator:

Group	Rights
Manager	A manager can create content and can see various information about the system. He/she is not allowed to: • Administer users Install modules and components Upgrade a user to super administrator or modify a super administrator Work on the menu option Site | Global Configuration Send a mass mailing to all users Change and/or install templates and language files
Administrator	An administrator is not allowed to: • Upgrade a user to super administrator or modify a super administrator Work on the Site | Global Configuration menu option Send a mass mailing to all users Install or change templates and language files
Super Administrator	A super administrator can execute all functions in Mambo administration. Only a super administrator can create another super administrator.

Table 4.5: Back-end User Groups

- Block User: Here you can block a user and forbid him or her access.
- Edit: With Edit you can modify a user.
- Delete: Delete allows you to delete a user.
- Force Logout: With Force Logout you can force the immediate logout of a user.

- Special Users: A special user is any user that has more rights than an author. At the moment, it is not possible to create your own user groups in Joomla!. The group, special users, is helpful in limiting content elements to this group. That can be very helpful if, for example, one wants to offer links to internal help files only to these special users.

Menu Manager

The individual menus are administered here. Joomla! has four different menus in the sample data (main menu, other menu, top menu, and user menu).

Each menu is coupled with a module, which is administered in the **Module Manager** (see Chapter 6). The four menus are shown to you in the Menu Manager workspace and in the menu bar (see Figure 4.38).

You can access the existing menus from the menu bar or by clicking the respective menu item icon in the Menu Manager. The editing steps are the same for all menus:

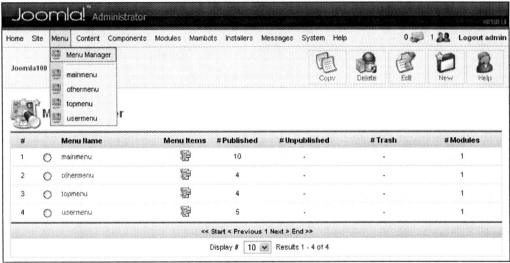

Figure 4.38: Menu Manager

Customize Existing Menu

Go to Site | Menu Manager | mainmenu (Figure 4.39). The first published menu entry on this list is shown as the starting page of your site. At the moment this is the front page. But you can make any other element the starting page:

Figure 4.39: The Main Menu in Menu Manager

New

This allows you to create a new menu. We will do this in the next section.

Edit

Here you can modify an existing menu, for example, the Links. Clicking on Links, takes you to the form for modification of menu elements as shown in Figure 4.40.

In the left area, you can set up the details and on the right the parameters. The number and the type of parameters depend on the type of the menu entry:

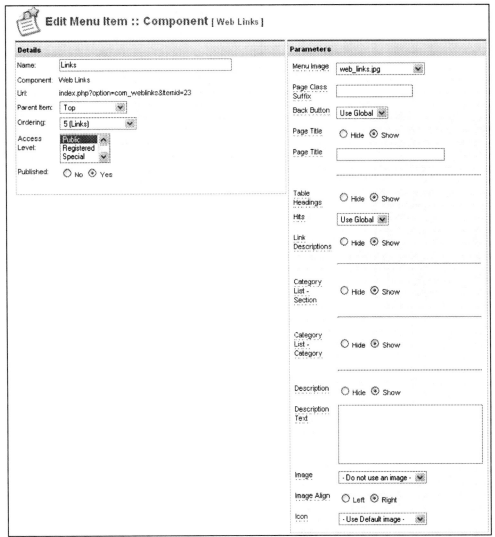

Figure 4.40: Edit Menu Item

Details

- Name: This is the name of the menu that appears on your site.

- Component: This gives you the type of content hidden behind the menu entry. This setting is specified while creating the menu entry. In our case, the web Links component is being addressed.

- Url: This is the part following the domain with which you access your site. In this case, it is index.php?option=com_weblinks&Itemid=23.

Parent Item: The parent item is the superordinate element to this menu. Top means at the top level; all other entries represent existing menu entries. If, for example, you arrange and store Links under News, the display in the Menu Manager (Figure 4.42) and the display on your site changes. On the site, the menu entry Links has now slipped into News. You first have to click News, in order to see the Links entry.

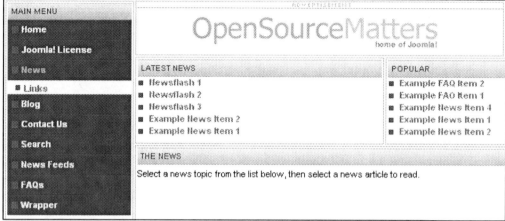

Figure 4.41: Tree Structures on the Site

This way your site can be structured like a directory tree very simply and effectively, as shown in Figure 4.42:

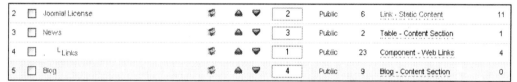

Figure 4.42: Tree Structures in Menu Manager

- Ordering: By clicking on the upward and downward pointing triangles you can modify the sort sequence within the menu. In the Ordering field you can do this in a listing. That way you don't have to keep clicking on the triangles.

- Access Level: You can decide whether this menu is to be made available to all visitors (Public), only registered users (Registered), or a special circle of users (Special).

- Published: You can publish or lock the menu here.

Parameters

- Menu Image: Here you can specify a picture to be displayed along with the menu. To do this, the image must be in the root directory of the Media Manager (/images/stories/). The position in which the picture is displayed depends on the template; in this case, it is displayed on the left, next to the menu entry.

- Page Class Suffix: Here you can specify a class from the CSS file of your template, with which this menu entry is to be formatted.

- Back Button: Here you can assign the global settings for the back button, display it explicitly, or hide it.

- Page Title: With this, you can display or hide the title of the page.

- Page Title: Here you can specify the page title as shown in the following figure. If you don't enter anything here, the name of the link is assumed:

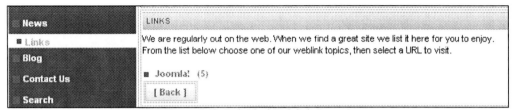

Figure 4.43: Individual Web link Area—1

- Table Headings: Here you can display or hide the heading above the listing.

- Hits: The hits on the links are displayed in the link list. You can change these in the global settings or via an appropriate selection.

- Link Descriptions: Here you can enable the description that is displayed under a link in the link list.

- Category List - Section/Category: If you click on Links, you can see the default text or your own text if specified in the parameters. This list can be turned on and off with two switches.

- Description: Here you can switch the general description of the link components on or off.

- Description Text: Here you can overwrite the standard text of the link components with individual text.

- Image: Here you can specify a picture from the root directory of the Media Manager (/images/stories/) to be displayed along with the text. Depending on the image align parameter, this picture is displayed on the left or right of the description text, as illustrated in Figure 4.44:

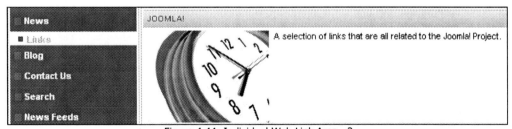

Figure 4.44: Individual Web Link Area—2

- Image Align: This is the setting for the alignment of the picture (see Figure 4.44).
- Icon: This is the icon that is displayed to the left of the list of links.

Publish

If you select one or more menu elements and click the Publish icon, they are published.

Unpublish

If you click Unpublish, marked entries are no longer displayed on the site.

Move

This is used for moving menu entries to a different menu. Select one or several menu elements and click Move. This opens a form listing the available menus (Figure 4.45). Select the menu into which you would like to move the marked menu entries:

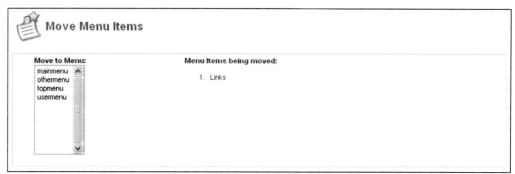

Figure 4.45: Move Menu

Copy

In order to copy menu entries, select one or several menu elements and click Copy. A form is opened, listing the available menus. Select the menu into which you want to copy the marked menu entries.

Trash

In order to throw menu entries into the trash can, select one or several menu elements and click on the trash icon. The marked menu entries are then dumped into the trash can.

Create a New Menu

Let's create a new menu with the name **Joomla_book** and a link to http://www.joomla.org/. Go to Menu | Menu Manager | New:

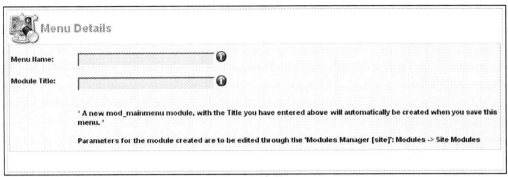

Figure 4.46: New

- Menu Name: The name of the menu. This name does not show up on the site, it only serves to make a connection between module and menu. I am selecting Joomla_book.

- Module Title: The name of the module as it appears on the website. I am selecting Joomla_book. After clicking Save, Joomla! produces a new menu with the given name (Figure 4.47):

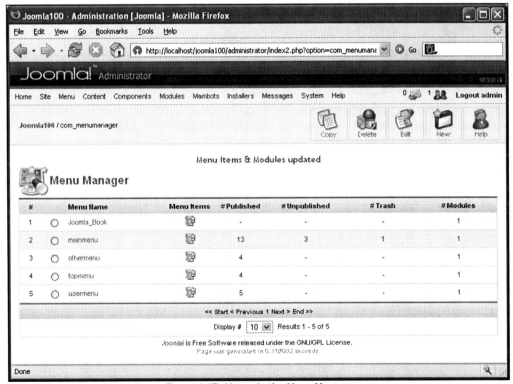

Figure 4.47: Menus in the Menu Manager

Now click the menu items icon or call up Site | Menu Manager | Joomla_book in the menu bar. You will see the overview mask about the content of the Joomla_book menu. Since no content is there yet, click New.

You can now select content from four different areas from the selection mask that appears on your screen (Figure 4.48):

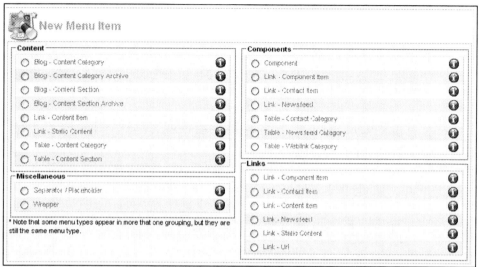

Figure 4.48: New Menu Item

Content

Content is divided into blogs, links, and tables. A **blog**, in the Mambo sense, is a list of entries with a hook and a read more link. A **link** refers directly to a certain piece of content. A **table** is a list of links. A **section** is a grouping element. Within a section there can be **categories**. You can find the meaning of the options in Table 4.6:

Option	Relevance
Blog - Content Category	Blog page that relates to a category (for example, latest news).
Blog - Content Category Archive	Blog page that relates to archived categories (no entries yet).
Blog - Content Section	Blog page that relates to a section (for example, news).
Blog - Content Section Archive	Blog page that relates to archived sections (no entries yet).
Link - Content Item	Link to a content element (for example, Sample News Item 2).
Link - Static Content	Direct link to a static content page. There is a static content page in the sample data (*Joomla License Guidelines*).
Table - Content Category	Link to a table that represents the content of a category.
Table - Content Section	Link to a table that represents the content of a section.

Table 4.6: New Menu Item—Content Options

Miscellaneous

Option	Relevance
Separator / Placeholder	Insertion of a hyphen into the menu.
Wrapper	Here an external page can be displayed within the site; for example, parts of your old site or an already existing guest book.

Table 4.7: New Menu Item—Miscellaneous

Components

Option	Relevance
Link - Component Item	A link to a component (for example, login)
Link - Contact Item	A link to an entry in the contact list
Link - Newsfeed	A link to a piece of news in the news section
Table - Contact Category	A link to a table that contains entries of a contact category
Table - Newsfeed Category	A link to a table that contains entries of a newsfeed category
Table - Weblink Category	A link to a table that contains entries of a weblink category

Table 4.8: New Menu Item—Components

Links

Option	Relevance
Link - Component Item	A link to a component (for example, login).
Link - Contact Item	A link to an entry in the contact list.
Link - Content Item	A link to a content item (for example, Sample News Item 2).
Link - Newsfeed	A link to a piece of news from the news section.
Link - Static Content	Direct link to a static content page. There is a static content page in the sample data (*Joomla! License Guidelines*).
Link - Url	Link to a URL (for example, `http://www.joomla.org`).

Table 4.9: New Menu Item—Links

In order to insert a link to a URL, you mark the last selection field Link - Url and click Next in the toolbar. You can specify the details and the parameters of the link in the form that opens on your screen (Figure 4.49):

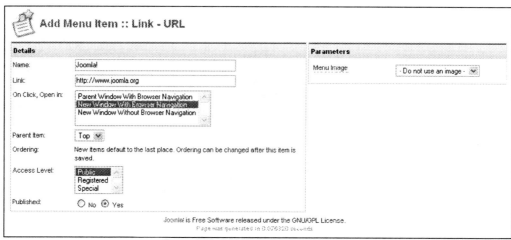

Figure 4.49: Add Menu Item :: Link - URL

- Name: Name of the link that appears in the menu (Joomla!).

- Link: The link to the page (http://www.joomla.org).

- On Click, Open in: What is to happen, if someone clicks on the link? Should the target be executed in the same browser window, a new browser window with navigation, or a new browser window without navigation?

- Parent Item: Should the menu entry be a submenu of a superordinate entry?

- Access Level: Should the menu entry be visible to Public (visitors), Registered, or Special groups?

- Published: Should the menu be published?

If you click Apply, your data is stored. By clicking on Save, the data is stored and the dialog is closed. Now you have created the menu and provided it with a link. Before it can be displayed, you have to publish the module in the Module Manager. Click Modules | Site Modules (Figure 4.50) and then Published:

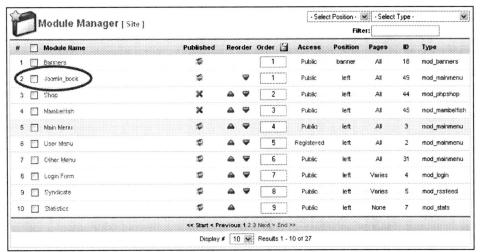

Figure 4.50: Site Modules

You can change the position of the menu with the help of the blue triangles. If you now call up your site, your new Joomla_book menu should be displayed above the Main Menu (Figure 4.51):

Figure 4.51: New Menu Joomla_book

On clicking the Joomla! link, a browser window with navigation should open and the project website should be displayed.

Installers Menu

All installers are summarized in the Installers menu:

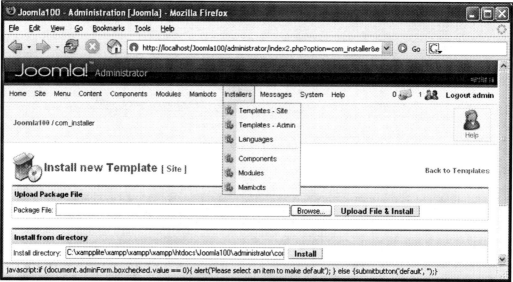

Figure 4.52: Installers

The menu branches out to installers for:

- Site templates
- Admin templates
- Languages
- Components
- Modules
- Mambots

Messages Menu

The Messages menu manages administrator messages. Joomla! has a small communication network that enables sending of messages within the administrators group. In addition, system messages are also delivered; for example, if someone has posted a new content element.

Inbox

The messages for the administrator are collected here. By clicking the New icon, you can send a new message to users who are permitted access to Joomla! administration.

Configuration

Here you can configure the communication system.

- Lock Inbox: You can lock your mailbox and thus suppress the receipt of messages. This is OK if you are the only administrator; otherwise you should leave your inbox open.
- Mail me a new Message: This feature is really useful. Joomla! sends the messages to the email address given in the user administration.

System Menu

The System menu consists of only one element. This is a global checking-in of all content elements in process.

Global Check-In

If an entitled user calls up the editing mode of a content element, then the Global Checkin element is checked out. Only the entitled user may work on this element. During processing, other users will see a lock icon in front of the name of the element. If the document is stored after the change, it is then automatically checked in again and the lock icon disappears.

If the user closes his or her browser window, or if there is a sudden break in their Internet connection, the element remains checked out and cannot be changed any more.

Here the Global Check-In comes into play. By clicking this menu option, all elements in process are checked in and you receive an appropriate list of the elements:

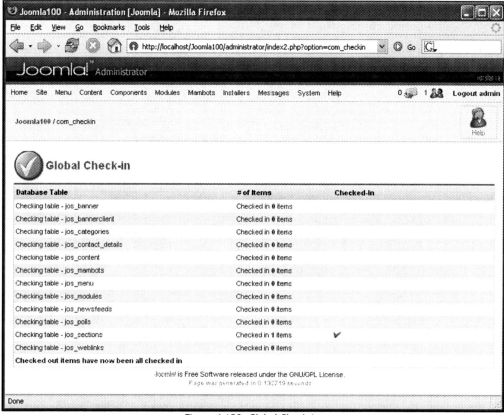

Figure 4.130: Global Check-in

The disadvantage of global checking-in is the fact that *all* elements get checked in. If one person is just about to change some particular element, this element is also checked in and someone else can also make changes to it at the same time. Be careful with this function and pay attention to who is online.

Summary

In this chapter we began customizing Joomla!. We began by experimenting with the different Joomla! templates. We configured Joomla! administration and also took a look at some of the Joomla! menus. We will continue with our tour of the Joomla! menus in the next couple of chapters.

5
Managing Content

This chapter discusses one of the most important functions performed by a CMS. This is, as you would have guessed, Content Management. The Content menu contains all content areas. Content is organized by the following structure in Joomla!:

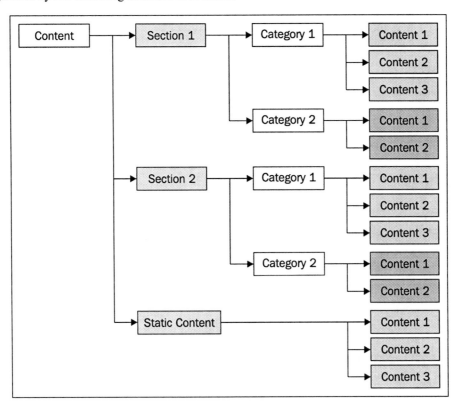

This structure can be compared with the directory tree on your hard drive. You can create as many sections and categories, and as much static content as you desire. If you archive individual elements, then the structure is completely transferred to the archive.

This fixed structure has advantages and disadvantages. The biggest advantage in my opinion is that a structure is predetermined and thus the administrator must keep a certain hierarchy. This makes it easier to grasp an overview of the website.

The disadvantage is that the two-stage structure cannot be changed and some administrators thereby feel limited when individualizing their website.

The Content menu makes different workspaces available in order to work on content and structures (Figure 5.1):

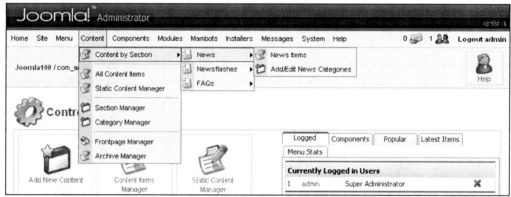

Figure 5.1: Content Menu

Content by Section

Content is sorted according to **Section**. The next step in the structure is **Category**; the actual content then follows (**Item**).

Section

Underneath the Content by Section menu, all available sections are shown. You can add as many sections as you want.

Category

Underneath each section you again find a listing of the existing categories, as well as the option to work on these categories.

Add/Edit Section Category

Here you can create a new category, by clicking New. Let us use the Joomlabook category as an example.

- Category Title: The title of the category that appears in the title line of the browser.

- Category Name: The name of the category that will be displayed on the site.

- Section: The section in which the category is to be created, in our case, News.

- Image: Here you can select a picture that will be displayed when the site is accessed. The picture has to be in the root directory of the Media Manager (/images/stories/). I have selected articles.jpg.

- Image Position: Here you can select the orientation of the picture.

- Ordering: Here the order of the category is determined. In this case it is a new element, which by default is integrated at the end. The sequence can be changed after it has been saved once.

- Access Level: Who has access to this element?

- Published: Should the category be published immediately?

- Description: This is the description of the category. If you selected the WYSIWYG editor in Site | Global Configuration | Site (refer the *Global Configuration* section in Chapter 4), a basic word processor will pop up:

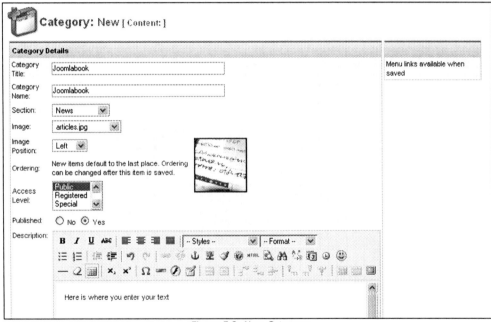

Figure 5.2: New Category

You can only specify parameters for this category after it has been saved once by clicking Save. You wind up in the Category Manager and will see the new Joomlabook category (Figure 5.3):

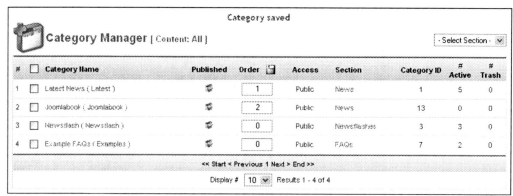

#		Category Name	Published	Order	Access	Section	Category ID	# Active	# Trash
1		Latest News (Latest)		1	Public	News	1	5	0
2		Joomlabook (Joomlabook)		2	Public	News	13	0	0
3		Newsflash (Newsflash)		0	Public	Newsflashes	3	3	0
4		Example FAQs (Examples)		0	Public	FAQs	7	2	0

<< Start < Previous 1 Next > End >>

Display # 10 Results 1 - 4 of 4

Figure 5.3: Category Manager

Content Item: After we have created a new category, we want to insert content into this category. Click Content | Content by Section | News | News Items.

You are now put into the Content Items Manager and can see the four standard entries of the Joomla! sample data.

Click New in order to be transferred to the content item workspace:

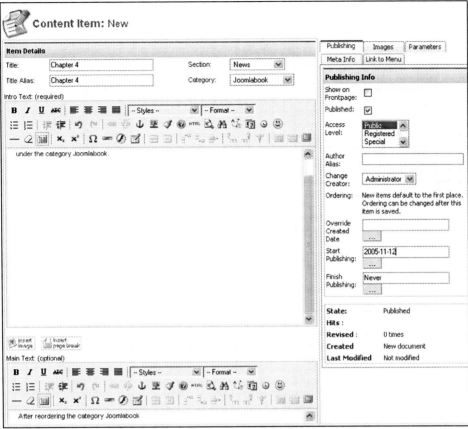

Figure 5.4: Content Item Workspace

You will see a form consisting of several areas. Actual content is located in the left panel; in the right panel are several tabs with different parameters. It is sufficient to fill out the left side at this time in order to write information.

- Title: Title of the item of information.

- Title Alias: Alias of the title.

- Section: Here you can select the section under which the message is to be displayed. Select News.

- Category: Depending on the section selected, the existing categories are shown. Select Joomlabook.

- Intro Text/Main Text: Here you enter your actual information. The intro text has to be filled out; the main text is optional. With one click on Preview, you can see a preview of your text in a separate browser window (Figure 5.5):

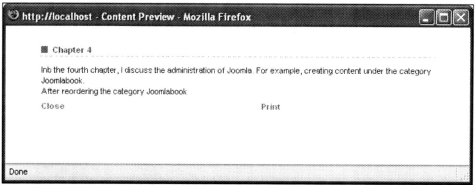

Figure 5.5: Content Preview

- In order to integrate the new information immediately into the Joomla_Book menu, you now click the tab Link to Menu:

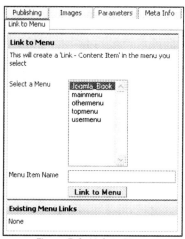

Figure 5.6: Link to Menu

You will see a list of the available menus.

If you select the Joomla_Book menu, enter Chapter 4 in the Menu Item Name field and click Link to Menu. The page is newly configured and you will see in the lower part of existing menu links that your information has been added to the menu. Click Save.

If you look at your site, you will notice that the Joomla_Book menu has an additional entry. After a click on the entry you will see your information:

Figure 5.7: The Created Information

All Content Items

The All Content Items menu leads you to the Content Items Manager:

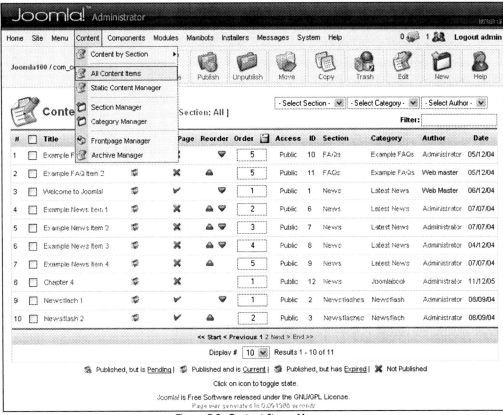

Figure 5.8: Content Items Manager

The Content Items Manager is the central configuration station for all types of content. You can filter the displayed content by section (area), category, and author in three option lists in the information area. In addition, you will find a search field, with which you can search the titles.

In the lower part is the navigation bar, with the assistance of which you can leaf through the contents. In the option list, you can select the number of entries you want to see. The setting that you entered in Site | Global Configuration | Site acts as the default. The list is sorted by title, section, category, and author.

There is a checkbox in front of the title, with which you can select those elements that you want to work on. If you select the checkbox in front of the headline, all elements of the list are selected.

- Title: The Title is a link to the edit mode for Content Items (Figure 5.4).
- Published: Published indicates whether the entry is published (green icon) or not (red cross). Besides these two symbols, the possibility also exists that the publication period has run out and the element is stored in the archives.
- Frontpage: Frontpage (see the *Frontpage Manager* section later on in the chapter) indicates whether the entry is published on the front page (green check mark) or not (red cross).
- Reorder: Reorder lets you move the entries within a section by clicking the blue arrows.
- Order: Order lets you execute this sorting by input of a number.
- Access: Access lets you see green public links. By clicking one of these links you can change the access rights between the three groups: Public, Registered, and Special. In addition there are also symbols for pending (waiting status) and expired (out of date).
- ID: ID is the record number in the MySQL table. This ID will show up again in the URL for this entry.
- Section: Section is the area to which this entry is assigned. You wind up in the Section Manager if you click this link.
- Category: Category is the category in which this entry is classified. Clicking the link takes you to the Category Manager.
- Author: Author gives the author of the entry. Click this link and you end up in the User Manager.
- Date: Date gives the creation date of the entry.

Static Content Manager

The Static Content Manager looks like the Content Manager. However, it does not have any fields for sections and categories.

Static content means something similar to a static HTML page. Normally, content elements and items of information are created and sorted into categories and sections within Joomla!. The content elements have a dynamic character, since they are usually displayed in a chronological order. Static content is fixed and refers to content that rarely changes and that has no chronological connection to other content elements. You can find a sample of static content in the sample data, for example, the license guidelines for using Joomla! (Joomla! License Guidelines):

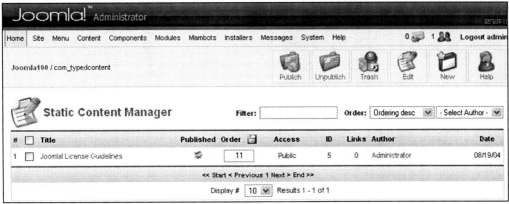

Figure 5.9: Static Content Manager

Click New and we'll run an example through the Static Content Manager by creating your imprint.

You will see an input mask, just like in Figure 5.9. This time, however, there will be a text field. Enter imprint as title or alias title and enter your address as text. Click Apply.

Content Parameters

This section discusses the different parameters associated with the content. These parameters are divided among five different tabs, Publishing, Images, Parameters, Meta Info, and Link to Menu.

Publishing

Parameters that have to do with publishing are defined with this.

- State: Current status (currently published).
- Published: Checkbox to change the status.
- Access Level: Access rights for the three user groups.
- Author Alias: Here you can enter a pseudonym for the author.
- Change Creator: Here you can change the creator of the information.

Figure 5.10: Publishing

- Override Created Date: At this point you can change the creation date of the item. Clicking on the three dots will get the graphic calendar to help you with the input of dates, as shown in Figure 5.11.

- Start Publishing: This serves to specify the start date of the publication. By default, content is published immediately. By clicking the three dots, a graphic calendar is displayed for input assistance (as shown in Figure 5.11).

- Finish Publishing: Here you can determine the expiration date of the content. The default is that content is *never* purged. Click the three dots to call up the graphic calendar again (as shown in Figure 5.11):

Figure 5.11: Calendar Element

- Content ID: The record number.
- Hits: How often the content has been accessed.
- Version: The document has the version number 1. Each time it is saved, the version number is increased by one.

Images

You can assign any picture from the Media Manager to any piece of content. If it is not available yet in the Media Manager, you can upload it while working on the content by clicking Upload:

Figure 5.12: Upload

You cannot, however, indicate a target subdirectory for this type of file upload. Select a subdirectory and click on a picture as shown. You will see a preview of the picture on the right side and now you just have to click Add. In the window below it, you can now see the filename:

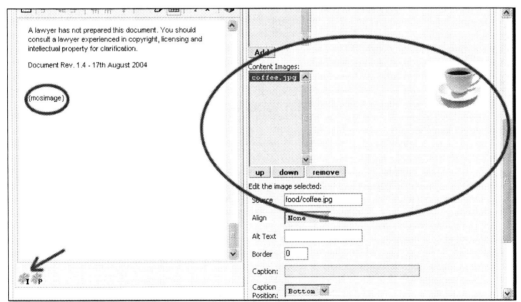

Figure 5.13: Mapping a Picture into the Text

If you click on it, the picture preview appears. You can assign as many image files as you wish. You still have to specify the position in the text where the picture is to be displayed. To do that, you need a Mambot with the name {mosimage}. Refer to Chapter 6 for more information about Mambots. Position the cursor at the position where the picture is to appear. Either type {mosimage} manually or click the insert images icon under the text window. You have to insert one {mosimage} command for each picture that you want to insert. The images will be displayed in the order that they are selected.

In addition to the insert image icon you will also see an insert page break icon. This is a {mospagebreak} Mambot that represents a page break. If you have text that you want to distribute over several pages, you have to insert this Mambot.

For the display on the site, Joomla! automatically produces a navigation bar to help you scroll through the content:

Figure 5.14: Navigation Bar

Parameters

In the Parameter tab you can overwrite the parameters that were defined in Site | Global Configuration for this content:

Figure 5.15: Parameters

Meta Info

In this tab you can enter a specific description and keywords for every page as metadata. The texts entered here are then inserted into the meta tags in the HTML source code of the message in addition to the metadata specified in the global configuration.

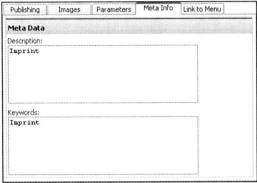

Figure 5.16: Meta Info

Link to Menu

Automatic links to a menu, for example, the Main Menu, can be created here (see *Static Content Manager* section). The site displays multipaged content (Figure 5.17 and Figure 5.18):

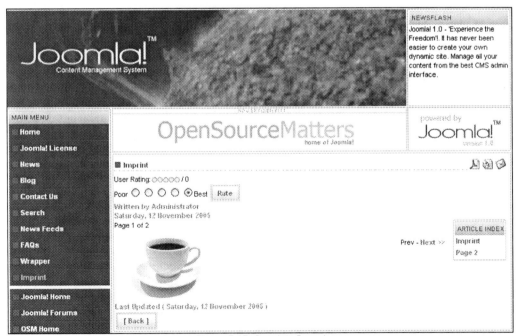

Figure 5.17: Imprint: Page 1

The evaluation and other parameters can also be faded individually.

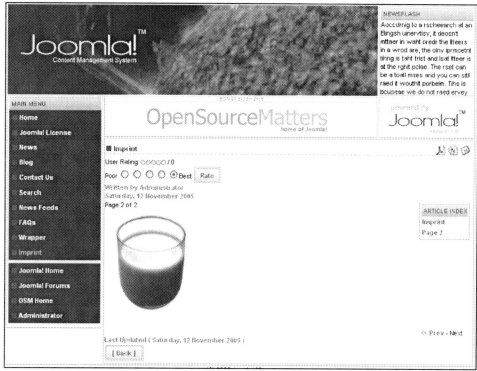

Figure 5.18: Imprint – Page 2

Section Manager

In Section Manager you can work on the sections. In the overview table, the information that you already know from the other lists is displayed, but in this case it is expanded to the number of total categories contained—how many are active and how many are in the trash can (Figure 5.19):

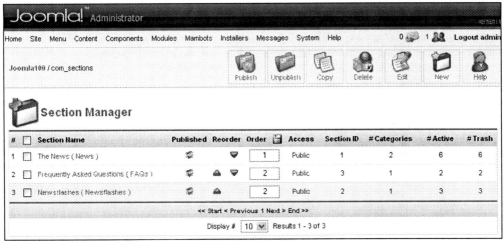

Figure 5.19: Section Manager

Category Manager

In the Category Manager you can work on categories. Here you will also see familiar information in the overview table: how many of the categories are active, and how many are in the trash can (Figure 5.20):

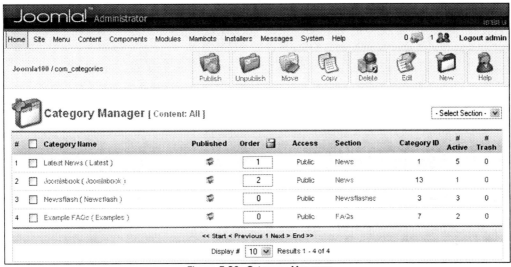

Figure 5.20: Category Manager

Frontpage Manager

The Frontpage Manager has a special task. The frontpage is the title page of your website. Selected content is here represented in blog form. Blog form means the representation of several pieces of information with their introduction text and a Read More link in several columns. You can select your content for the frontpage from all of the content, regardless of category and section. Whether content appears on the frontpage is specified by you in the Content Manager.

Figure 5.21: Frontpage Manager

The Frontpage Manager as illustrated above has the same structure as the Content Items Manager (Figure 5.8). You can also sort the individual content items within the Frontpage Manager.

Archive Manager

The idea of archives is not to delete outdated content, but to preserve it for posterity:

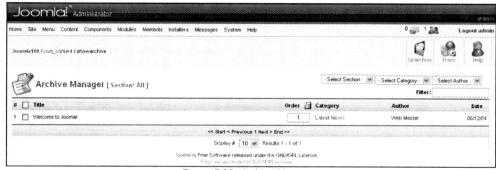

Figure 5.22: Archive Manager

Laid out like the Content Items Manager (Figure 5.8), the Archive Manager (Figure 5.22) collects all content that is archived by clicking the Archive icon.

Archives can be displayed by the Menu Manager in, for example, a New Archives menu. In addition, there are the following possibilities, as illustrated in Figure 4.48 of Chapter 4:

- Blog - Content Category Archive: Display of a particular archive category
- Blog - Content Section Archive: Display of a section

Summary

We discussed content organization and document management in Joomla! in this chapter. We went about adding, editing, archiving—in short, managing—content and categories. We now move to the next chapter, which will cover the building blocks of Joomla!, Components, Modules, and Mambots.

6

Components, Modules, and Mambots

This chapter discusses what is probably the most important topic in the book, the Joomla! components, modules, and Mambots. It is possible to run a Joomla! page without understanding these features, but knowing the possibilities of inbuilt and additional components, Modules and Mambots brings the full power to your Joomla! driven website. Let us start with the inbuilt features.

Components Menu

In software development, a component means a program that contains business logic, is accessible through defined interfaces, and sometimes also has a user interface. Imagine a simple component acting like a black box: You put something in the front and something comes out of the back; you don't have to know what happens inside. What matters is that you can use the black box for completely different purposes.

Components can be designed very generally and bundled into handy packages. This idea of a software component is similar in Joomla!. Business logic, such as banner administration or a forum, is written generally and in Joomla! works in concert with all the templates and the Joomla! administration.

Installing and Uninstalling Components

Anyone can write a component, package it according to certain rules, and integrate it as per Joomla! installation into his or her website:

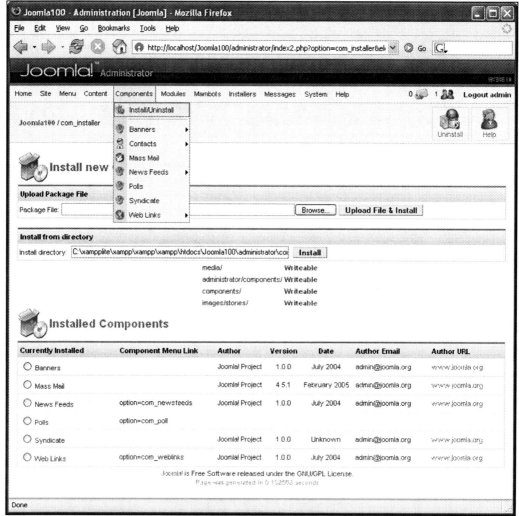

Figure 6.1: Install/Uninstall

The installation, as with the template files, is executed either by file or FTP upload of the component package.

The necessary database tables are created during the installation. The installation fields indicate whether the necessary directories for the installation, media/administrator/components/, components/, and images/stories/ are provided with write rights.

Installed Components

In the Installed Components workspace, you can see a list of components installed by default.

- Currently Installed: Name of the component
- Component Menu Link: Necessary parameter in the URL to access the component; only components addressable from the homepage need this link
- Author: The author of the component
- Version: The component version
- Date: The creation date
- Author Email: Email address of the author
- Author URL: Website of the author

Banner

The banner component makes the display of advertising banners on your site possible. Banner switching with Joomla! is accounted for, on the basis of bought banner impressions. Each time your site is accessed, another banner is displayed. Every display counts as an impression. The banner is clickable and links to the site of the customer.

The banner component offers customer and banner administration. By default, the so-called full banner is sent. A full banner is 468 x 60 pixels large and should not substantially exceed 20 KB in file size. The format is .gif, .jpg, or .png.

Let's walk through a banner switch. Create or copy a banner with the dimensions of 468 x 60 pixels as shown:

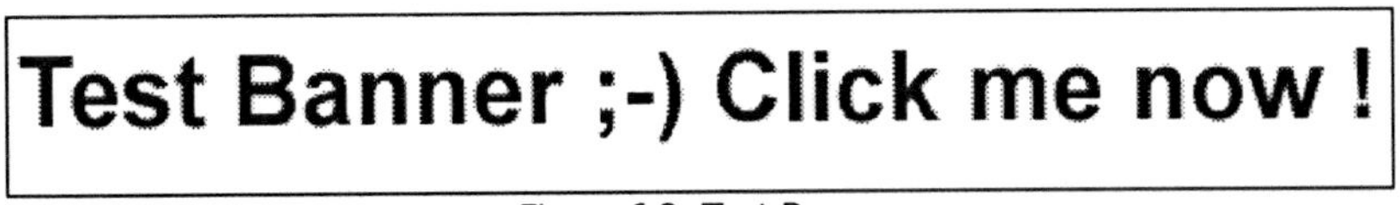

Test Banner ;-) Click me now !

Figure 6.2: Test Banner

Manage Clients

Before you can switch a banner, you need a customer. If you click Components | Banner | Manage Clients | New, you are opening a new customer account. Store it by clicking Save.

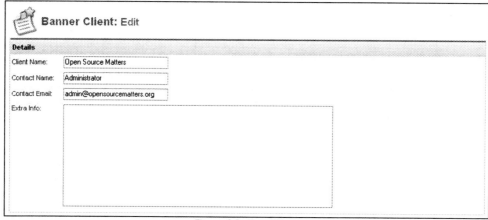

Figure 6.3: New Client

The Banner Client Manager, where you wind up, now displays your new customer as well as the number of active banners of this customer.

Manage Banners

In order to assign a banner to the customer, click on Components | Banners | Manage Banners. You can see the Banner Manager, which gives you an overview of the existing banners as shown:

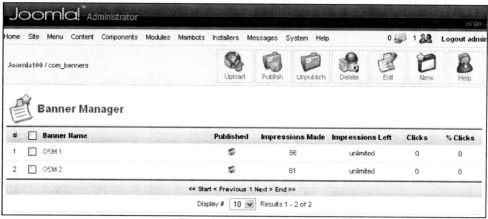

Figure 6.4: Banner Manager

- Banner Name: Name of the banner
- Published: Whether the banner is published or not
- Impressions Made: Number of impressions to date
- Impressions Left: Number of remaining impressions

- Clicks: Clicks on the banner
- % Clicks: Proportion of impressions to clicks

In order to switch to a new banner, you first click on the upload icon. A small upload window opens for uploading banners. The banners don't emerge in the Media Manager, but are stored in the directory /image/banner/. If you want to delete a banner again, that can only be done currently by an FTP client. After you have uploaded the banner, click New and fill out the banner details as shown in Figure 6.5:

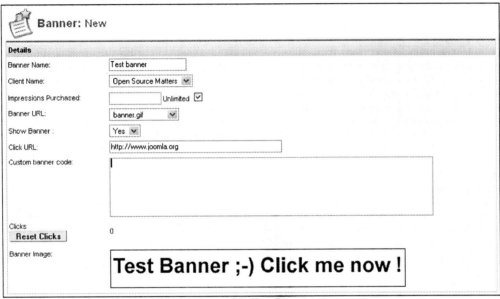

Figure 6.5: New Banner

- Banner Name: Give the banner a meaningful name so that you will recognize it in the Banner Manager.
- Client Name: Select the client from the list of current clients.
- Impressions Purchased: Enter the number of purchased pageviews or check the Unlimited box.
- Banner URL: Select the newly uploaded banner from the list of the existing banners. After the selection, you will see a preview of the banner in the lower area.
- Show Banner: Should the banner be published?
- Click URL: Enter the URL of the site to which the banner is supposed to be linking.
- Custom banner code: Here you can enter a special banner code from affiliate programs.

Since this mask is also designed for the editing of banners, you will find an indicator of the clicks already executed and a reset button, which sets the counter back to zero.

After clicking the Save icon, your banner should be in rotation and displayed on the site:

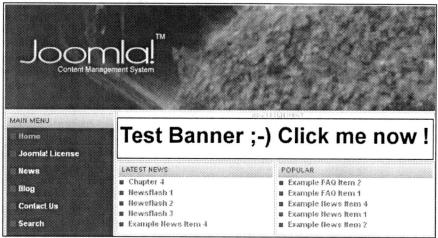

Figure 6.6: Client Banner on the Homepage

Contacts

It is often difficult for a customer surfing your site to contact you. Many employees normally work in different departments in companies and often only one address (for example, info@company.com) is shown on the homepage or on a form and the customer has no idea who receives it.

To avoid this, Joomla! makes it possible to specify contact categories. You can register contact persons for your company. Joomla! then produces a contact form for every coworker on the site.

Manage Contacts

Click Components | Contacts | Manage Contacts. You will see the Contact Manager and a contact from the sample data as shown:

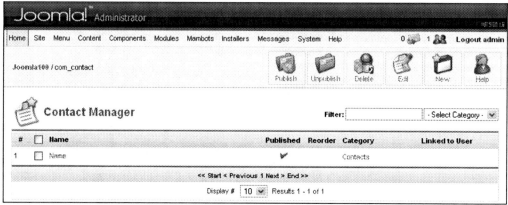

Figure 6.7: Contact Manager

Checkmark the sample contact and click Unpublish. You can create a new contact with New as shown in Figure 6.8.

- **Category:** Select the contact category here. At the moment, the sample category Contacts is available.

- **Linked to User:** With this option you can connect a contact with a user account. Since I have already created an account for myself, I can now select it.

You can populate the remaining fields with the appropriate address data and add some text as miscellaneous information. In order to store it, click on the save icon:

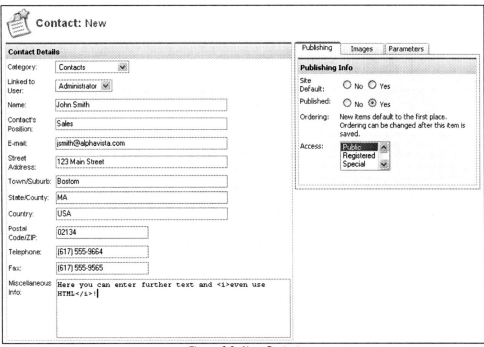

Figure 6.8: New Contact

Since we did not publish the sample entry, there is currently only one contact in the system. There is no necessity to show categories. Because of this, the Contact link branches immediately to that one entry. If you publish the sample entry again, the following window pops up:

Figure 6.9: Contact Category List

The existing contact categories are displayed here. After clicking on the category, you get a table with the existing contacts:

Figure 6.10: Contact List within a Category

If you now click on the name, you get the contact form:

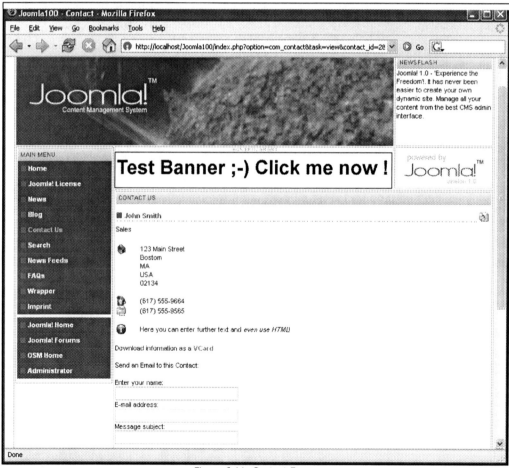

Figure 6.11: Contact Form

I'm sure you noticed the tabs when you created the contact. In the Publishing tab (as illustrated in Figure 6.8) you can specify the default contact (Site Default).

In addition, you can specify the publication, ordering, and access rights:

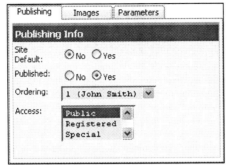

Figure 6.12: Publishing

Under Images, as shown in Figure 6.13 you can assign a picture to each contact. Photograph your staff and let your customers know what the guy they are writing to looks like:

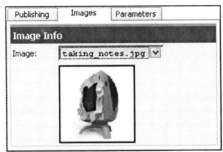

Figure 6.13: Images

Under Parameters, the contact form can finally be completely individualized. You can even change the icons next to the telephone numbers. The available icons are in the /images/M_images/ subdirectory and cannot be accessed via the Media Manager.

Contacts Categories

In the Category Manager for contacts, you can create new categories and modify existing ones:

Figure 6.14: Category Manager

An editing form pops up after clicking the Edit icon or the category name:

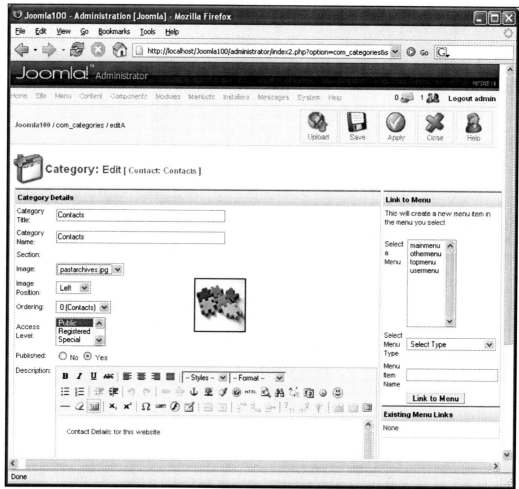

Figure 6.15: Edit

You can assign a picture here and you can make changes to the description with the help of the WYSIWYG editor. In the space on the right, the category can immediately be assigned to a particular menu (Select Menu Type). You can also decide whether you want to have the table listing or a listing of all categories first.

Mass Mail

Delight your users with mass mail! As cynical as this sentence sounds in the age of massive spam emailing, mass mailing is the best way of contacting one's registered users. The Mass Mail component gives you the tool to do it.

- Group: Here you can select the user group to which the mass mailing is to be addressed.

- Mail to Child Groups: If you put a checkmark here, the subgroups of the selected user groups are also addressed.

- Send in HTML mode: Check this if you want to send the mass mail in HTML format. HTML mail is becoming more and more popular. You should, however, keep in mind that many email clients can switch the HTML display off. For different reasons, some users may not even like HTML mail.

- Subject: This is the subject of your email.

- Message: This is the actual text.

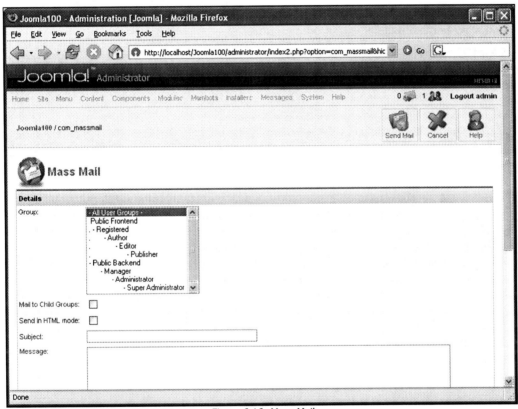

Figure 6.16: Mass Mail

For mass mailing, set the mail settings in Site | Global Configuration | Mail correctly. If you want to send a mass mail from your local environment, but are not running a mail server, then you can also register the SMTP server of your mail provider in the mass mail settings.

News Feeds

News feeds are a terrific thing. The ever-growing information abundance on the Internet makes it necessary to test effective organizational methods. If you regularly have to visit twenty web pages to check what's new, it takes up too much time. With fifty or hundred it is absolutely hopeless to try to keep an overview. News feeds are an attempt to solve this problem. What they are and how they are produced is covered in the *Syndicates* section.

With the News Feed component you can merge feeds from other pages into your pages. To do that, a Category Manager and a Content Manager are at your disposal. The sample data already has several categories and numerous news feeds incorporated. Integrate your own news feed. You can use a search engine for this purpose or look for the small XML button at the sites that you visit.

Manage Newsfeeds

Click on Components | News Feeds | Manage New Feeds | New.

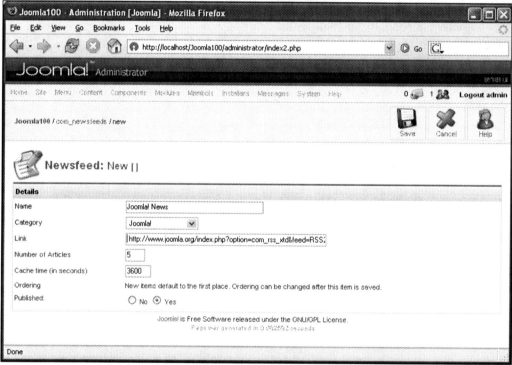

Figure 6.17: New News Feed

- Name: This is the name of the news feed that appears on your page.
- Category: Select a suitable category from the existing ones.
- Link: This is the link to the news feed.

- Number of Articles: This refers to the number of articles that are to be merged.
- Cache time (in seconds): How long should the break between checks for new items be (in seconds)?
- Ordering: This is the sequence new news feeds will start at, by default. The sequence can be changed after it has been saved once.
- Published: Should it be published immediately?

Your new news feed, as long as you have Internet access, is displayed on your site:

Figure 6.18: News Feeds on your Website

However, should you wish to read newsfeeds in languages with non-ASCII modified latin characters (German, Polish, Czech, Croat, Turkish, and so on), there is a problem with umlauts in Joomla! version 1.0.0. In order to repair this, make the following changes in the `[PathtoJoomla!]/components/com_newsfeeds/newsfeeds.html.php` file:

Line 274

```
<?php echo htmlentities( $currChannel->getTitle() ,ENT_QUOTES,'utf-8'); ?>
```

Line 284

```
<?php echo htmlentities( $currChannel->getDescription() ,ENT_QUOTES,'utf-8'); ?>
```

Line 317

```
<?php echo htmlentities( $currItem->getTitle() ,ENT_QUOTES,'utf-8'); ?>
```

Line 322

```
$text = htmlentities( $currItem->getDescription(),ENT_QUOTES,'utf-8' );
```

If you now install the newsfeed of any site that uses umlauts, you will see them correctly.

Manage Categories

Here you can administer the news feed categories. The administration functions are similar to the Contacts Category Manager shown in Figure 6.14.

Polls

The integrated poll module makes it possible for you to publish polls on your site. One poll is already included in the sample data as illustrated below:

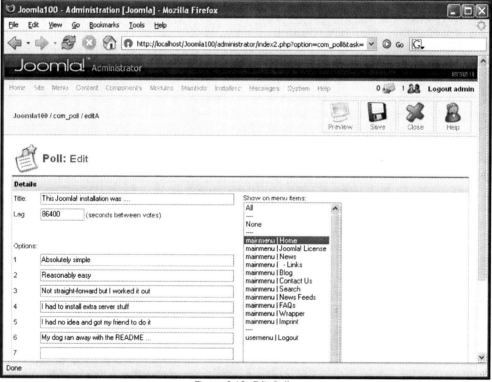

Figure 6.19: Edit Polls

- Title: This is the title of your poll.
- Lag: This determines the time in seconds that has to elapse before another selection can be made. This lag offers some kind of protection from the falsification of survey data.
- Options: Here you can enter up to twelve answer options.
- Show on menu items: You can select in which area of the site the poll is to be displayed. Multiple options are possible by holding down the *Control* key and clicking the left mouse button.

Click Preview to get a preview of your poll. To display it on your site, make sure that polls are provided in the current template. Now see the poll on your site:

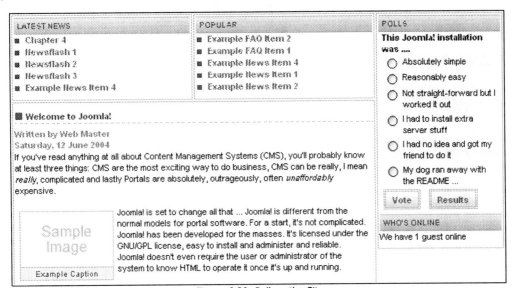

Figure 6.20: Poll on the Site

If you try the poll out and select an answer, an analysis appears:

Figure 6.21: Poll Analysis on the Site

The poll itself is no longer displayed, since by default it was attached only to the front page. Attaching the poll to the individual pages can be configured in the **Module Manager** (see the *Site Modules* section).

Syndicates

The parameters for producing news feeds can be specified in the syndicate component.

A news feed is an XML file that adheres to current standards (Listing 6.1). You can create this file by clicking the RSS 0.91 option on your site, as illustrated:

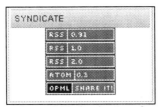

Figure 6.22: Syndication of
News Feeds

This file is not intended to be read, but serves as an exchange format between two programs. Normally one doesn't transfer the file, but only hands over the appropriate URL; in this case, http://localhost/Joomla100/index2.php?option=com_rss&feed=RSS0.91&no_html=1. The file creation and the visual preparation are handled by the reading program.

Listing 6.1: XML-News Feed in RSS 0.91 Format Created by Joomla!

```
<?xml version="1.0" encoding="ISO-8859-1" ?>
<!-- generator="FeedCreator 1.7.2" -->
<rss version="0.91">
<channel>
<title>Joomla!book</title>
<description>Joomla! syndication</description>
<link>http://localhost/Joomla100/link>
<lastBuildDate>Sun,18 Sep 2005 13:10:30</lastBuildDate>
<generator>FeedCreator 1.7.2</generator>
<image> <url>http://localhost/Joomla100/images/M_images/joomla_rss.png</url>
<title>Powered by Joomla! 1.0</title>
<link>http://localhost/Joomla100</link>
<description>Joomla! site syndication</description>
</image>
<item>
<title>example page</title>
<link>http://localhost/Joomla100/index.php?option=com_content&task=view&id=1&I
temid=9</link>
<description> Epsum factorial non deposit quid pro quo hic escorol. Olypian
quarrels et gorilla congolium sic ad nauseum. Souvlaki ignitus carborundum e
pluribus... </description>
<pubDate>Fri, 16 Sep 2005 18:56:41 +0100</pubDate>

</item>
_ additional items
</channel>
</rss>
```

The title and text of the latest news messages are located in the file, as well as other information: for example, the time of production, from which site the messages come, and direct links to the pages.

Joomla! can create news feeds and support the following standards:

- RSS 0.91/1.0/2.0
- ATOM 0.3
- OPML SHARE IT

The content of the feeds can be influenced as follows:

- Cache: Should the feeds be cached, to avoid them being recreated for every request?
- Cache Time: Here you can specify how long the data should be cached (in seconds).
- # Items: How many entries should be transferred to the feed?
- Title: What is the title of your feed?
- Description: What should the description of your feed be?
- Image: What picture link should be assigned to the feed? It might make sense to use the logo of your company.
- Image Alt: What should be displayed if the receiving terminal cannot read pictures?
- Limit Text: Should the text to be transferred be limited to a certain length?
- Text Length: How long should the text be?
- Order: How should the news be ordered?
    - Frontpage Ordering: The same as on the front page
    - Oldest first: The oldest first
    - Recent first: The most recent first
    - Title Alphabetical: Alphabetically by title
    - Title Reverse-Alphabetical: Reverse alphabetically by title
    - Author Alphabetical: Alphabetically by author
    - Author Reverse-Alphabetical: Reverse alphabetically by author
    - Most hits: By maximum number of hits
    - Least hits: By minimum number of hits
- Live Bookmarks: These are a function of the Mozilla Firefox browser. These are dynamic bookmarks that display information from feeds instead of static text. If you are working with Firefox, select RSS 2.00 from the list, and store the parameters.

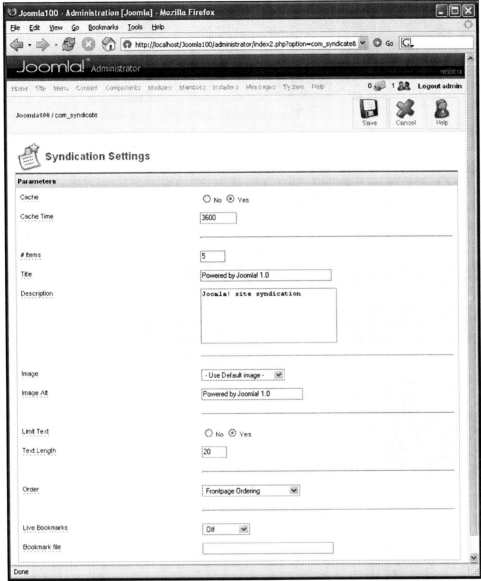

Figure 6.23: Syndication Settings

If you visit your homepage with Firefox, you will see a bright orange XML display in the right lower corner of the browser with the news feed from your site. Here you can view your news messages by clicking this item as shown:

Figure 6.24: Live Bookmark Offer with
the Firefox Browser

If you look in your bookmarks later, you will still see the headings of your messages:

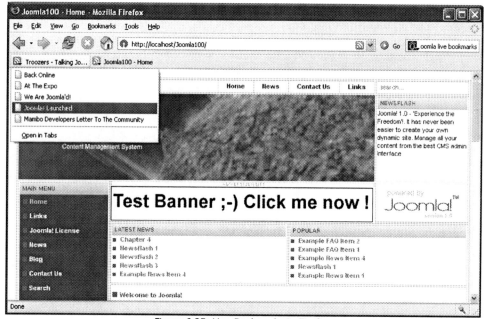

Figure 6.25: Live Bookmarks in Firefox

Weblinks

Here you create a link list that you can integrate into your site. Joomla! offers categories and counts the hits on the links. In the user menu, you can let your registered users suggest links that should be included in this list. These suggested links wind up in the weblinks items list and still have to be published.

Weblink Items

You can enter individual links here as shown:

Figure 6.26: Edit Weblinks

- Name: Name of the link that is displayed on the site.
- Category: Selection of an available link category.
- URL: The URL of the link.
- Description: Here you can enter a detailed description of the link.
- Ordering: Ordering of links.
- Approved: Has this link been approved?
- Published: Should the link be published?
- Target: Should the link should be displayed in a new window (with or without navigation) or whether it should be displayed in the same window.

Weblink Categories

The link categories are administered in the respective **Category Manager**:

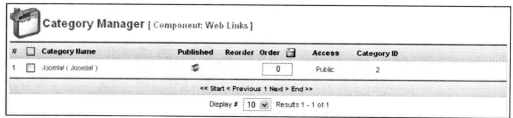

Figure 6.27: Categories

Module Menu

A module is simpler than a component. It is an independent code snippet that is inserted and interpreted by another part of the program.

Because of the capabilities of the PHP script language, modules can collect data from all kinds of sources. These could be sources on your own site—say, the last five articles—or the weather, foreign exchange rate, Amazon, or an e-bay web service.

A module contains business logic and a user interface. Unlike most components, it does not have its own administration area. The template of your site calls and starts the different modules directly.

Since modules are independent programs, they can perform some particular function in an area of the template, for example, display a banner. A template doesn't do anything, but groups many different modules in a visually appealing way. The module structure has an advantage because you can easily expand your site.

Since you can use templates both for your site and for Joomla! administration, there are also various modules for each of these templates.

Install/Uninstall

Here you can install file packages for modules by file upload or from a directory:

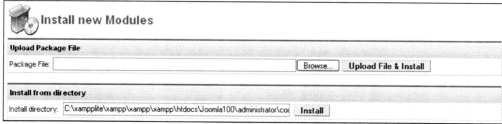

Figure 6.28: Install/Uninstall Modules

For uninstalling, select the module and click Delete. Below the installation area, you can see a list of the installed modules with the origin of the modules and other information.

Site Modules

The Module Manager is the central place for the administration of modules:

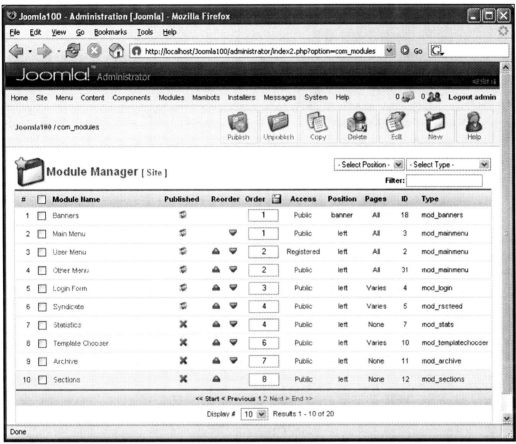

Figure 6.29: Site Modules

- Module Name: This is the name of the module and heading on the site.
- Published: This shows whether the module is published or not.
- Reorder: Here, with help of the blue arrows, you can change the order. With this you can determine, for example, whether the Joomla_book menu should be displayed above or below the Main menu.
- Order: Direct ordering, by specifying the position and a single click on the icon next to Order can spare you excessive clicking of the blue arrows.

- Access: This refers to the access rights for this module (Public, Registered, and Special).
- Position: The Position is a specification for the template. It defines where this module should be displayed. There are eight positions within a template:
  - Banner (advertising area)
  - Left (left page)
  - Right (right side)
  - Top
  - user1 (user defined 1)
  - user2 (user defined 2)
  - user3 (user defined 3)
  - user4 (user defined 4)

  You can filter the list of modules by position for a better overview with the help of the drop-down list in the upper area.
- Pages: This shows whether the module is shown on all or only designated pages.
- ID: The record number from the database.
- Type: There are different types of modules. The mod_mainmenu type, for example, appears several times, since every menu belongs to this type. The individual menus differ only in the parameters.

In order to have a better overview, you can filter the information by these types with the help of the option list within the upper area. In addition, there is still another filter field with which you can filter the information by search words. These filter mechanisms are quite helpful.

Joomla! comes packaged with 21 of these modules as standard. These modules, to a large extent, function uniformly. Besides the input for name, you also have to decide on which pages your module is displayed and what position the module takes up in the template. The parameter list is particularly important with modules; therefore we will particularly emphasize parameters during further demonstration of the modules.

All Menus (mod_mainmenu)

The mod_mainmenu module is used for all menus. There are vertical (*main menu*) and horizontal menus (*top menu*). With vertical menus, the option of a **flatlist** is offered. A flatlist is simply an enumeration of individual points.

- Menu Class Suffix: Here you can enter a special CSS class for the visual organization of the menu.
- Module Class Suffix: Here you specify a special CSS class for the visual organization of the module (menu content).
- Menu Name: This is the name of the menu.
- Menu Style: Here you specify whether the menu should it be vertical, horizontal, or flatlist.

- Enable Cache: Here you specify whether the content of the menu be should cached in order to reduce load time.

- Show Menu Icons: Here you specify whether the menu icons should be displayed. The format of the icons depends on the respective active template.

- Menu Icon Alignment: Here you specify position of the menu icons as left or right.

- Expand Menu: Here you specify whether the menu entry should always be expanded, even if one clicks on another entry. This function is only meaningful with interlocked menu structures:

Figure 6.30: Menu Nesting

- Indent Image: Which icon is to be represented with the substructures of a menu entry? You may take the icons from the template, use the Mambo default values, provide each hierarchical level with its own picture, or not use any icons.

- Indent Image 1-6: You can define icons for six hierarchical levels here.

- Spacer: With horizontal menus, a separator (which you determine here), should be placed between menu entries.

- End Spacer: With horizontal menus an end character can be shown at the end of menu entries. If you want that, specify it here.

Banner

This module controls the display of banners. You can use the record ID of the customer (banner client) as a parameter and thereby make sure that only banners of this customer are displayed. In addition, you can assign a CSS class to this name. In this case, it would have to be an addition to the class table, for example, table.moduletable. This enables an individual organization of the module (module class suffix).

Login Form

The login module makes two different views available. If one is not yet logged in, one gets a Login Form. Depending on the settings in Site | Global Configuration | Site, it's possible to register again:

Figure 6.31: Login Module

After successful authentication, the display changes to the Logout option:

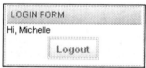

Figure 6.32: Logout Module

The parameters of the Login Form include:

- **Module Class Suffix:** Here you can enter a special CSS class for the visual organization of the menu.
- **Pre-text:** Text that you enter here appears before the form in the login mode.
- **Post-text:** Text that you enter here appears at the end of the module in the login mode.
- **Login Redirection URL:** Here you can determine the URL to which the user is forwarded after a successful login.
- **Logout Redirection URL:** Here you specify the URL to which the user is sent after a successful logout.
- **Login Message:** Should a message in a JavaScript box be displayed after a successful login?
- **Logout Message:** Should a message in a JavaScript box be displayed after a successful logout?
- **Greeting:** After login, the module changes its appearance and displays a greeting text and a logout button. Here can you decide what you want this text to read ("hello, username").
- **Name/Username:** Here you determine whether the user is addressed with his or her real name or with his or her username in the greeting text.

Syndicate

In the syndicate module, different news feed formats are offered as shown in Figure 6.22.

You can specify which standards you are offering and whether you want to use standard pictures or individual pictures in the parameters. The content of the news feeds offered is given by the entries on the front page.

Statistics

The statistics module is deactivated by default. If you activate it, you must still select the pages on which the statistics are to be displayed. The module supplies information about your server and its site:

Figure 6.33: Statistics Module

The parameters of the Statistics module are:

- Server Info: Here you can specify whether the server information is displayed or not.
- Site Info: Here you can specify whether the site information is displayed or not.
- Hit Counter: Here you can specify whether the visitor counter is integrated or not.
- Increase Counter: Here you can specify the initial value of the visitor counter.

Template Chooser

This module allows the visitor to the page to select from various templates. By default, it is deactivated and assigned to the site:

Figure 6.34: Template
Chooser Module

The parameters for this module are:

- **Max. Name Length:** This is the length of the template name in characters that is shown in the option list. If the name is longer, three dots are attached.
- **Show Preview:** This allows you to switch on or off the template preview.
- **Width/Height:** This is the width and height of the preview picture in pixels.
- **Module Class Suffix:** Specify the name of a CSS class here. It has to be an addition to the class `table`, for example, `table.moduletable`. Thus you can configure the module individually.

Archive

The Archive module, by default, is deactivated. If you activate it, you must select the pages on which it is to be displayed.

It supplies information about the contents of your archive (Figure 6.35). The display is grouped by month:

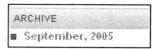

Figure 6.35: Archive Module

The parameter for this module is:

- **Count:** Here you specify the number of displayed months.

Sections

The `Sections` module is deactivated by default. If you activate it, you must select the pages on which it is to be displayed. It lists the existing sections:

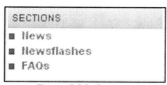

Figure 6.36: Sections
Module

Related Items

The `Related Items` module indicates other content that is related to this content. The relationship is based on the keywords specified in the metadata. All keywords of recently displayed content are compared with those of other published content. If, for example, you register the keyword "law" in the Joomla! License Guidelines in the static pages and also in your created imprint, the license guidelines are shown as a related item when you request the imprint:

Figure 6.37: Related
Item Module

Wrapper

The `wrapper` module wraps external content that is not produced by Joomla! within an `iframe`. An **iframe** is an HTML element and represents a scrollable area within a web page:

Figure 6.38: Wrapper-Bound Page

With the help of this module you can integrate complete pre-existing HTML pages from other servers into the content area of Joomla!.

The parameters for this module are:

- URL: Here you can specify a standard URL. The specification of the page that is to be shown, however, usually takes place in the menu allocation (see Figure 4.48 in Chapter 4).

- Scroll Bars: This allows you to show scrollbars in the iframe. You have a choice between yes, no, and automatic (displayed if necessary).

- Width/Height: Width and height of the iframe in percentage or pixels can be specified.

- Auto Height: This allows you to adjust the height be automatically.

- Auto Add: By default, an http:// is inserted before a URL if no http:// or https:// is found. This function can be turned on and off here.

Polls

Here the functionality for the display of polls is switched on or off. The polls themselves are configured in the polls component (see the *Polls* section). You can decide here whether the content of the module should be cached or not.

Who's Online

The Who's Online module indicates who is currently on the site. A distinction is made between guests and registered users:

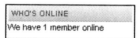

Figure 6.39: Who's
Online Module

The parameters for this module include:

- Display: Here you decide on the display of the module. You have a choice between:
  - Number of guests, number of users
  - User names of the registered users
  - A combination of the two choices shown above

Random Image

With this module, randomly selected pictures from a file can be displayed in the order of your choice. This module is activated by default, but not assigned to any pages.

Figure 6.40: Random
Image Module

Before you can see it on your site, you must assign the desired pages by clicking the Edit icon. The parameters for this module include:

- Image Type: Here you can specify the type of picture (.jpg, .png, or .gif). You can specify only one type at a time.
- Image Folder: Here you have to enter the directory in which the pictures are stored. I have selected /images/stories.
- Link: If you enter a URL here, the picture becomes clickable. The link target is the URL that you have specified here.
- Width (px)/Height (px): Width and height of the displayed pictures in pixels. If you specify nothing here, the pictures are displayed according to the default.

Newsflash

The Newsflash module shows random hooks from dynamic content:

Figure 6.41: Newsflash
Module

The parameters for this module are:

- Category: Here you can specify, by selection from a list, whether content items are to come from a special category or from all categories.
- Style: Here you can select between a column representation (horizontal) and the vertical representation shown in Figure 6.41.
- Show images: Here you can specify whether pictures that are contained in content should be displayed or not.
- Linked Titles: If you set Item Title to Yes, you can specify here whether this title should be linked to the content page.
- Read More: Integrate the read more link.
- Item Title: Here you can decide whether you want to integrate the title of the (news) message.
- No. of Items: Here you determine the number of pieces of content to be displayed at the same time.
- Enable Cache: Here you can specify whether the content should be cached.

Latest News

With this module the latest (newest) messages are displayed (Figure 6.42). By default, this is placed at the user1 position. You can also put it in another position, for example, to the right.

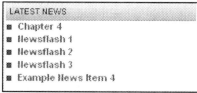

Figure 6.42: Latest News Module

The parameters for this module include:

- Module Mode: Here you can decide whether you want to show dynamic (Content Items only), or static content (Static Content only), or both, in the list.

- Frontpage Items: When you are in the Content Items only mode, you can specify whether elements from the front page should also be included here.

- Count: Here you determine the number of elements that can be displayed.

- Category ID: If you enter the record numbers of the categories that are to be displayed, separated by commas, you force content to be selected from only these categories.

- Section ID: Here you can enter the record numbers of the sections that are to be displayed, separated by commas. Thereby, the content selection is made only from these sections.

Popular

The most popular messages are displayed with this module.

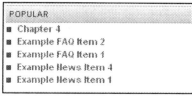

Figure 6.43: Popular Module

The parameters for this module are similar to the ones discussed for the Latest News module.

Search

The Search module appears only as an input field in the standard template. The two templates provided with Joomla! do not convert these parameters. In order to demonstrate the configuration options, I have selected the *JavaBean* template from the old Mambo version.

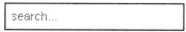

Figure 6.44: Search Module

The parameters for this module are:

- Box Width: Size of the text box in characters: at the moment, it is 30 characters.
- Text: Here you enter the text that is displayed in the search field.
- Search Button: Here you can decide whether you want to have a search button or not.
- Button Position: If you selected a search button, you can specify the position here (Right, Left, Top, and Bottom).
- Button Text: Here you decide on the description of the search button.

Administrator Modules

Under the menu option Modules | Administrator Modules, you can see the Module Manager with the same structure as in the case of Site modules. This time, however, modules are applied within the administration area:

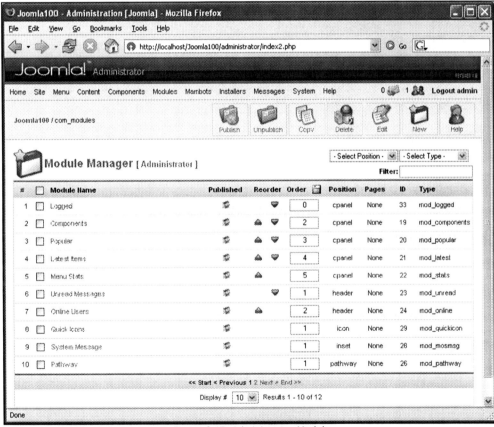

Figure 6.45: Administrator Module

Logged

This module shows a list of the currently logged-in users at the cpanel position, that is, as a tab in the control panel.

Components

The Components module lists the installed components as a tab in the control panel.

Popular

The Popular module presents a list of the most visited content items as a tab in the control panel.

Latest Items

The Latest Items module offers a list of newest content items as a tab in the control panel.

Menu Stats

The Menu Stats module displays statistics about the allocation of the individual menu elements as a tab in the control panel.

Unread Messages

The Unread Messages module informs you about the number of unread administrator messages in the place header, that is, the top right.

Online Users

The Online Users module indicates the number of logged-in users in the place header.

Quick Icons

The Quick Icons module offers icons for fast access in the control panel.

System Message

The System Message module is responsible for the display of system messages.

Pathway

The Pathway module is responsible for the display of the paths.

Toolbar

The Toolbar module determines whether to display the toolbar.

Full Menu

The Full Menu module is responsible for the display of the Joomla! Administration menu.

Copying a Module

Imagine that you wish to display two different random pictures. One module should display pictures from listing A and a second module pictures from listing B. In such a case, you simply select the random images module by marking the checkbox before the name and click Copy.

A new module with the name of Copy of Random Image appears in the list. Change the settings as you desire and you have a new module:

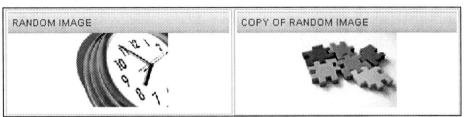

Figure 6.46: Copying of a Module

If you deactivate the Latest News and Popular modules, and put the two picture modules in the user1 and user2 positions, the new modules are displayed in the content area of the template above the messages, or the front page.

Mambots Menu

The name originates from Mambo times (Mambo Bot = mambot). The Joomla! team decided to keep this name. **Bot** is a short form for the word robot. A Mambot thus is a kind of Joomla! robot. One can compare Mambots with a Joomla!-specific script language. We have already come into contact with built-in Mambots when we inserted pictures into content elements.

Mambots are always of a certain type. For example, in order to position the picture in the content element, you wrote {mosimage} in the text. This calls the mos_image Mambot during the representation of the page, which ensures that the assigned picture is shown.

Installing New Mambots

New Mambots are installed in exactly the same manner as components, templates, and language files, via the menu option Mambots | Install Mambots—either by uploading or via directory installation.

Site Mambots

In the Mambot Manager, you will find nine *Content*, four *Editor*, and six *Search* Mambots:

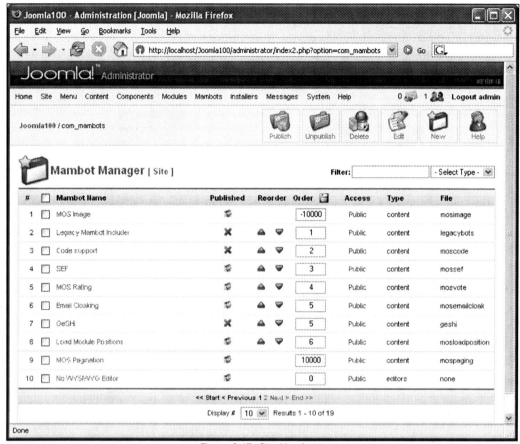

Figure 6.47: Site Mambots

Mambots have few to no changeable settings, since they are mostly programmed and optimized for a very special purpose.

- **MOS Image (content):** This Mambot displays the picture in the content elements on the site with the {mosimage} command (see the *Content Parameters* section in Chapter 5).

- **Legacy Mambot (content):** The Legacy Mambot offers support for older Mambots from version 4.5.x onwards.

- **Code Support (content):** The Code Support Mambot formats source code; thus content elements that contain source code can be formatted with the {moscode} command.

Listing 6.2: Deployment of the moscode Mambot

```
<code>{moscode}
  if ($number > 0){
  echo $number;
  } else{
  $number++;
  }
{/moscode}</code>
```

- SEF (content): SEF stands for **Search-Engine Friendly**. This Mambot produces the search-engine-friendly URLs for content elements. If you use the associated feature, this Mambot must be activated.

- MOS Rating (content): This is the Mambot that provides the evaluation bar about the content. If you want to use this, it must be activated.

  E-mail Cloaking (content): This Mambot changes an email address entered into a content element as hagen@sit2000.de to the form
  <a href=mailto:hagen@sit2000.de> hagen@sit2000.de</a>.

- GeSHi (content): The GeSHi Mambot formats source code like moscode. GeSHI, however, understands syntax highlighting and provides impressive listings on the site, if you merge the source code to be formatted into < pre > </pre > HTML tags. The GeSHi Mambot, which structures and colors the code, then highlights the source code:

Listing 6.3: Deployment of the GeSHi Mambot

```
<pre>
  if ($number > 0){
  echo $number;
  } else{
  $number++;
  }
</pre>
```

- Load Module (content): The Load Module Mambot makes it possible to load modules within content. It is called with {mosloadposition user1}, for example.

- MOS Pagination (content): The MOS Pagination Mambot takes care of page breaks in content elements. It is simply inserted into content in the same way as the MOS Images Mambot. Besides a simple word wrap, you can also define various headings and lemmas.

Syntax

```
{mospagebreak}
{mospagebreak title=page title}
{mospagebreak heading=first page}
{mospagebreak title=page title titleheading=first page}
{mospagebreak heading=first page title=page title}
```

- No WYSIWYG Editor / TinyMCE WYSIWYG Editor (Editor): You can control the activation of these two Mambots via Site | Global Configuration. Thus the WYSIWYG editor is activated in many description texts.

- MOS Image Editor Button / MOS Pagebreak Editor Button (Editor-XTD): These two Mambots generate the two buttons below the editor. By clicking on these buttons, a {mosimage} or a {mospagebreak} is inserted into the text.

Search Mambots

The `search` Mambots for content, web links, contacts, categories, sections, and news feeds can be activated as needed. They influence the behavior of the `search` module.

Summary

Now that we know how to customize Joomla! to our specific needs, we can concentrate on extending our website using a wide range of Joomla! extensions. We will be covering a number of Joomla! extensions in the next few chapters. So let's started...

7

Forums, Comments, and Calendar

We have covered the almost inexhaustible range of Joomla! extensions in the previous chapter. As beautiful as the standard version is, soon you will be searching for components, modules, and Mambots with which you can extend your website. Due to the modular structure of Joomla!, it is easy to create extensions. The following are six popular extensions:

- A forum
- The ability to post comments
- A calendar
- A picture gallery for photographs
- Creating multilingual pages
- An online store

The Joomla! website at `http://developer.joomla.org/` contains lots of components, modules, Mambots, templates, and language files that you may require.

> The scope for creating additional extensions exists, but commercial extensions for Joomla! are also available. Before you buy one of these, you should carefully assess your requirements and check out modules suitable for your application. You can also take part in the further development of these modules.

Forum

Forums are used to display and administer a number of topics where users with common interests can post messages. Such a forum is called a **board**. **Simpleboard** is one such board from *Two Shoes M- Factory* (`http://tsmf.net/`).

Times are changing fast. When this Joomla! book was being written, Simpleboard reached its Version 1.1. With that version, the component was very stable and reliable. A few weeks later, Jan de Graaff, decided to move Simpleboard to Joomlaboard as a Joomla! Project.

The version numbering is exactly the same, because the functionality is exactly the same. This is done to avoid confusion between the components. Starting from the next release of Joomlaboard, Mambo and Simpleboard will not be supported anymore.

The current version now (Jan 2006) is Joomlaboard 1.1.2 together with Joomla 1.0.7.

To learn the functionality, you can use the Simpleboard component described here. For production use on an online website, use always the most recent stable releases!

What can Simpleboard do?

One big problem with open-source software is that often the manual provided with the software turns out to be inadequate. Due to this, one should gain as much information about the software as possible, before installing it. The following functions are available for the different types of users:

- Full integration into Joomla! administration
- Adding access rights to forums
- Editing posts and viewing previous posts of a topic
- Specifying a minimum time span between posts to secure the forum from flood attacks
- Forum categories for building a structure with an overview
- Customizing appearance with the CSS template editor

The administrator functions available directly from the forum include:

- Modifying, deleting, and moving posts
- Locking and unlocking topics (that is, preventing further posts to a topic)
- Positioning a topic at the beginning of the topic list

The functions for all visitors include:

- Writing of posts
- Use of smileys and BBCode for text formatting without knowledge of HTML
- Two different views of the posts (flat or threaded)

The functions for registered users are:

- Private user profile
- Email notifications of new posts in a topic
- Creating a signature that can be automatically added to every post
- Uploading files and pictures to a post

Installation of Simpleboard

The developers of Simpleboard recommend the following preconditions for installation:

- A version of PHP of 4.3.2 or higher (the forum works with PHP version 4.1.0 and up)
- MySQL version higher than 4.0

Our local version of XAMPP Lite fulfills both conditions. Download the `com_simpleboard-1.1.0-stable.zip` file. This version was originally developed for mambo 4.5.2, but also works great with Joomla! 1.0.

Click Installer | Components in the menu bar. Scan your computer for the file and click Upload File & Install. The installer loads the package onto your server, unpacks the individual files, adds the necessary tables to the database, and then gives you further information:

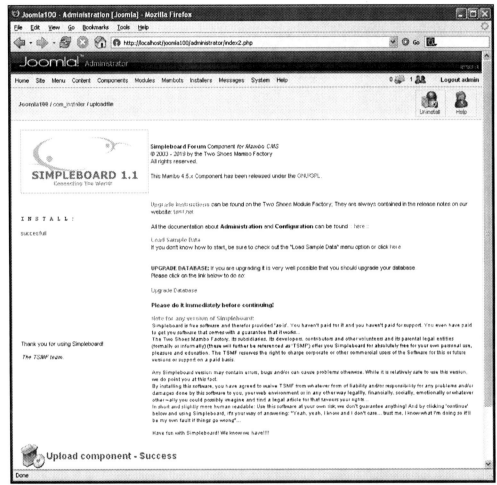

Figure 7.1: Successful Installation of the Forum Component

That's it! The component is installed when you see the Upload component - Success message. The database tables have been created and your Joomla! administration has been customized accordingly. Click Continue, thank the Joomla! development team for this wonderful installer, and thank *Two Shoes M-Factory* for its forum! You can see the new component, the Simpleboard forum, among the installed components.

Uninstallation

Select the component and click Uninstall. The component and data are now permanently deleted.

Simpleboard Administration

After installation, there is a new entry in the Components menu. Click Components | Simpleboard and you will see the Control Panel of your forum component. There are eleven icons giving quick access to the forum features:

Figure 7.2: Simpleboard Control Panel

There is a PAYPAL button on the bottom right of the Control Panel. Try to make a small donation if you are satisfied with the forum. A lot of work has been invested in such components, and programmers have to eat and pay the rent! They are pleased when someone acknowledges their work.

Simpleboard Configuration

Here you specify the basic configuration of your Simpleboard component:

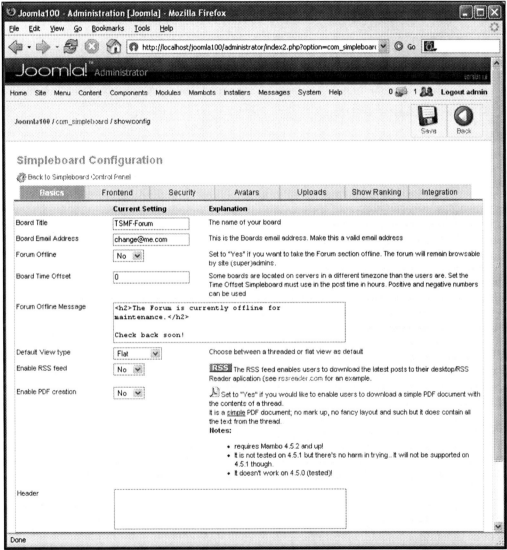

Figure 7.3: Simpleboard Configuration

Descriptions of the seven tabs that run along the top of this screen are as follows:

Basics

The Basics tab has the following settings:

- **Board Title / Board Email Address:** Enter the name of your board and your board's email address.
- **Forum Offline:** A bit like Joomla! itself, you can disable the forum here and supply an appropriate message in the Forum Offline Message field.
- **Board Time Offset:** You can change the time base here.
- **Default View type:** You chose from the two possible views for forum postings (Flat or Threaded).
- **Enable RSS feed:** You can add an RSS button on the forum page. This creates an XML file for a news feed of the newest forum posts.
- **Enable Pdf creation:** With this you can produce a PDF document from every forum entry.
- Enter a **Header** so that it appears in the header area of the forum.

Frontend

There are four blocks of parameters for changing the 'look and feel' of the forum. You can stick with the standard settings, or you can enable or disable display areas, and specify many other useful things.

Security

By default, the board is set up so every visitor can read and write. Flood protection is disabled and a moderator is sent an email whenever a new post is added. You can leave the default settings as they are.

Avatars

Avatars are small pictures that can be attached to a user and displayed alongside his or her posts in the forum. A library of existing pictures is available and you can make changes to settings related to user upload, physical size of images, and file sizes.

Uploads

Each user can upload a file or picture with each post. Both are displayed with the user's post. In this tab, you can adjust what exactly you want to permit. You should also add PDF to the permitted file types.

Show Ranking

Depending on their number of posts, each user is given a particular rank and picture. Thus, other visitors can differentiate 'Fresh Boarders' from 'Expert Boarders'. In this tab, you set up the names of the individual stages and the number of posts it takes to move up a rank.

Integration

Here you can integrate various components into Simpleboard. For example, the Discuss mambot enables a comment link and adds an appropriate entry into the text of the content element.

You can post a comment after opening the content elements. This comment is treated like a topic in a forum and you can skillfully shift discussions about content into the forum.

Forum Administration

Here you set up forums and forum categories. Click New and you will see a form with three tabs:

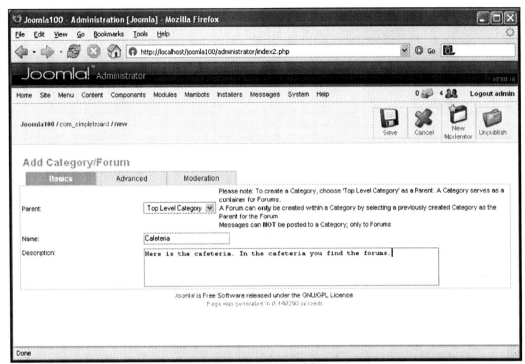

Figure 7.4: Add Forums and Categories

- **Basics**: Before setting up a forum, you have to create a category, let's say with the name Cafeteria, and give a basic description for it.
- **Advanced**: Here you specify the access rights for the category.
- **Moderation**: This tab does not affect categories, but is available as this form is used for creating both categories and forums.

Save the category by clicking Save and this category will show up as unpublished in your overview:

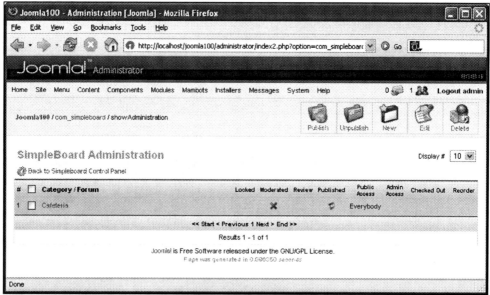

Figure 7.5: New Category

Repeat the procedure to create another forum. Call it Tips & Tricks and enter a description. Select the recently created Cafeteria as the assigned category. Click Save.

There are now two entries in your overview. Publish both by clicking Publish and the basic version of your forum is completed:

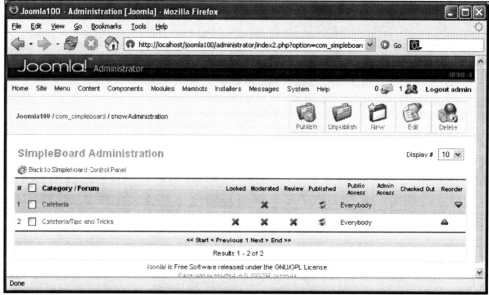

Figure 7.6: Publication of a New Forum

Merge the newly created forum with the main menu, so users can get there via a link from your website.

Click Menu | Main menu and then New.

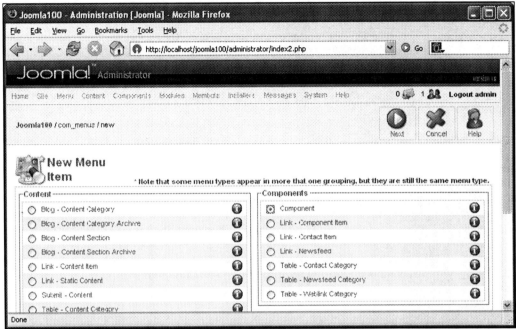

Figure 7.7: New Menu Entry of a Component

In the following dialog, select Component, as shown in Figure 7.7, and click Next. Name the new menu entry as Forum and select Simpleboard forum in the component list. Keep the access as Public and click Save. If you go to your website and reload the page, there will be a new entry entitled Forum at the bottom of the main menu. Click on it to start your new component:

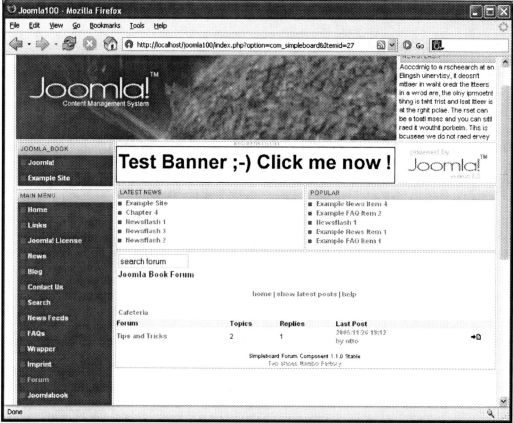

Figure 7.8: Forum on the Website

User Administration

Here you can change existing user profiles. The list is still empty. Create a profile (see the *User Front End* section) or write a post so you'll have a few entries in the list:

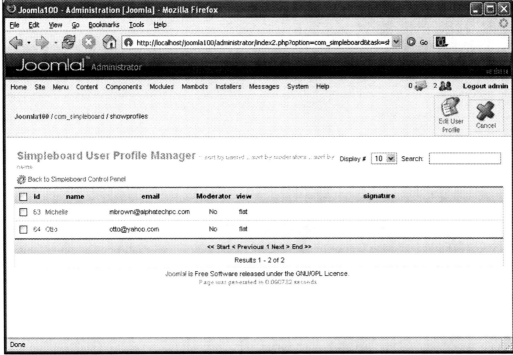

Figure 7.9: Simpleboard User Profile Manager

You can work on profiles by clicking the Edit User Profile icon.

Uploaded Files Browser

In the file browser, you can administer the uploaded files that users have attached to the postings. You can delete a file (Remove Completely) or jump to the appropriate post in the forum (Open Message):

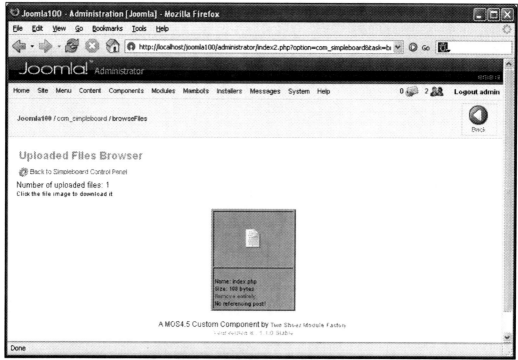

Figure 7.10: Simpleboard Uploaded Files Browser

Uploaded Images Browser

In the images browser, you can administer pictures that were uploaded with posts. You have the same options as in the files browser (see Figure 7.10).

Edit CSS File

Like Joomla!, the forum also contains templates. You can modify the appropriate CSS file from Joomla! administration:

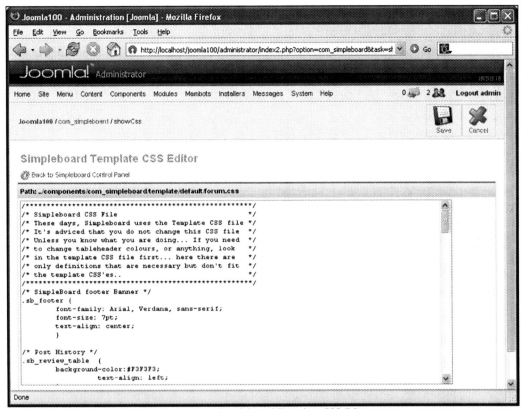

Figure 7.11: Simpleboard Template CSS Editor

You can find additional templates on the *Two Shoes M-Factory* website.

Prune Forums

Forums exist for discussions. They are not productive when there are many topics but few answers. The Prune Forums function enables you to delete topics that have no responses. You have to select the forum and the number of days you want it to remain active.

Prune Users

This function synchronizes the users of the Joomla! user administration with those of the Simpleboard component. For example, when users are deleted in Joomla!, they are also deleted in Simpleboard after applying this function.

Support Websites

You can find various forums, downloads, and items of news about the forum component at the *Two Shoes M-Factory* website.

Load Sample Data

Clicking this button loads sample data into your forum. Sample data is always useful for practice. This function is only available after installation. You can also find a link to the sample data on the web page that appears after installation (see Figure 7.1).

Update Database to Version 1.1.0-Stable:

If you have installed an older version of Simpleboard, you can update your database structure by clicking on this icon. In our case, we are using the latest version of Simpleboard.

User Front End

Visitors can post topics when you have merged the forum with your website (see the *Simpleboard Administration* section). By default, a new forum is left empty, which can be confusing for inexperienced users. You can start working on this new forum by posting a greeting message. The first post is the topic (Caption).

The integrated editor is unfortunately not Mambo's WYSIWYG editor, but an editor based on **Bulletin Board Code** (**BBCode**). This code is an unofficial standard on web forums. First click on the Forum link in the main menu, then on Tips & Tricks in the forum list, and finally on ::post new topic::. You can write a posting in the form that pops up on your screen:

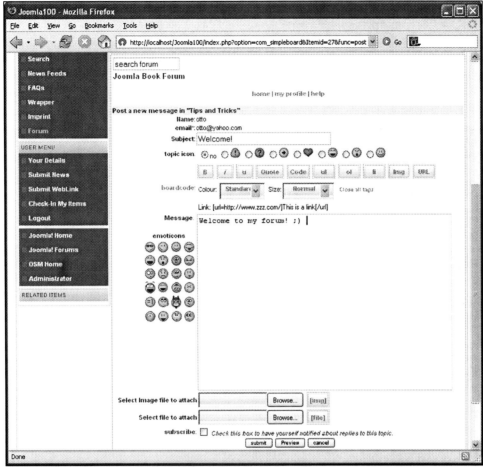

Figure 7.12: Creating a Forum Post

The buttons with letters correspond to the HTML tags of the same name:

- B: bold
- i: italic
- u: underline
- Quote: quote from another posting
- Code: code
- ul: unordered list
- ol: ordered list
- li: list item
- Img: image
- URL: Link

If you move your mouse cursor over the buttons, the text directly above the text-area field changes, and the help text related to the button is displayed. You can add pictures and files to your post by entering the path in the appropriate input field. There is a subscribe checkbox below this field. Check it if you want to be notified by email about responses to your post.

Click submit after you have entered some text in the editor. The post is stored and you have the option of moving on to different places of the forum via links. After a few seconds, the program will redirect to your post:

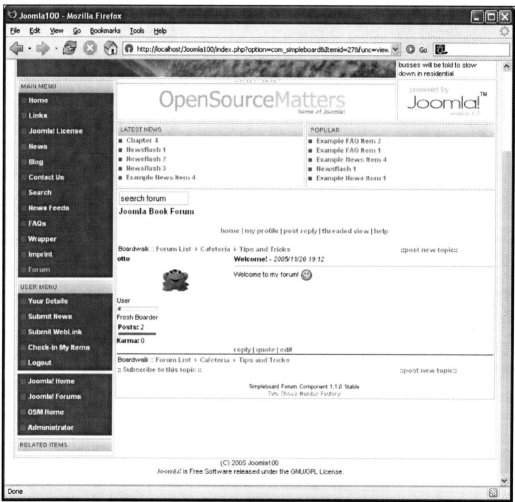

Figure 7.13: Forum Posting

You can display the topic tree as a PDF file by clicking on the pdf link (Figure 7.14).

All users including you can respond to this post. Write a short response, perhaps under another user name. The new post is displayed under your first post. If you click Tips & Tricks, you will wind up in the topic overview (Topics) and your first heading will be a Welcome! greeting:

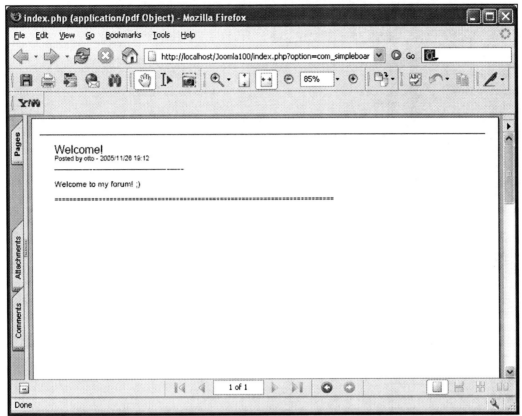

Figure 7.14: PDF view of a forum entry

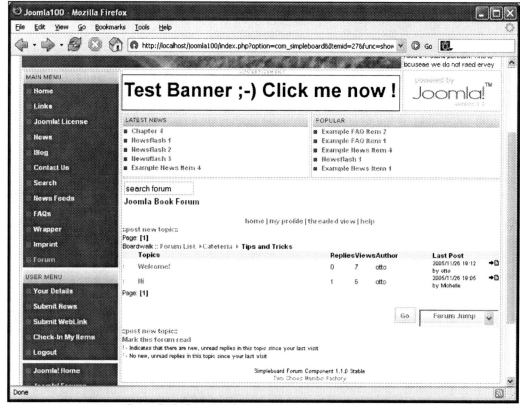

Figure 7.15: Captions of the Tips & Tricks Forum (flat view)

Here you can see that users have accessed this post thirteen times and there is a response to it. The last response was written by Michelle on 2005/11/26 at 19:05.

In the link bar above the forum there is a link reading flat view or threaded view. Flat view shows the number of replies, views, and the most recent post in one row. However, in threaded view, the Topics column contains hyperlinked titles that indicate the relationship of replies to the parent post. This overview has a tree structure, which uses more space, but it is easier to follow the replies to the parent post:

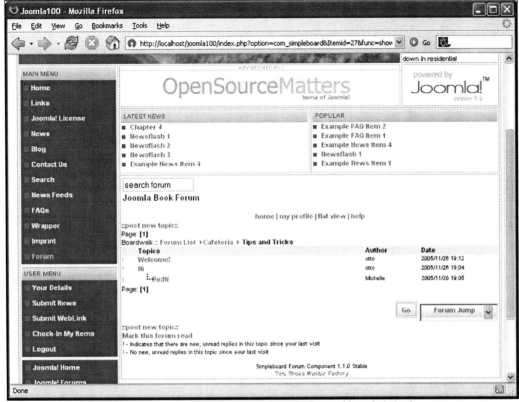

Figure 7.16: Captions of the Tips & Tricks Forum (threaded view)

See how the display changes when you click each of these links.

Set Up a User Profile

Open the forum on your website, click my profile, and fill it out as you wish.

- Preferred view: Select flat or threaded view.
- Ordering: Specify how the messages should be ordered.
- Signature: Define the text that will be automatically inserted at the end of your posts.
- Avatar: Upload a picture or choose one from the list of available avatars:

Figure 7.17: Forum Avatars

Simpleboard Module

Naturally, there are modules available for the Simpleboard component. For example, there is a module that displays the last five forum postings on your website.

Installation

Download the `mod_simpleboard5.zip` file and install it by clicking Installers | Modules. After installation, a new module named `mod_simpleboard` appears in the module list. By clicking Modules | Site Modules, you can name the new module and determine the pages on which it is to be displayed. In this example, it is called 'forum posts' and is published on all pages on the right side of the template area. The last five forum posts are displayed on the web page:

Figure 7.18: Simpleboard
Module

Comments

If you prefer interactive websites and are interested in your visitors' opinions, it would be great for your users to be able to comment on content items. This is possible with Arthur Konze's **AkoComment** component.

Installation

Download the com_akocomment20.zip file from http://www.joomlaresource.com/joomla_downloads/Download/Joomla_Components/Akocomment20/ and install it from the Installers | Components menu:

Figure 7.19: Installation of the AkoComment Component

Subsequently, download the `cb_akocommentbot.zip` file and install it using the mambot installer:

Figure 7.20: Installation of the AkoComment Mambot

Now activate the Mambot!

Since this component did not yet work perfectly with PHP5 at the time of this writing (September 2005), you have to delete the following lines in the [Joomla!]/administrator/components/com_ akocomment/toolbar.akocomment.php file.

```
line 36 default:
line 37 //MENU_Default::MENU_Default();
line 38 break;
```

Administration

There are three menu entries in the menu Components | AkoComment:

View Comments

Here you can edit comments that have been posted by users. Since at this moment there are no comments present, this area is still empty.

Edit Settings

Here you can specify settings in four different tabs, General, Layout, Posting, and Notification.

General

This tab has the following settings:

- Main Operating Mode: Here you can decide whether comments should always be displayed or if only the Mambot command {moscomment} is present in the content.

- Sections available: With automatic display, you can select which group of content elements automatically gets comment windows.

- Autopublish Comments: Here you can specify whether comments are approved automatically and thus appear immediately on the page.

- Anonymous Comments: Here you can specify whether or not to allow anonymous comments.

- Comment Window: Here you can choose if the comment window should appear in the same or in its own window.

Layout

This tab has the following settings:

- Comments Sorting: Should the oldest or the most recent comment be shown first?

- Form Position: Should the form be positioned below or above the comments?

Posting

This tab allows you to decide the following settings:

- BB Code Support: Should BBCode for simple formatting be supported?

- Picture Support: Should pictures be permitted as part of the comments?

- Smiley Support: Should smileys be displayed?

Notification

This tab has the following settings:

- Notify Admin: Specify if an email should be sent to an admin when a new comment is posted.

- Admin's Email: Specify the email address of the user to which the admin message is sent.

Edit Language

Here you get a text area field for the modification of text.

Front End

When you go to your website, you will see a comment window under the content elements that corresponds to your settings.

Here your visitors can post comments about your content to their heart's desire:

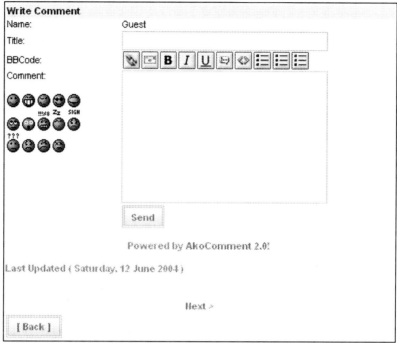

Figure 7.21: Comment Window

Calendar

A calendar is useful for websites where, for instance, many appointments are scheduled. There is a popular component available for Joomla! with the unspectacular name **Events** (http://mamboforge.net/projects/events/).

Installation

Download the com_events-1.2.zip file and install it from the menu option Installers | Components. You will receive a message that the component has been installed. This is followed by further instructions. In addition, a new component named Events appears in the component list.

Configuration

Click Components | Events. You will see three menu entries: Manage events, Manage event categories, and Events config.

Events Config

Here you can specify the admin's email address, determine which users can post events, format the date and time, and customize the layout. The first tab handles the parameters for the component:

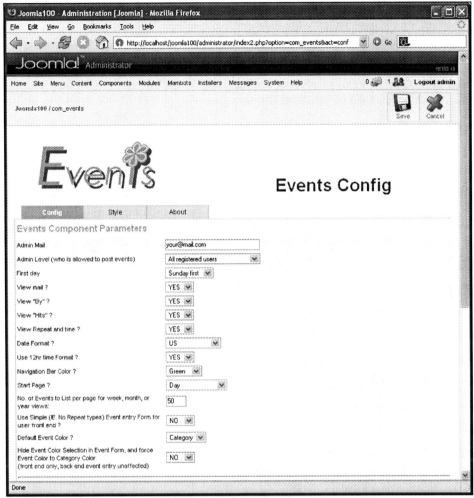

Figure 7.22: Event Component Parameters

- **Admin Mail:** Change the email address to your own.

- **Admin Level:** Specify whether registered or special users are allowed to post events.

- **First day:** Specify the day (Sunday or Monday) on which the week should begin.

- **View mail ?, View "By" ?, View "Hits" ?, View Repeat and time ?:** Assign various display options for individual appointments.

- **Date Format:** Change the format of the date if required. I use a format that displays in the following way: Sunday, 27 March 2005.

- **Use 12hr time Format:** Chose between the twelve-hour and twenty-four-hour clock.

- **Navigation Bar Color:** Select the color of the navigation bar.

- Start Page: Select the type of display that is to be default for the calendar (day, week, month, year, monthly list, categories, or a search field).
- No. of Events to List per page for week, month, or year views: Enter the number of events that are to be displayed on the first page of the list.

The second tab, Style, contains a CSS editor for customizing the layout. A button here lets you enter the default values back into the CSS file.

Manage Event Categories

Before entering an event, you need a category. Go to Components | Manage event categories in the menu bar and click New:

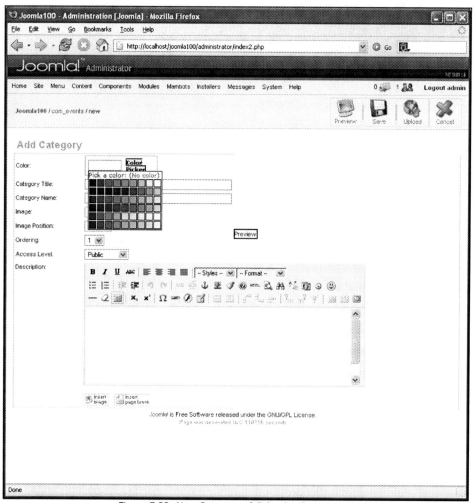

Figure 7.23: New Category of Calendar Component

You can set up a category here. Each category has a different color so it is easier to recognize in the calendar. In addition, you can assign and position a picture from the Media Manager. You can also upload a picture on the spot just by clicking the upload icon. The picture is saved in the /images/stories/ subdirectory. You can add a description for the components using the WYSIWYG editor. After you finish editing, click Save to store your changes.

Once this is done, you still have to publish the category in the Events Category Manager.

Manage Events

This allows you to enter your preferences. Click Components | Events | Manage events in the menu bar, and then click New. You will see a form with four tabs:

- Events: Here you specify a title, a category, and a description for the event. The WYSIWYG editor is again at your disposal to help with the description. You can also set up a place, a contact, and some additional information:

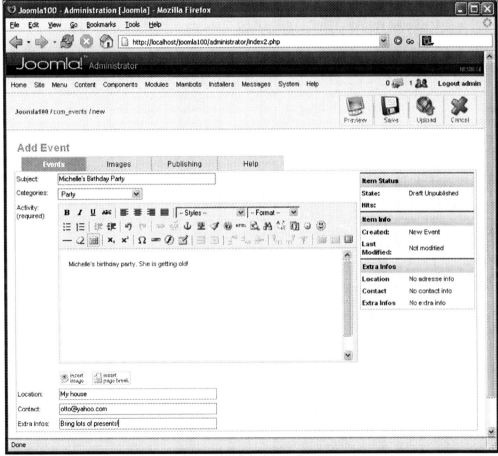

Figure 7.24 Schedule an Event

- Images: Here you can assign a picture from the Media Manager to the event just as for Content Items:

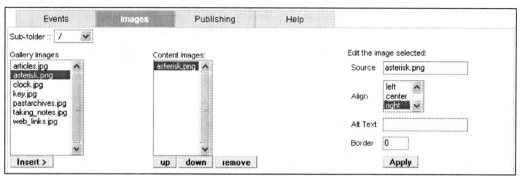

Figure 7.25: Assign Picture

- Publishing: It is easy to enter the dates of events. Click on the button with three dots and a calendar pops up. Here you can select the first and last day of the event:

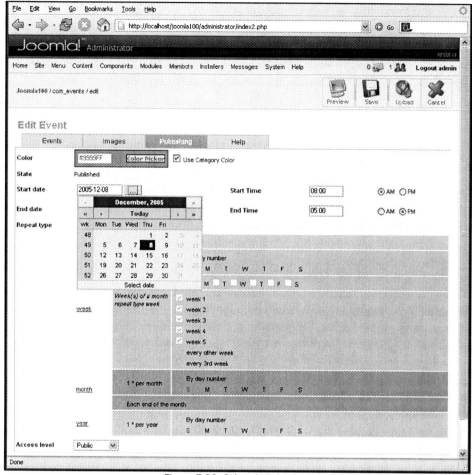

Figure 7.26: Select Appointment

In addition, you can scroll through months and years by clicking on the « and » symbols.

The Start Time and End Time have to be entered in a twelve-hour or twenty-four-hour format (hh:mm) depending on the settings in Event Config.

Another convenient feature is the repeat options for appointments:

- o **Every day:** Select this option for an event that is repeated on one other or several days. A new event will be entered for each of the days with the same start and end time.
- o **Every week:** This option makes it possible to choose the day of the week on which the event takes place.
- o **Several days in one week:** This option lists several events that occur on different days of the week.
- o **Weeks:** With this option, you can repeat events based on weeks, for example, every two weeks.
- o **Month:** Here you can select a day of the month for the repeat with this option.
- o **At the end of the month:** The event is on the last day of every month as long as the last day falls in the period specified by the start and end date.
- o **Year:** This option lets you select a day of the year to repeat the event.

- • **Help:** In this tab, specification of the event date is explained in detail. One-day events that extend beyond midnight can be set up here.

> Be careful with the special case of a one-day event that ends after midnight.
> When a one-day event begins, for example, at 19:00 and ends at 3:00, the start and end dates must both be set for the same *date,* which must be the date *before* midnight.

To show a link to the calendar from the site, you have to merge the calendar component into the main menu. Click **Menu | Main menu** and **New**, select **Component** in the subsequent dialog, and then click **Next** (see Figure 7.7).

Name the new menu **Calendar** and select **Events** in the component list. Leave the access as **Public** and click **Save**.

If you reload your website, there should be a new entry at the bottom of your main menu (**Calendar**). Clicking on it will start the new component:

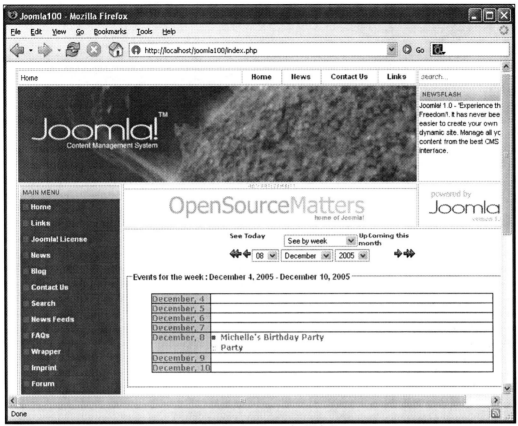

Figure 7.27: Events on the Website

User Front End

When you log in to the website, you may or may not enter appointments depending on the settings in Event Config.

If you have permission, two links appear below the calendar: enter appointments and my appointments. The enter appointments link leads to the same interface as in Joomla! administration, inclusive of help text. From the my appointments link, you can see the appointments that you have entered under this user name. Next to each are Modify and Delete links:

Figure 7.28: Your Events on the Website

Click on the event name to see a corresponding form displaying the details of the event. To modify the form, click on the highlighted pencil icon:

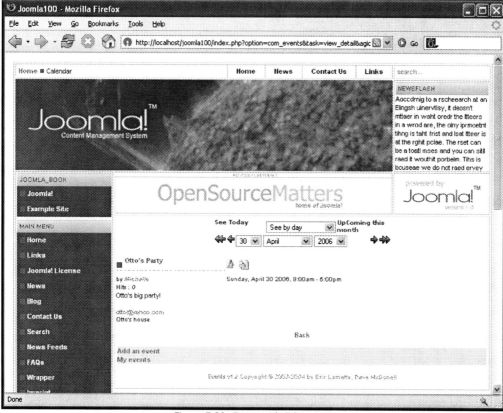

Figure 7.29: Event with Editor Icon

Module

For the Event component, a module displays the current month on the website.

Download the mod_events_cal-1.8.zip file and install it from the menu option Installers | Modules. After the installation, a new module named mod_events_cal appears in the module list.

Click Modules | Site Modules. You can rename the new module (Events Calendar), and specify the pages on which it is to appear. In this example, it is called Appointments and is published on all the pages in the right side of the template area:

Figure 7.30: Event Module

The month is now displayed on the site with differently colored days indicating events.

Event Mambot

The Event Mambot is always ready to browse appointments via the search module.

Download the `bot_events_search-1.1.zip` file and call it up from the menu bar by clicking Installers. Select the file and click Upload File & Install button. Search Events shows up in the list of installed Mambots.

Click Mambots | Site Mambots in the menu bar and publish the newly installed Event Mambot.

When you now enter something in the search field of your website, appointments and events are also searched and are shown in the results list if a match is found.

Figure 7.31: Search Function in the Front End with Installed Event Mambot

Summary

We created and configured a new forum for Joomla! using Simpleboard (now Joomlaboard). We also made our site more interactive with a Comments extension. We also installed and configure a calendar for our web site. In the next couple of chapters we will discuss a few more extensions including an image gallery and online stores.

8

Image Gallery and Document Management

This chapter will cover file storage. Files can be pictures or documents. Both are more or less important and could be stored on the website by the users themselves or by the administrator.

In the case of documents, people often need descriptions and hints about which files contain what and where they are stored. In the case of picture, people often wish to look at the pictures as a slideshow, to make comments, to rate, to send e-cards, and so on before they download them.

For both cases we have different possibilities and therefore, different components—for example, the picture gallery. There are several gallery components available. Every project has its own advantages and disadvantages. We have chosen the project zoom gallery and the project DOCMan. The zOOm Gallery has a lot of features and shows what is possible. DOCMan is the *standard* for Document Management for Mambo/Joomla!.

Gallery

You often find pictures, sculptures, montages, and similar artistic works in a gallery. In principle, a gallery is a collection of images. The Internet is becoming more visually rich nowadays and a picture, after all, says a thousand words.

There are many areas suitable for galleries. For example, if you want to create an association's website, you might want to photograph your association meetings and your members. Why not put these pictures at the disposal of the visitors or registered users of your site using a gallery?

zOOm Media Gallery

Mike de Boer from Rotterdam, Netherlands, developed this component. You can download the current version, join in the discussion on the forum, and check out a demo of the component at `http://www.zoomfactory.org/`.

Installation

Download the `com_zoom_251rc1.zip` file. Install the file from the Installers | Components menu option. A message about where the component was installed, and instructions about how to make it work, are displayed after installation.

Figure 8.1: Installation of zOOm Gallery

Click Continue and you will see a new component with the name zOOm Media Gallery Admin in the component list.

Administration

In the Components menu, you will find a new zOOm Media Gallery menu option. The gallery administration area consists of six icons displayed one below the other:

Figure 8.2: Administration

If you roll your mouse cursor over the icons, a tooltip appears showing their name.

Gallery Manager

As is the case with all content, a certain order is necessary. For pictures, the hierarchical levels are called **galleries**. Click Gallery Manager and then New Gallery.

New Gallery

You need to fill in the following information here:

- Parent gallery: Just like the Joomla! menu entry system, you can nest galleries to your liking. To do this, you must select the parent gallery here.
- Title: This is the name of the gallery that will appear on the website.
- Keywords: These keywords are considered while searching.
- Description: The description you entered is shown on the gallery's page.

189

The input form for a new gallery is divided into two tabs.

Properties

In the Properties tab, specify the properties of the gallery:

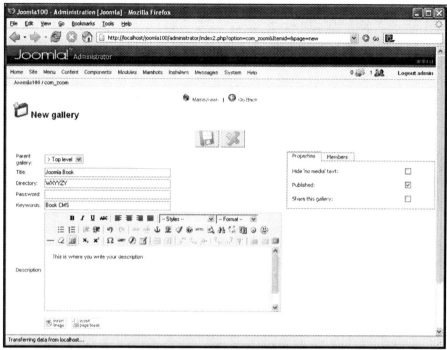

Figure 8.3: Create a New Gallery

The options available under Properties are:

- Hide 'no media' text: If there are no pictures in the gallery, the no media text is displayed. If you don't want this text, click the checkbox.
- Published: This is where you release the gallery.
- Share this gallery: Check this, if you want to allow other users to upload pictures from the front end.

Members

In the Members tab, you enter the access rights for the gallery.

- Public Access: All users of the website can access the pictures.
- Members Only: Only registered users can access the pictures.
- User Name: Only the named user can access the pictures.

On clicking Save, you will see a message box indicating that the gallery has been created and you are automatically sent to the list of existing galleries. If you want to edit a gallery, select it via the check box and click Edit.

Media Manager

The Media Manager under this option gives you the ability to comfortably manage your images. Depending on the available image administration libraries, you can even rotate and flip the images. You can upload files in different ways:

- single (ZIP-)file: Presumably, you will first want to upload an individual file. The principle is always the same. File location, gallery, name, keywords, and description text are specified as shown in the picture:

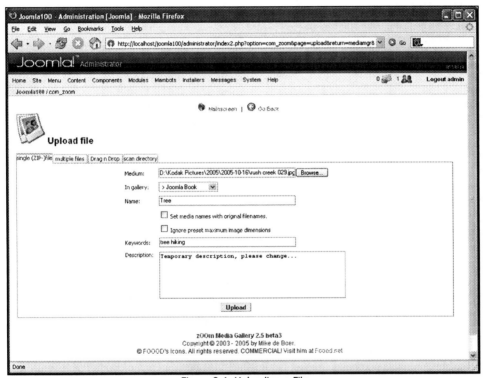

Figure 8.4: Uploading a File

- multiple files: The form for individual files is shown several times so you can upload several pictures at once.

- Drag n Drop: You can start a Java applet with which you can transfer several files at once by clicking Drag n Drop if you have the Java plug-in in your browser or have the Java Runtime Environment installed on your computer (http://java.sun.com/products/plugin/),:

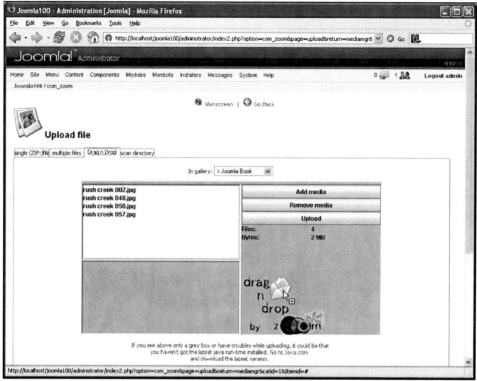

Figure 8.5: Java Applet for File Upload

With the Java applet you can also add files using a normal file dialog or via Drag n Drop from your File Manager. You have to assign the same description to all pictures.

- scan directory: You can search whole directories for pictures and upload them together.

Zoom Thumb Coder

Here you can create thumb codes. Various extensions for the zOOm Gallery—for example, the `zoom Thumb` Mambot—are available. Similar to the `Image` Mambot, it merges pictures from the zOOm Gallery into your contents. You can create the necessary codes with the `{moszoomthumb imgid=2}` menu option. If you put this code in a static content item, for instance, then the picture from the gallery will appear in that content on the website.

Settings

The Settings dialog is divided into several tabs.

System

When working with pictures, issues that always crop up are size and overview. Having thumbnails (small picture previews) displayed, a bit like table of contents, on a page has become standard on the Internet. The advantage is that users get a rough overview of the pictures without downloading them. By clicking on the preview of a picture, the corresponding large version is opened. The System tab allows you to enter the system configuration values to achieve this.

> Depending on your server configuration, it is possible that the multiple upload option will not work, but soon there will be a version that can do this error-free.

Media

To view thumbnails, the preview pictures have to be produced automatically. It is not that simple and can be performed in several ways.

The zOOm Media Gallery offers four possibilities. Two external programs, **ImageMagick** (`http://www.imagemagick.org/`) and **NetPBM** (`http://netpbm.sourceforge.net/`) must be installed on the server, and two libraries, **GD1** and **GD2** must be compiled into the PHP module. Since you have no influence on the selection of the software installed on a rented server and both require major system resources, the first two options are just a matter of luck. With a local installation under Windows or Linux, you can download and install the programs yourself.

The third program, the **GD1 library** (`http://www.boutell.com/gd/`), has the advantage that it is already contained in PHP. There are different versions of PHP and GD. Fortunately, the setup routine recognizes whether GD is the latest version and selects it automatically. GD has less functionality than the first two programs, but can produce `.jpg` previews.

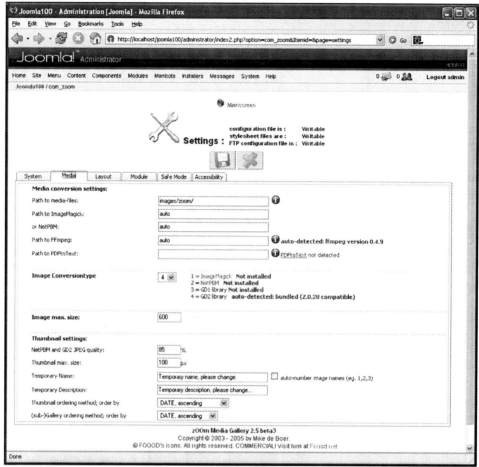

Figure 8.6: Settings—Layout

- **Path to FFmpeg:** Here you give the path to ffmpeg, a command-line program that converts files from a video/audio or picture format into another format. It also supports recording and encoding from a TV card in real time.

- **Path to PDFtoText:** Here you give the path to a program that converts PDF to text.

- **NetPBM and GD2 JPEG quality:** Here you specify the compression ratio as a percentage.

- **Thumbnail max. size:** Here you determine the size of the preview picture in pixels.

- **Temporary Name:** Here you type in a default name.

- **Temporary Description:** Here you can specify a standard description.

Layout

Here you can specify various stylistic parameters for your gallery:

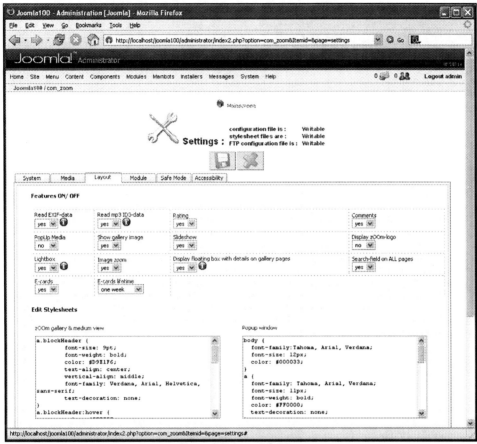

Figure 8.7: Layout Settings

The parameters decide the number of thumbnails on a page and the display or lack of display of, for example, comments, postcards, keywords, search fields, and so on. In addition, the zOOm Media Gallery CSS file can be customized here and a method for sorting the thumbnails can be selected.

Safe Mode

The PHP language has a "safe mode" in which certain actions, for example, file write access, are forbidden (`http://aspn.activestate.com/ASPN/docs/PHP/features.safe-mode.html`).

If safe mode is switched on, no files can be uploaded and file uploads are necessary for the gallery. Therefore, you can simply specify your FTP access instructions here and PHP then uses the built-in FTP functionality for uploading pictures.

Accessibility

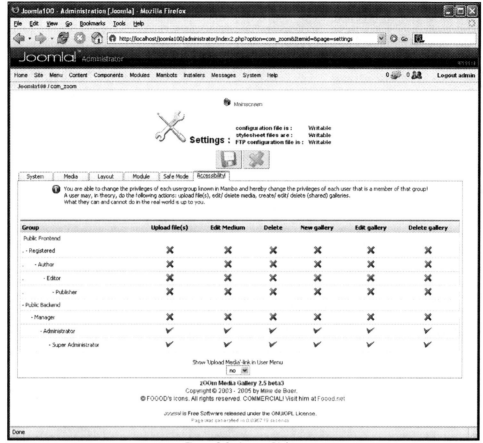

Figure 8.8: Access Rights

Here you select the default access rights for the following:

- Upload of images
- Editing of images
- Deletion of images
- Creation of a gallery
- Editing of a gallery
- Deletion a gallery

And choose whether to show the upload link in the user menu.

Optimize Tables

This cleans the database tables used by the gallery. Occasionally such housekeeping may be necessary, for example, when users upload files and interrupt the process before it is finished. This creates entries in the database, although the matching pictures never got there.

Update zOOm Media Gallery

This link leads to Mike de Boer's website from where you can install the latest updates for the gallery.

Integration of the Gallery into your Website

Now you have to merge the gallery with the main menu so that it is displayed on your website. Click Menu | Main menu and then New. Select Component in the subsequent dialog and click Next (see Figure 7.7 in Chapter 7).

Give a new name to the menu entry (picture gallery) and select Zoom Media Gallery Admin in the component list. Leave the access on Public and click Save.

If you exit your web page and reload it, a new entry (picture gallery) is located in your main menu at the bottom of the page. Clicking on it will start your new component. Depending on your choice of settings, you will see your photo galleries with a preview of the pictures. Click on the gallery link to see the previews for all pictures. If you click on a preview picture, a new page with the original picture and the information you entered is opened. Below the picture, there is a space for comments.

User Front End

Depending on the access rights set, you may create galleries and upload files. A similar interface to the one described in the *Administration* section, is at your disposal. You get to this interface via the user system link.

Lightbox

Lightbox is a personal selection of pictures displayed when you click the Lightbox icon. You can insert individual pictures and whole galleries into the Lightbox. You can find the Lightbox icon above the picture.

E-Cards

You can send pictures and a message as an e-card to a friend's email address by clicking the link to your card in the email. You can specify the expiry date of the e-card in the administration settings.

Comments and Ratings

Every image can have comments and ratings. You can configure this function in settings.

The rating of the data can be displayed in separate modules.

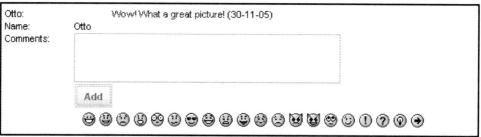

Figure 8.9: Ratings and Comments

Modules for the zOOm Media Gallery

There are various modules for your gallery. For example, to show random pictures, the last five, the most visited, those with the most comments, and even a scrolling module that lets you scroll random pictures. Look around Mike de Boer's site and try out a few modules.

Document Management/Download Area

If you upload files to your website and administer them in various user groups, and you want to offer these files with individual descriptions and optional licenses for downloading, then there is only one component for you: DOCMan (`http://www.mambodocman.com/`). With it, you can manage various kinds of documents (files) and make them available for download.

Because of its ability to create categories and user groups, you can offer a different download area for different user groups. DOCMan is also suitable for closed work groups with the relevant documents made available in a central place.

Installation

Download the docmanV13_RC_1.zip file and install it from the Installers | Components menu.

Figure 8.10: Installation of DOCMan

In the Component menu, you can now see the new entry DOCMan and a number of submenus. If you select the main DOCMan menu option, you are in the DOCMan's control panel (Figure 8.11). You can go directly to the DOCMan functions using the nine icons.

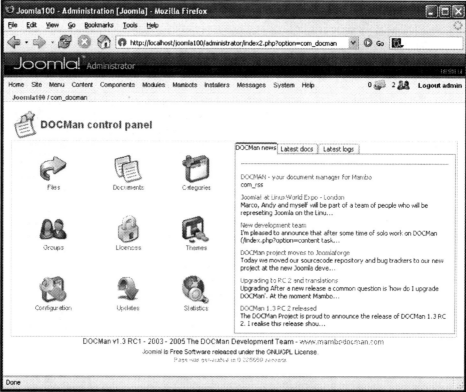

Figure 8.11: DOCMan Control Panel

Administration

I will go through the administration briefly on the basis of a concrete example. We want to offer files that are subject to certain licenses for download on the website. Before the visitor downloads the file, he or she must confirm the license by means of a checkbox. A group of users is to be responsible for the files and an administrator should be able is to notify this group via email.

Categories

We begin with a **category**. Make one and name it Constitution. To do that, click on the Category icon in the DOCMan control panel and afterwards on New.

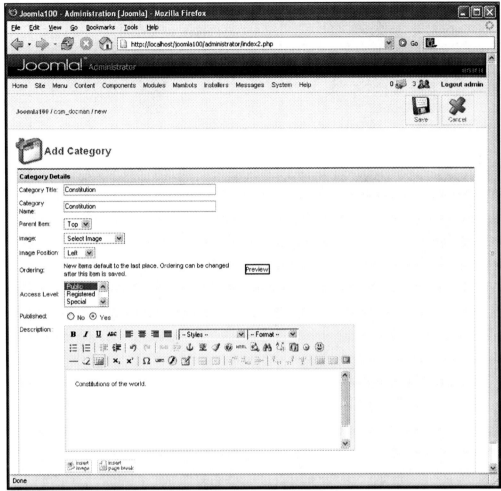

Figure 8.12: New Category—Constitution

Assign all parameters and store the new category.

Group

A group of users, which is responsible for a file, is specified here. All group members need a user account in your Joomla! system. For example, set up a group of politicians (Figure 8.13).

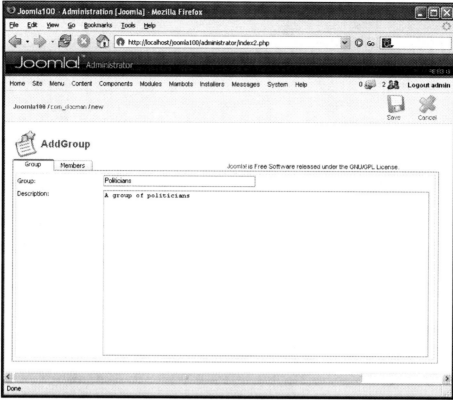

Figure 8.13: New Group—Politicians

If you click on the Members tab, you can select the members of the group from your population of registered users (Figure 8.14).

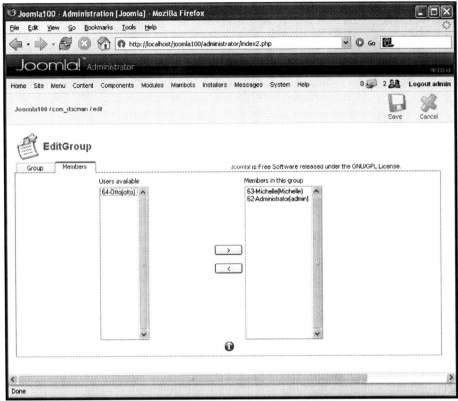

Figure 8.14: Member Allocation—Group Politicians

With one click on the Save icon, you save the group. This newly created group is now in the group list. In the right area of this list, you will find an Email symbol. You can send a message to the group by clicking on this symbol.

Files

To be able to assign a document or a download to our group, we naturally need a file. Select a suitable file from your server. As the first step, you have to decide how this file is to be offered on your server. You can upload from the local server, upload it from another server, or refer to a file on another server via a link.

The first option allows you to upload a zip file. You can check the batchmode checkbox. Then DOCMan extracts the zip file and stores all the files in the server's file system. If you want to upload a zip file, don't check it.

With the second upload option, you must enter the URL of the desired file and the file name that this file is to receive on your server. DOCMan then loads this file on the server, without taking a detour through your computer. We require the first case (Figure 8.15).

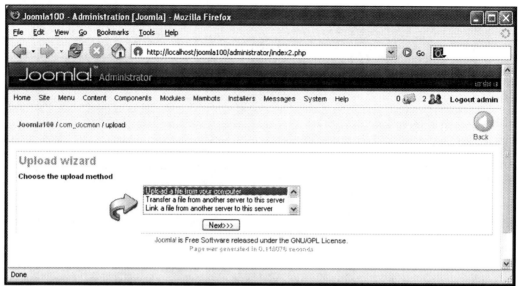

Figure 8.15: File Upload in DOCMan

By clicking on the Next>>> button, you arrive at an upload dialogue. Select the desired file. If you want to upload several individual files in a zip file, you can mark the Batch Mode checkbox (batch processing). The zip archive is unpacked and every file is available individually (Figure 8.16).

Figure 8.16: File Upload II in DOCMan

After the upload, you receive a success message and a query whether you want to upload any other files, go to document processing, or display the uploaded files. Select the last option and let it show you the uploaded files (Figure 8.18).

Figure 8.17: Upload Options

The third option immediately jumps into document administration, where the desired link is provided with the desired parameters for display on the website.

And that is exactly where we want to be.

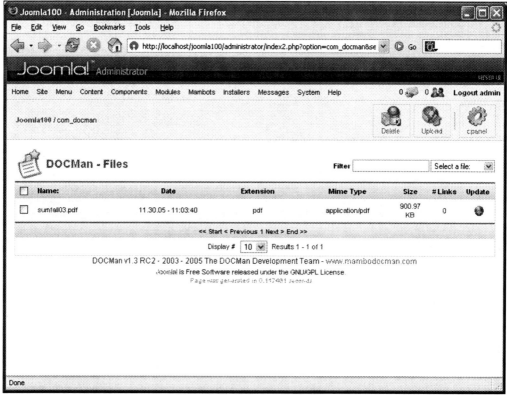

Figure 8.18: List of available Files

Icon info

With a computer that runs the Linux operating system, you have to pay attention to directory authorizations. The default DOCMan directory [pathtoJoomla!]/dmdocuments must be writable for the web server otherwise the upload of pictures does not work. Use the chmod command or the appropriate function in your FTP program and set the directory attribute to 0777. On the command line, it would look like this:

```
chmod 0777 [pathtoJoomla]/dmdocuments
```

If possible, set this directory up outside of the publicly accessible area of your web server. If this directory is publicly accessible and, in addition, its name is known, the files contained in it can be downloaded directly.

Documents

Now that we have a group, a category, and a file, we can interconnect all three objects. Open the document administration by clicking on the Documents icon in the DOCMan control panel and click on the New toolbar icon.

Document

Here you can enter a detailed file title, a picture for the document from the media manager, the desired downloadable file, a category, a date/time stamp, and a detailed description (Figure 8.19).

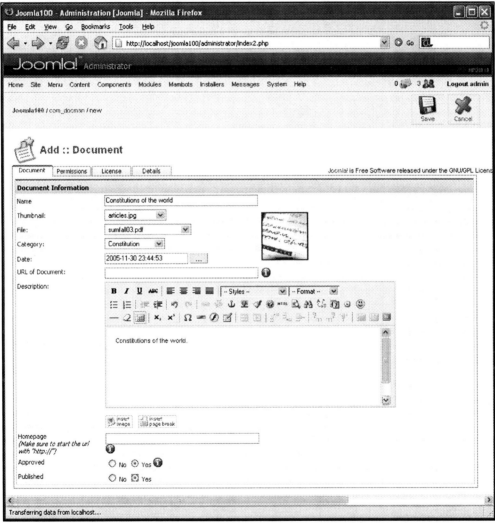

Figure 8.19: DOCMan Documents—Document Tab

Permissions

In the Permissions tab, you specify who may access the file (Everybody) and who is responsible for it (Publisher) (Figure 8.20).

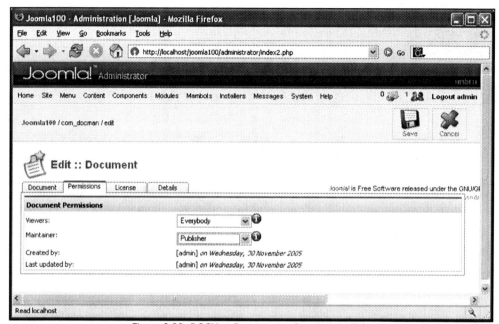

Figure 8.20: DOCMan Documents—Permissions Tab

License

Now we still have to worry about the license issue. Click on the License tab, select your license, and specify that this license must be explicitly acknowledged (Figure 8.21).

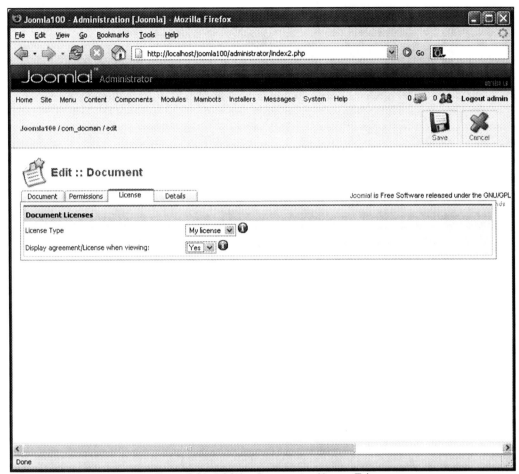

Figure 8.21: DOCMan Documents—License Tab

Details

Last but not the least, in the Details tab you can also specify a website that is important in connection with this file (Figure 8.55).

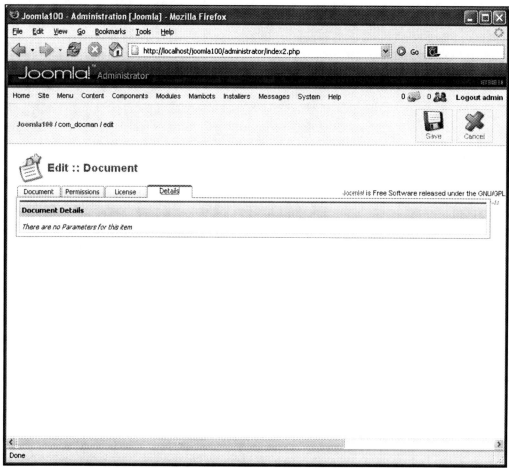

Figure 8.22: DOCMan Documents—Details Tab

After you have documented the download, click on the **Save** icon and store the data. You wind up back into the **Documents** directory. Publish your document and release it by clicking on the red crosses in each case (Figure 8.23).

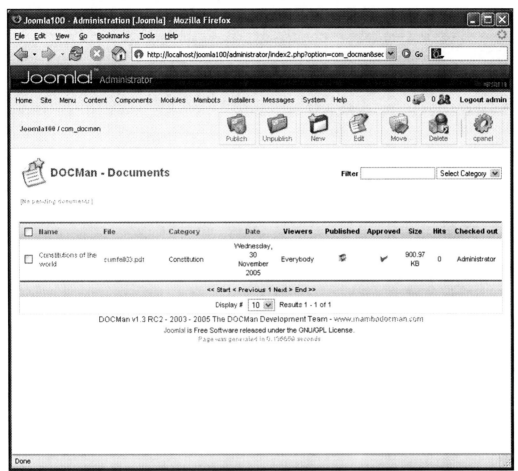

Figure 8.23: Document list

Licenses

In the License Manager you can formulate your personal terms of license. You can administer and later assign to your downloads as many licenses as you want (Figure 8.24). Write a license here that you want to have acknowledged by the visitor.

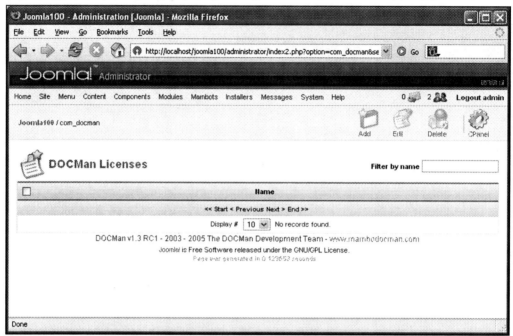

Figure 8.24: Administration of Licenses

Themes

In the themes area, you can edit the HTML and CSS files of DOCMan and install new themes just as with the site templates (Figure 8.25).

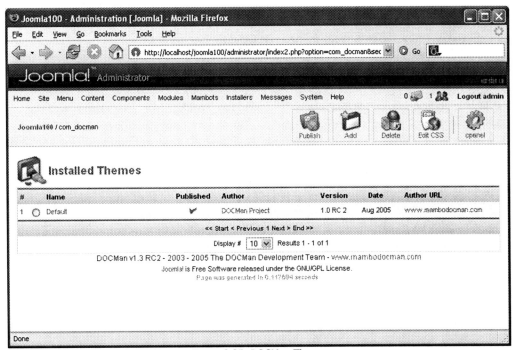

Figure 8.25: DOCMan Themes

Configuration

You can leave the parameters at their default settings. You can load zip, RAR, PDF, and text files up to one megabyte on the server for this application. All registered users may upload files, publishers may release the files, and visitors to the site are allowed to download them. You can change these and many other attributes in DOCMan configuration.

By clicking on the Save icon, you can store your attributes; clicking on the cpanel icon takes you back to the DOCMan control panel.

Updates

Clicking on this icon initiates a search for possibly existing updates and an appropriate message is displayed.

Statistics

Here you can see the 50 most frequently downloaded files.

Integration into the Website

After this job you can now merge the DOCMan component into your website. When you install DOCMan component, it creates automatically a menu entry called Docs. You can change it by renaming the menu option or setting on a new one. For the new installation you add a further menu option to the main menu in the **Menu Manager**, check off **Component**, click on the **Next** icon and enter the appropriate descriptions in the following form.

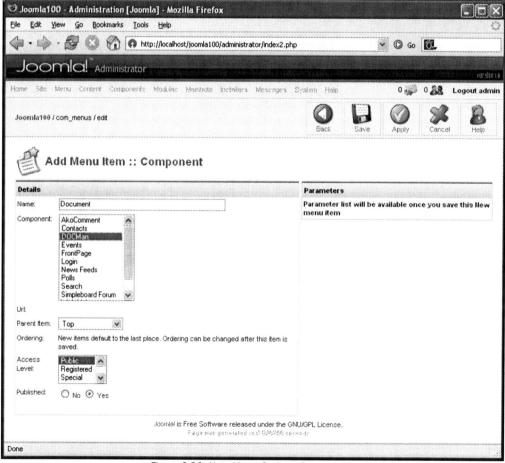

Figure 8.26: New Menu Option—Documents

After clicking on the Save icon, your Main Menu has a new link to your document area. First you will see the available categories and by clicking on the category name, you arrive at the Documents directory (Figure 8.27).

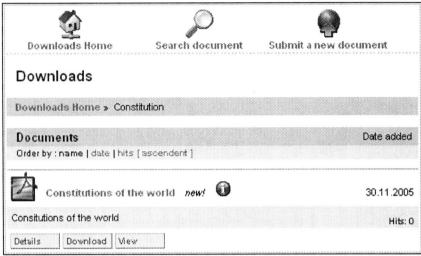

Figure 8.27: DOCMan on the Website

Before you can download a file, you have to acknowledge the license assigned to the file.

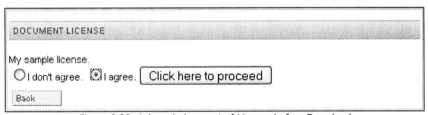

Figure 8.28: Acknowledgement of License before Download

Modules

There are various modules available for DOCMan. In order to display the most downloaded files on the website, download the mod_mostdownV10_RC_2.zip file and install it from the Installer module. Release the module, change the name to something else if you want to, and set it up in a place of your choice.

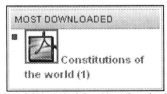

Figure 8.29: DOCMan Module—Most Popular Downloads

Mambots

For the icing on the cake, you still need a search Mambot so that the descriptions of your downloads also become scanable. Download the `bot_searchv10_RC_2.zip` file and install it from the Mambot installer. Publish the `DOCman Search` Mambot and try a search (Figure 8.30).

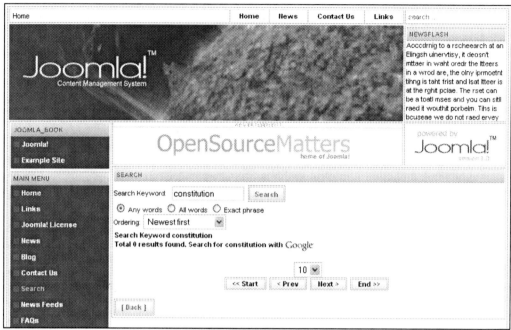

Figure 8.30: DOCMan Search Mambot

Summary

In this chapter we discussed the managing of downloadable files in the Joomla!-powered website using the zOOm gallery and DOCMan. We now proceed to the next chapter where we will discuss the internationalization of Joomla! and set up our own online store.

9
E-Commerce and I18N

In this chapter, we will talk about two very important extensions for e-commerce and internationalization. E-commerce systems are always in demand and Joomla! has something to offer here in the shape of VirtueMart. If you have a regional target group for your site, it is necessary that you understand the language of the target group and build the site in that language. The MambelFish Joomla! extension will help you out here.

Online Store

The **VirtueMart** component offers a complete store system for your Joomla! installation. VirtueMart emerged from Mambo's phpShop after the separation of Mambo and Joomla!. Mambo phpShop in turn is based on phpShop version 0.8.0.

We will describe a few features in order to give you an impression of the efficiency of this Shop system:

- Unlimited products and categories with unlimited nesting depth
- Sale of downloadable products, such as MP3s, videos, and software
- Additional attributes of products (for example, size and color)
- Ability of auction pricing
- Ability to import from CSV files
- A welcome form displays current statistics, for example, the number of customers and orders
- Administration from the Internet
- Different currencies and countries
- Different shipping addresses for customers
- Different tax rates
- SSL encryption
- Various payment options (for example, credit cards and PayPal)

On the basis of these features you can already see that a store system is a large project. Even if the goods are relatively simple to organize, you are dependent on interfaces when it comes to the latest in credit card payments.

A store requires constant care of the inventory, sale prices and special sales, customer care, fast processing of the orders and shipments. Here as well, VirtueMart for instance offers the option of informing the customer when an order was dispatched, and overview forms for the store administrator.

Installation

The installation is pretty simple. Load the virtueMart_1.0.1-COMPLETE_PACKAGE file into a directory and unzip it. In this package are all components, modules, and mambots that you need for a successful store. First install the com_virtuemart_1.0.1.tar file from the Installers | component option. After the upload, you are asked whether you want to have an empty store or one with example data (Figure 9.1).

Figure 9.1: Greeting Form after Installation

The first time, decide on the sample data and click on the Install SAMPLE DATA button. The installation of the sample data can take a few seconds, so don't interrupt the subsequent processing. When all of the tables have been created, the administrative interface of the store (Store Control Panel) is displayed:

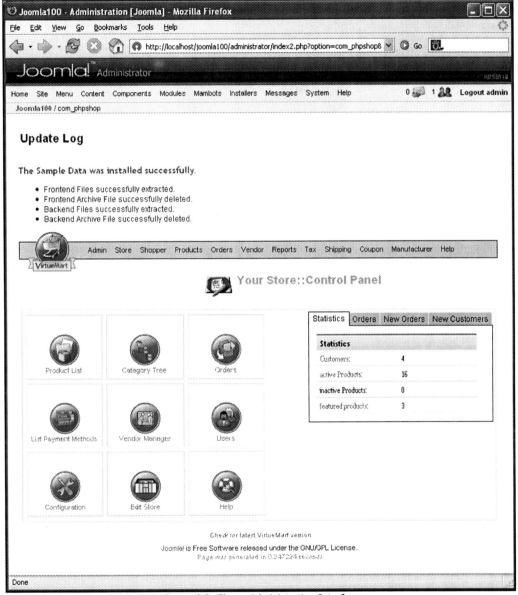

Figure 9.2: Shop—Administration Interface

Look the menus over. The structure corresponds to the Joomla! system. You have a menu system with twelve menus in the top area, nine icons in the main window for quick access to the most used menu options, and in the right area, tabs with current information about orders and customers. You need at least one module to make the store work properly. Install the `mod_virtuemart_1.0.1.tar` file from the Modules installer. Go to the module list, look for the new module and publish it. If you now go to your website and reload the display, the module with the sample data should appear (Figure 9.3).

Figure 9.3: Shop Module
on the Website

You now have the minimum configuration of the store and it is already functional. If you click on the categories, you will see the sample products:

Figure 9.4: Sample Products

You can already see from the Nice Saw that price comparisons are possible (You Save $2.00). The customers can appraise the articles. By clicking on the article name, you arrive at the detail area (Figure 9.5). You can buy this saw in three sizes and three performance levels. In addition, the availability is reported to you (1-4 Weeks). If you sign yourself on in the front end, you can evaluate this item.

Figure 9.5: Product Details

Configuration

You can accomplish the individual configurations in the following way. Go to the administrative interface of the store by clicking on the Components | VirtueMart menu option.

Work on Store Data

First go into the Store | Edit Store menu. Here you can enter all of the necessary information about your store by using three tabs. You can even upload your logo here! Remember to enter the correct currency and symbol and, of course, your correct email address.

Figure 9.6: Store Data

Add Tax Rates

Now call up the tax rate listing in the Tax | List Tax Rates menu. Add all the tax rates for your store from the Tax | Add Tax Rates menu. In each case, you can assign these tax rates to a country.

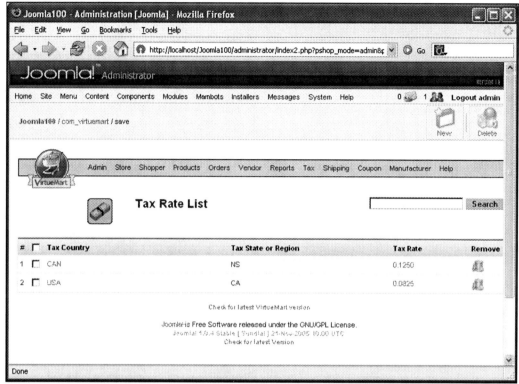

Figure 9.7: Tax Rate List

Configuration

In the Admin | Configuration menu you can specify details for all the relevant areas of your store from numerous tabs and in various submenus. The individual parameters are self-describing. In order to use, for example, the downloadable goods feature, you have to activate it in the Downloads tab (Figure 9.8).

You can also configure various included interfaces for delivery systems.

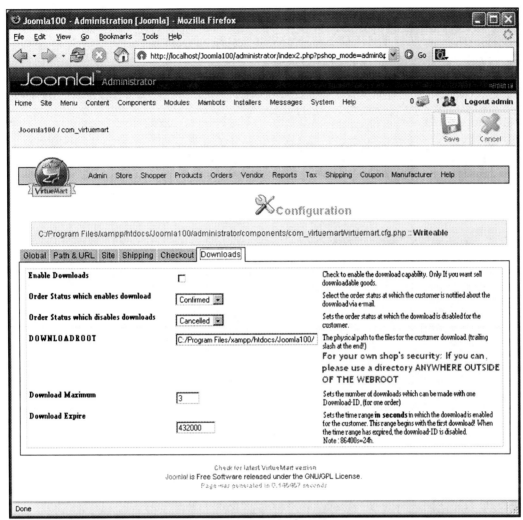

Figure 9.8: Store Configuration

Product Categories

You can see an overview of the existing store categories in the Products | Categories | List Categories menu option. From Products | New Category | Add Category you can add the categories that you need. You can structure, sort, and delete categories as in the Menu Manager. Remember to publish newly created categories:

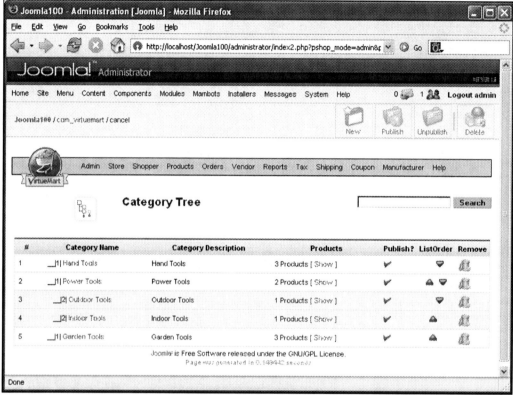

Figure 9.9: Product Categories

Now we are finally at the actual product. In Products | Add Product you can set up your items. You can specify all of the relevant product data by means of five tabs. You can also upload product pictures, define weights and measures, and define the availability of the items and related articles, all of which are then shown in the store:

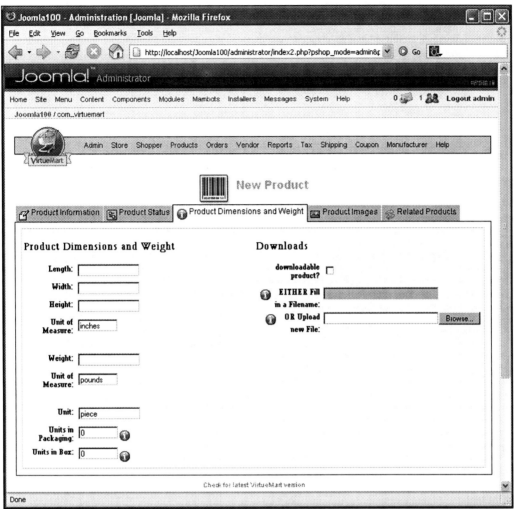

Figure 9.10: Product Entry Form

You can see the entire product list from the Products | Products Listing menu option. Here you can edit, publish, copy and delete the items.

Joomla! Configuration

You have to pay attention to a few things in the global configuration of Joomla! so that the store functions properly.

- Users must be able to register themselves (Allow User Registration). The store uses the registration for the order process.

- Activation of user accounts via an email link must be deactivated (New Account Activation).

- The store uses the email configuration from Joomla!'s global configuration.

- **Search Engine Friendly (SEF)** links function well in principle; now and then, however, there can be errors. If you want to be safe, do not use this feature.

You can learn more about configuration in the VirtueMart tutorial at
`http://mambo-phpshop.net/documentation/User_Manual/index.html`.

The Order Process

The customer selects the desired articles and puts them in the shopping cart by clicking on the Add to Cart button. The shopping cart is shown in the standard module. By clicking on the Show Shopping Cart link, the customer can see a detailed listing of the items with prices per unit. Here they can change the order quantity and remove the item again from the shopping cart.

Figure 9.11: Shopping Cart with Two Items

By clicking on the Checkout button, the multi-level ordering procedure begins. The number and shape of the stages depends on the configuration of the store.

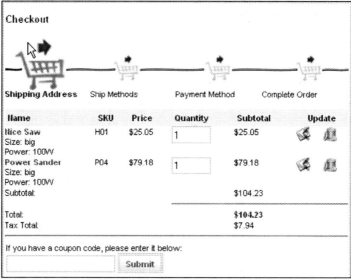

Figure 9.12: Check-out Procedure

The customers have to register themselves. If they already have a user account, they can authenticate themselves with their user name. If they don't have a user account yet, they can set one up with the form on the same page.

The customer can redeem a coupon in this dialogue and specify the billing and shipping addresses.

If you have a coupon code, please enter it below:

Submit

Please select a Shipping Address!

Billing Information
Company:
Full Name: Michelle Brown
Address: 123 Some Street
          Novato, 94947
          USA
Phone: 415-555-1234
Fax:
Email: otto@yahoo.com
(Update Address)

Shipping Information :
Add a new Shipping Address.
⊙   - Default (Same as Billing)

Next >>

Figure 9.13: Billing and Shipping Addresses

After clicking on the Next button, the customer has to specify the desired dispatch and payment terms (Figures 9.14 and 9.15).

Figure 9.14: Set Up Shipping Method

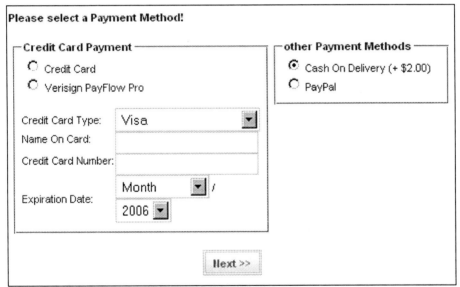

Figure 9.15: Set Up Payment Terms

In the next step, the customer gets a summary of the data he or she entered for examination and confirmation. With each step, the progress of the process is also shown visually above the shopping cart symbol. Here the customer can also enter written additions to the order in a form field.

Figure 9.16: Final Check before Ordering

If everything is correct, the customer clicks on the Confirm Order button and thereby releases the order. A confirmation screen with a link to a page with all of the relevant order data is displayed:

Figure 9.17: Order Confirmation

Order Administration in the Back End

After the customer has placed an order, it shows up in the store's administration interface in the Orders | List Orders menu option.

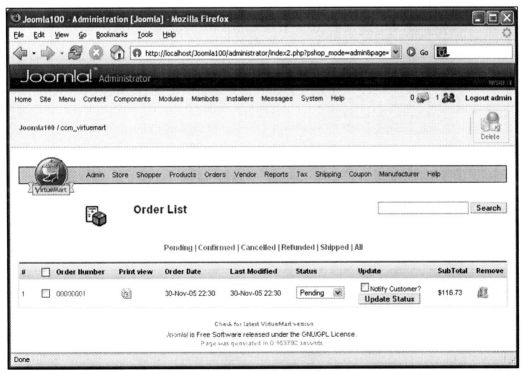

Figure 9.18: Order List

You can now communicate the progress of the order to your customer via email. Select the appropriate status, mark the Notify Customer check box, and press the Update Status button. The customer gets an email notification of the status change and the order moves into the appropriate list in your order administration.

With this, both you and your customers have a good overview of the status of the orders.

As store administrator, you naturally need detailed information about the activity in your store. In the report menu, you can create variable lists at variable times.

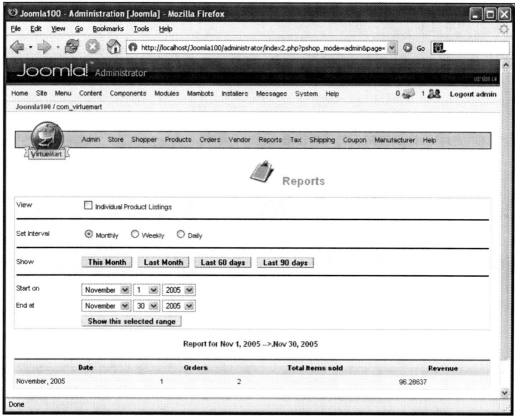

Figure 9.19: Reports

Modules

Various modules are contained in the shop package. Install them from the module manager and try them out.

Mambots

A store of course also needs a search mambot. In order to use this functionality for VirtueMart, you have to install the `virtuemart.searchbot_1.0.1.tar` file that is also contained in the Shop package from the Mambot Installer.

Joomla! Internationalization

If you want to reach target group with your site, you should understand the language of the target group and build the site in that language. If you want to address an international audience, you should use English as the standard language. Regardless of which language you choose, you need a customized language file. As a base, it's best to take what is already available.

Installation of a Different Language File

For example, if you want to reach a German target group, download the `jos100germani.zip` and `jos100germanf.zip` files. The `i` stands for informal and `f` for formal language. These language files were created by the **German Translation Team (GTT)** under the project direction of Antonio Cambule.

Log on to Joomla! administration as described earlier and click Site | Language Manager | Install. Now click Browse and select the `jos100germanf.zip` file. Click Upload File & Install. If all rights are correctly set, you will receive the message:

Upload language – Success

After one click on the Continue link, you will see the available languages. Besides English there is also German Formal - Sie and a bit of information about the creator of the language file (at the time of publication, the translation team still operated the mamboGTT.de website). In the other zip archive is the German version with the German Familiar - Du mode of address. If you want, you can install this version as well.

The green checkmark for the standard language, however, is still for English. If you want to select the German option, click Publish, which is on the right, above the Language Manager. The icons that finalize actions and dialogs are always in this position:

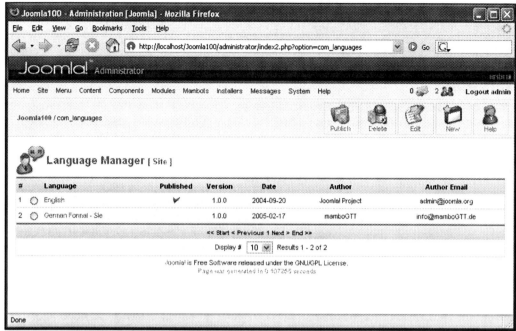

Figure 9.20: Language Selection

Translation of a Menu Entry

Your front end is now in German. Go to `http://localhost/joomla100/` and take a good look at the search field and the login module. Click the Search link in the main menu.

This page displays both German and English languages. Everything that is programmed to function automatically, like the search procedure or the login procedure, is in German; everything else is in English.

Why? The answer is quite simple. Only the words and sentences that are programmed in can be translated. A large part of the page, however, consists of entered content. This content appears in the language in which it was entered. In our case, the sample data was provided in English.

Before you try to translate the sample page, look at the buttons in the Language Manager. Besides Publish, there are New, Edit, Delete, and Help. Joomla!'s online help can be accessed by clicking the Help button.

With the New button you can install new language packages and with Delete you can erase them. But the Edit button is really interesting. Select the language that you want to see and click Edit. The Language Editor opens and you can make changes online, as shown in Figure 9.21:

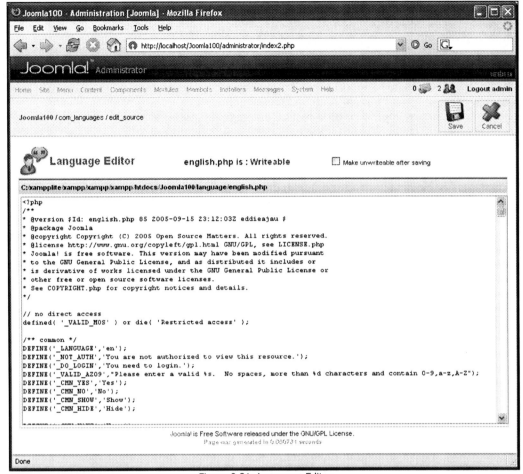

Figure 9.21: Language Editor

Browse through the language file for a while. You will get a feel of the Joomla! functions by doing this.

At present, the language file is writable, thus alterable from PHP or any other tool. If you are of the opinion that the translation was successful and you want more security, simply mark the appropriate checkbox to make the file read only. The write rights are now revoked for this file and granted next time for memory procedures only. In order to restore the original rights situation, you have to change the file rights from your FTP client or from a shell with the chmod command. Click Save or Cancel to exit the Language Editor.

What do you have to do in order to change the Search menu entry into Suchen or to rename the Main Menu into Hauptmenü?

Exit the Language Editor and click Menu | mainmenu. You are now in the Menu Manager. Click the Search link as shown in Figure 9.22 and edit it in the form that appears on your monitor as shown in Figure 9.23.

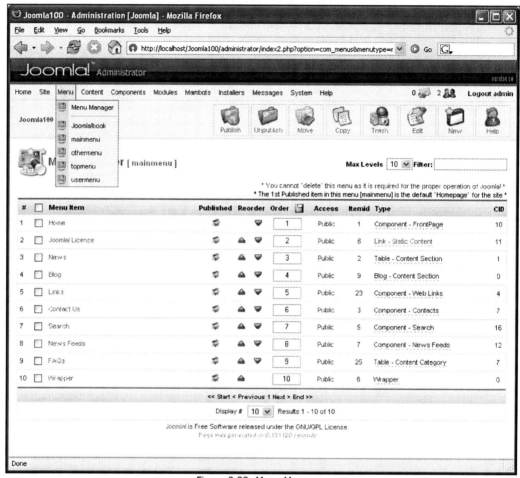

Figure 9.22: Menu Manager

Simply replace the word Search with Suche and click Apply. You will now see Suche on the Main Menu of your site!

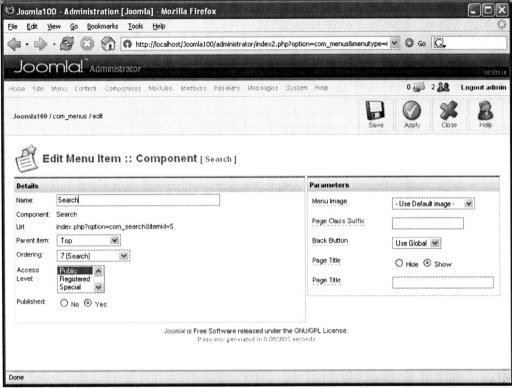

Figure 9.23: Change Item Menu

Multilingualism with MambelFish

In Europe, there is a demand for multilingual websites. Up to now, creating a real multilingual site with Mambo, for which this component was originally created, was not possible. You could select from many front-end language files, but the website had only one language. With an ingenious component from Alex Kempkens (a member of Joomla!'s development team and expert consultant for this book), it is now possible to produce real multilingual websites.

The first version of Joomla! will not have multilingual web pages included as standard equipment either. The next version of Joomla!, which will presumably be on the market when you are holding this book in your hands, will have a multilingual administration area, and there will probably be an international Joomla! version, into which the MambelFish component will be integrated.

The **MambelFish** component makes it possible to produce a multilingual website. This topic is quite complex and using this component is not easy. Even though there are a number of options for offering multilingual websites, the language aspect is always difficult. A web page consists of standard sentences, which are translated into language files. These language files are also used in MambelFish. Furthermore, a standard language is specified in Global Configuration. According to requirements, users can select several target languages.

But what happens to the content?

Here, MambelFish takes the rocky but logical route of translating all dynamic content in the translation manager into an appropriate target language. This includes the menu descriptions and different categories. The content is not translated automatically; instead, you have to produce every content element in the target language.

This has the following advantages:

- Every part of your website is available in all languages.
- The user can see the entire website in a different language by a click of the mouse.

Installation of MambelFish (Component and Module)

Download the `mambelfish_1.5.zip` file and install it from the menu option Installers | Components. After installation, you will see a message indicating that the component has been installed. In addition, you will see an extensive greeting text with a notice that various files have to be patched one by one.

You can find the patch files in the `[pathtoJoomla]\administrator\components\`
`com_mambelfish\patch\4.5.2` directory. Copy all files and subdirectories, including the contained files, into your Joomla! `[pathtoJoomla]` master directory:

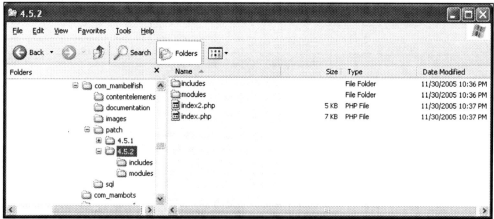

Figure 9.24: MambelFish Patches

The existing Joomla! files are overwritten with this action. The patched files are necessary to make the language functionality available everywhere in Joomla!.

For immediate results, install the appropriate module. Download the `mbf_module.zip` file and install it from the menu option Installers | Modules. After installation completes, you will see a message announcing that the module was successfully installed.

If you now check your website, you will see an empty box with the heading MambelFish at the bottom left hand corner. This is because you have not configured the component yet.

MambelFish Configuration

After installing MambleFish, install all languages that you want to offer from the Site | Languages | Install menu. At this time, the German and the English language file would have to be installed, with German selected as the default. For now, I will leave it like this.

To make the languages available for MambelFish, you have to enter the appropriate values in Components | Mambelfish | Language Configuration. The dialog has two tabs: Languages and Frontend.

Languages

This tab displays all the installed languages. You can select all languages and overwrite the default descriptions. In addition, you can specify the correct character set (ISO) and an image file to be displayed in place of the name, for example, a flag. You can also specify the order that languages should be displayed in the module.

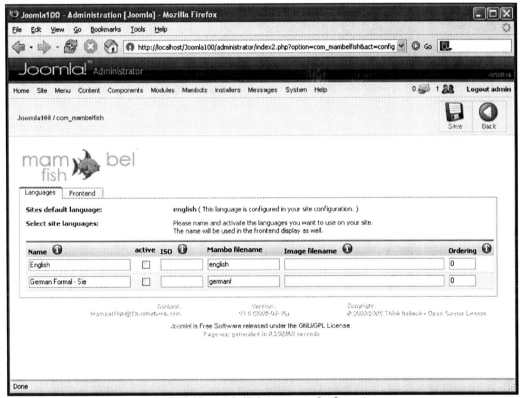

Figure 9.25: MambelFish Language Configuration

Now on the web page, the module offers both languages:

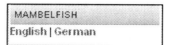

Figure 9.26: Language
Selection

If you click on the language links, you will notice some differences. The most common one is the notice: Sorry this content is not available in your selected language.

Since we are working with Joomla! sample data, they must be translated. Now let's look at the second tab.

Frontend

The settings for the website are defined in the following figure:

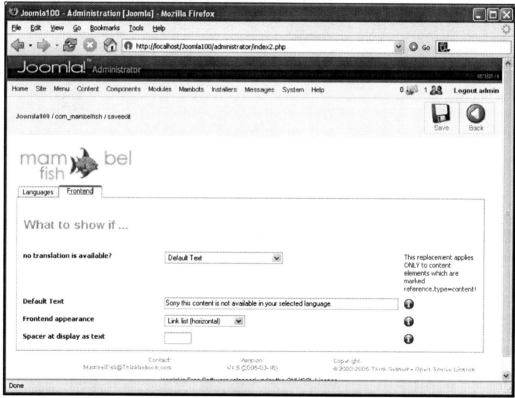

Figure 9.27: Language Configuration in Frontend

Two things need to be addressed here. First, what should happen to the display of content elements if no translation is available, and second, how should language entries in the module be displayed? For elements that have not been translated, there is an option to display alternative text.

This alternative text can be chosen in the next field presented to you. The second option is to display the original text. The third option also offers the original text, however, with additional information.

The front-end layout takes place either horizontally or vertically and either as text or as an image. A separator can be entered in the field below it, for use with horizontal layout. By default, it is the pipe symbol (|).

Translation with MambelFish

It is very easy to translate a web page using the MambelFish component. From the Components | Mambelfish | Translation menu, you come to the translation area of the component. You get an empty window when you first access this area. Select No translation as language and Categories as content elements. All categories, Joomla_book as well as others, are now displayed. Now select the language. The display without translation changes accordingly.

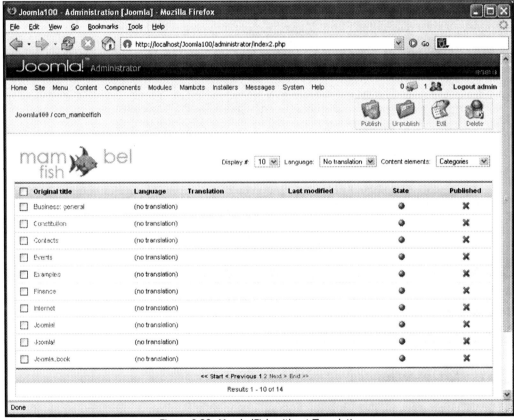

Figure 9.28: MambelFish without Translation

Click on the Joomla_book link. You will get an edit form as shown in Figure 9.29.

If you enable the WYSIWYG editor, pasting by mouse-click may not work. If this is the case, use the *Shift + Insert* or *Ctrl + V* key combination.

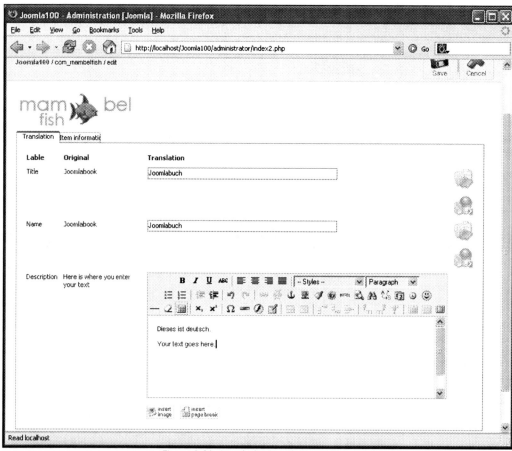

Figure 9.29: MambelFish with Translation

Click Save to translate the first part of your website. The date of the translation appears in the categories list. Publish the category by clicking on the red cross.

Select English as the language in the Language field and repeat the process.

If you select All Languages in the option list, translations are visible:

☐ Joomlabook	(no translation)	Joomlabuch	2005-11-30 22:54:09		✖
☐ Joomlabook	German	Joomlabuch	2005-11-30 22:51:53		✿
☐ Joomlabook	English	Joomlabook	2005-11-30 22:52:43		✿

Figure 9.30: Display of Translated Categories

Repeat the process with a Content item. The Examples is used as an example:

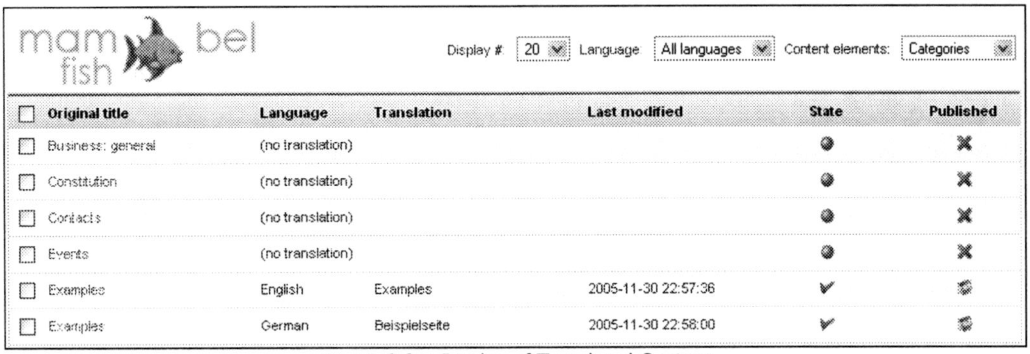

Original title	Language	Translation	Last modified	State	Published
Business: general	(no translation)				
Constitution	(no translation)				
Contacts	(no translation)				
Events	(no translation)				
Examples	English	Examples	2005-11-30 22:57:36		
Examples	German	Beispielseite	2005-11-30 22:58:00		

Figure 9.31: Display of Translated Content

The text on your website now appears in the language you selected. You can translate your entire website using this method. It is a lot of work but the result, especially for a business application, is respectable and competent.

Mambot for MambelFish

MambelFish Mambot can browse the translated pages using the search module.

Download the `mbf_searchbot.zip` file and click Installers | Mambots in the menu bar. Select the file and click Upload File & Install. The list of installed Mambots displays multilingual content searchbot.

Click Mambots | Site Mambots in the menu bar and publish the newly installed multilingual content searchbot. When you enter text in the search field on your website, the translated elements are scanned and displayed in the result list if a match is found.

Integrate your Own Components into MambelFish

By copying a table description in XML format into the `[pathtoJoomla]/administrator/components/com_mambelfish/contentelements/` directory, you can merge all components into the MambelFish system. You can find an XML file for the sample components in Listing 9.1 given below.

Based on this description, MambelFish integrates the data that has to be translated into the administration interface. MambelFish can be controlled by assigning the value `0` or `1` to the `translate` attribute.

Listing 9.1: joomlabook.xml

```
<?xml version="1.0" ?>
<mambelfish type="contentelement">
  <name>joomlabook</name>
  <author>Hagen Graf</author>
  <version>1.0</version>
  <description>example from the Joomla!book</description>
  <reference type="joomlabook">
    <table name="joomlabook">
     <field type="referenceid" name="id" translate="0">ID</field>
```

```
        <field type="titletext" name="text" translate="1">Text</field>
      </table>
    </reference>
</mambelfish>
```

Summary

This chapter covered extensions for two very important features, namely VirtueMart for e-commerce and Mambelfish for internationalization. We discussed the installation and configuration of these two extensions. This brings to the end of the discussion on Joomla! extensions. In the next chapter, we will proceed to creating our own templates.

10
Your Own Templates

In order to customize the appearance of your site to your company colors, you have to modify an existing template or create a new one. In this chapter you will learn the basics of Joomla! template production.

Corporate Identity

Corporate Identity (**CI**) refers to the self-image and the appearance of an enterprise. This appearance, the identity, either results from the enterprise's tradition or could be completely invented in a newly created establishment. This identity is important to give the customer a feel for the enterprise and to enable recognition. The visitors to your website should recognize your enterprise on the first visit.

Corporate Identity includes:

- Corporate Image (price, product, and advertising strategy)
- Corporate Design (visual appearance)
- Corporate Communication
- Corporate Behavior (behavior of coworkers with each other and to the outside world)

These areas need to be considered while developing a website. In this chapter, we will examine Corporate Design. At a minimum, it consists of a logo, a character font, and the house colors that the enterprise uses.

HTML/XHTML, CSS, and XML

The abbreviations HTML/XHTML, CSS, and XML stand for Internet technologies that Joomla! works with. The **World Wide Web Consortium** (http://www.w3.org/) standardizes these technologies.

HTML/XHTML

The World Wide Web is based on **HTML**, a page-description language. It is not a programming language, but a text-description language.

Every text consists of structures like headings, lists, bold and italic areas, tables, and much more. HTML works with so-called **tags**. A tag has an opening and a closing form. For example, a first-level heading looks like this:

```
<h1>This is a heading</h1>
```

The tags are interpreted in a browser and the text is displayed according to their meaning.

HTML is easy to learn and a tutorial can be found at `http://www.w3schools.com/html/`. HTML is not being developed any further and the successor to HTML is XHTML version 1.0.

CSS

Cascading Style Sheets (CSS) are an extension to HTML. CSS is not a programming language, but a vocabulary for defining the format properties of HTML elements.

With the help of CSS commands, you can determine that first-level headings should have, say, a character size of 18 points in the Arial character font, are not bold, and have a spacing of 1.9 cm to the next paragraph.

Such options are not possible with pure HTML and were not necessary while developing it. With the progressive commercialization of the Internet, additional formatting possibilities do become more important.

CSS data can be included in HTML in the following three ways:

In the Central HTML File

The CSS commands are defined in the head section of the HTML file:

```
<head>
   <title>title of the file</title>
   <style type="text/css">
     <!--
       /* ... this is where the CSS commands are defined ... */
     -->
   </style>
</head>
```

In a Separate CSS File

If the CSS commands apply to several HTML files, they can be stored in a separate file and the path to this file can be specified in the HTML head section. This is the version that Joomla! uses:

```
<head>
  <title>title of the file</title>
  <link rel="stylesheet" type="text/css" href="formate.css">
</head>
```

Within an HTML Tag

CSS commands can be integrated within an HTML tag:

```
<body>
    <h1 style="... CSS command ...">...</h1>
</body>
```

Combinations

These three methods can be combined without any problem in an HTML file. It is, for instance, possible to overwrite CSS commands in a central HTML file that applies to all pages with the subsequent source code of an HTML page. It is better to use the central file because overriding it results in unclear structures.

XML

The **Extensible Markup Language** (**XML**) is a universe in itself. It represents a metalanguage in which other languages are formulated. To a certain extent, it is the mother of all languages. For our purposes, you need XML as the description language for the metadata of the templates that you want to create. These metadata are primarily important for the template installer and the display in the Template Manager. In principle, these data consist of opening and closing tags. For example:

```
<name>Joomla_book</name>
```

One difference between HTML and XML is that in XML no tags are predefined. For this reason, one is free in the organization of the structures and naming of tags.

Create Your Own Templates

Now we want to create our own template. There are several things to consider before we have a finished template package.

Concept

Before you start working, you have to create a concept. The work starts with a sketch or a diagram, especially when producing templates. Whether you create this sketch with programs like Adobe Photoshop (http://www.adobe.com/products/photoshop/), Microsoft Paint, which comes with Windows, the open-source program Gimp (http://www.gimp.org/), or with a piece of paper and markers, is up to you.

Fixed Size or Variable Size

You can create two kinds of templates: templates that adapt their structure to the size of the browser window and templates that have a fixed size. An example for the first flexible layout is if you have 2048 pixels on your screen and the browser window is maximized, then your page is stretched accordingly. It can look strange if you use graphics and non-scalable elements like logos and signatures in your template. You have no control of what it is going to look like.

The other variation is to decide on a certain resolution and to position all elements exactly on the pixels in the template. The advantage is that your web page always looks the way you want.

Unfortunately, you do not know the default screen resolution of your page. Your page fills the screen with a resolution of 800 x 600 pixels. On a large screen with 1400 x 1050 pixels, it occupies about a third of the screen surface and looks a little lost.

There is no real solution for this dilemma. You have to weigh the pros and cons and make a decision.

If you prefer the fixed size, you should select a size that looks presentable on most screens, which are 800 x 600 pixels. Since the browser has a scroll bar on the right side and the browser window is framed, the available width is even smaller, so you have a maximum of 780 pixels to work with.

Structure

You are dealing with structured data and first have to determine a general allocation. Joomla! normally uses a structure shown in the following figure:

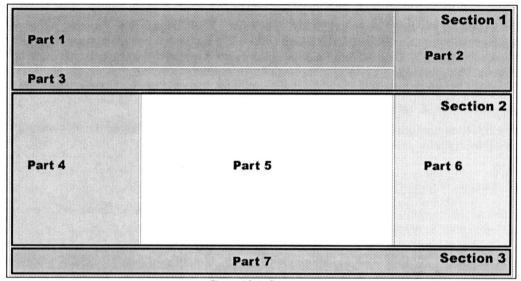

Figure 10.1: Structure

Section 1:

- Part 1: This is where your logo or a picture and the page name go.
- Part 2: This is where the search field is.
- Part 3: Here is the linked navigation path (Breadcrumbs).

Section 2:

- Part 4: The most important menus are shown in the left column.
- Part 5: The actual page content goes here.
- Part 6: The right column is a place for additional menus.

Section 3:

- Part 7: The bottom part is the footer.

HTML Conversion

Now you have to convert the concept into HTML. Depending on the program with which you created it, there is a possibility that the picture can be automatically converted to HTML code. You can also do the conversion manually in a text editor, in an HTML editor like Macromedia Dreamweaver (http://www.macromedia.com/software/dreamweaver/), or in one of the numerous free HTML editors (http://www.thefreecountry.com/webmaster/htmleditors.shtml).

The source code of the HTML conversion looks like Listing 10.1. The code is kept simple and does not correspond to the XHTML standard in the head section.

Listing 10.1: HTML Basic Structure

```
<html>
  <head>
    <title>Untitled Document</title>
  </head>
  <body bgcolor="#FFFFFF" text="#000000">
   <table width="780" border="1">

     <!-- Part 1 -->
     <tr>
        <!-- Area 1 -->
        <td colspan="2" height="89" bgcolor="#F5C228"> </td>
        <!-- Area 2 -->
        <td width="178" height="120" rowspan="2" bgcolor="#FFCC33">  
        </td>
     </tr>

     <tr>
        <!-- Area 3 -->
        <td colspan="2" height="33" bgcolor="#FFCC33"> </td>
     </tr>

     <!-- Part 2 -->
     <tr>
        <!-- Area 4 -->
        <td width="197" height="233" bgcolor="#F5EE28">   </td>
        <!-- Area 5 -->
        <td width="389" height="233"> </td>
        <!-- Area 6 -->
        <td width="178" height="233" bgcolor="#FFFF33">   </td>
     </tr>

     <!-- Part 3 -->
     <tr bgcolor="#FFCC33">
        <!-- Area 7 -->
        <td colspan="3" height="40"> </td>
     </tr>
    </table>
   </body>
</html>
```

If you open this source code in a browser, the structure looks similar to our concept (see Figure 10.1). You must store this source code in a file named index.php.

To see the division better, the table is drawn with a border (`border="1"` attribute). Here you can give your creative juices free reign when it comes to colors and logos.

File Structure of the Template

Now it's time to think about certain conventions. The template has to be stored in a special directory structure. If required, you can work directly with your local Joomla! installation. If that is too unclear, you can also store the template in an arbitrary place on your hard drive. You have to adhere to the following file structure:

`/templates/[name of the template]/`

`/templates/[name of the template]/CSS/`

`/templates/[name of the template]/images/`

The name of the template cannot contain blanks and other special characters. Later, the template installer has to create a directory from this name. Depending on the operating system, exotic combinations of characters can cause problems; also, the name should be meaningful. For example, if you make the `template chooser` module available on your website, this name will be offered to your visitors in the selection list. I am using `joomla_book` as my template. Various files with certain names have to be present in the template directories. Besides the image files of your template, all other file names have to agree with the defaults.

- `/templates/joomla_book/index.php`: This is the basic version of the HTML file that we created earlier. It has to have the `.php` ending, since the dynamic Joomla! module element, which we will insert later, has to be interpreted by PHP.

- `/templates/joomla_book/template_thumbnail.png`: A preview picture of your template for selection in Joomla! administration and in the template chooser module will be available. Preview pictures have a format of approximately 227 x 162 pixels.

- `/templates/joomla_book/templateDetails.xml`: This file represents the construction manual for the 'template installer'. Here you specify the location where the files are to be copied. During the upload, PHP picks this file out and copies the files to the correct place. For the example template, you can use the file from Listing 10.2 and provide your own data. You have to surround every file that you use in the template with an opening and a closing XML tag.

```
<files>
    <filename> ... enter the filename of a file in the TemplateRoot directory ...
    </filename>
    <filename> ... for every file a filename-Container </filename>
</files>
<images>
    <filename> ... enter the filename of an image in the images-directory ...
    </filename>
    <filename> ... for every file a filename-Container </filename>
</images>
<css>
    <filename>css/template_css.css (Name of the CSS file)</filename>
</css>
```

The other containers of the XML file provide the description of the template. Here the complete functional listing of the XML file:

Listing 10.2: templateDetails.xml

```xml
<?xml version="1.0" encoding="iso-8859-1"?>
<mosinstall type="template" version="4.5.2">
    <name>joomla_book</name>
    <creationDate>03/23/05</creationDate>
    <author>Hagen Graf</author>
    <copyright>GNU/GPL</copyright>
    <authorEmail> hagen@aubkunden.de </authorEmail>
    <authorUrl>http://www.alternative-unternehmensberatung.de</authorUrl>
    <version>0.1</version>
    <description>… description</description>
    <files>
        <filename>index.php</filename>
        <filename>template_thumbnail.png</filename>
    </files>
    <images>
        <filename>images/logo.png</filename>
    </images>
    <css>
        <filename>css/template_css.css</filename>
    </css>
</mosinstall>
```

- `/templates/joomla_book/css/template_css.css`: This is the CSS file of your template and the organization of the CSS file is open to you. However, there are standard descriptions for various side elements. You can find a table of these elements in the Appendix. For your first attempt, you need an empty CSS file with this name.

- `/templates/joomla_book/images/[user-defined picture files]`: Here you can store arbitrary image files, which will be used in your template. The installer then copies the files into the 'image' sorter.

First Trial Run

You can see and access your new template in Joomla! administration once you have reconstructed all the structures in the `[pathtoJoomla!]/templates/` subdirectory:

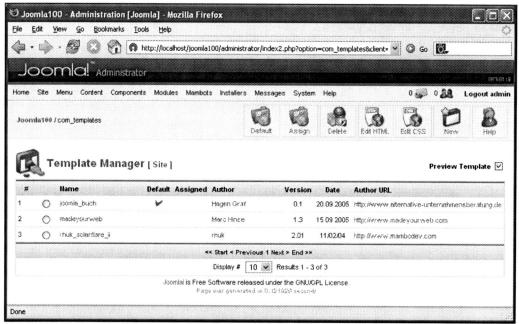

Figure 10.2: New Template

When you open your website, you will see the structure as shown in Figure 10.1. Unfortunately, no content is shown yet. Since this content is produced dynamically, you have to integrate it piece by piece into your new template.

Integration of the Joomla! Module

The integration of the Joomla! module takes place by means of PHP commands that are embedded into the HTML code. If you insert the following lines in place of the title tag in the head section of the index.php file, the favicon and the title of the page are displayed:

```
<head>
  <?php mosShowHead(); ?>
</head>
```

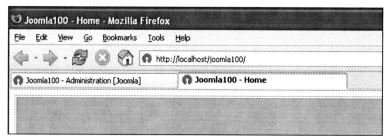

Figure 10.3: Favicon and Page Title

If you view the source code of this page, you will notice that Joomla! has written the entire metadata, which you had entered in Administration, into the HTML code.

Listing 10.3: Joomla! Metadata

```
...
<head>
<title>Joomla 1.0.0 - Home</title>
<meta name="description" content="Joomla - the dynamic portal engine and
content management system" />
<meta name="keywords" content="Joomla, joomla, test, test" />
<meta name="Generator" content="Joomla! - Copyright © 2005 Open Source
Matters. All rights reserved." />
<meta name="robots" content="index, follow" />
<link rel="alternate" type="application/rss+xml" title="Joomla 1.0.0"
href="http://localhost/Joomla100/cache/RSS2.0" />
<link rel="shortcut icon" href="http://localhost/Joomla100/images/favicon.ico"
/>

... <link
href="http://localhost/Joomla100/templates/joomla_book/css/template_css.css"
rel="stylesheet" type="text/css"/>
</head>
...
```

Since this has worked so well, we will waste no time and get to the other relevant PHP modules
that deal with functions. For example, the function mosLoad-Modules() expects the location of the
module (right, left, user1...) as parameter. You can assign this place in the 'Module Manager'.
The function then displays all modules with the appropriate parameter.

The following listing shows the complete source code of the index.php file with PHP modules:

Listing 10.4: index.php with Joomla! Modules

```
<html><head>
<?php mosShowHead(); ?>
</head>
<body bgcolor="#FFFFFF" text="#000000">
<table width="780" border="1">
  <!-- Part 1 -->
  <tr>
    <!-- Area 1 -->
    <td colspan="2" height="89" bgcolor="#F5C228"> </td>
    <!-- Area 2 -->
    <td width="178" height="120" rowspan="2" bgcolor="#FFCC33">
    <?php mosLoadModules ( 'user4' ); ?>
    </td>
  </tr>
  <tr>
    <!-- Area 3 -->
    <td colspan="2" height="33" bgcolor="#FFCC33">
    <?php mosPathWay(); ?>
    </td>
  </tr>
  <!-- Part 2 -->
  <tr>
    <!-- Area 4 -->
    <td width="197" height="233" bgcolor="#F5EE28" valign="top">
    <?php mosLoadModules ( 'left' ); ?>
    </td>
    <!-- Area 5 -->
    <td width="389" height="233" valign="top">
    <?php mosMainBody(); ?>
    </td>
    <!-- Area 6 -->
    <td width="178" height="233" bgcolor="#FFFF33" valign="top">
    <?php mosLoadModules ( 'right' ); ?>
    </td>
```

255

```
    </tr>
    <!-- Part 3 -->
    <tr bgcolor="#FFCC33">
        <!-- Area 7 -->
        <td colspan="3" height="40">
        <?php include_once( $GLOBALS['mosConfig_absolute_path'] .
        '/includes/footer.php'); ?>
        </td>
    </tr>
</table></body></html>
```

If you open the home page with the changed HTML code on a local server, you will see dynamic content. Your new template is filled with data. You are now working with pure HTML code and the results look as if they could benefit from some visual improvement:

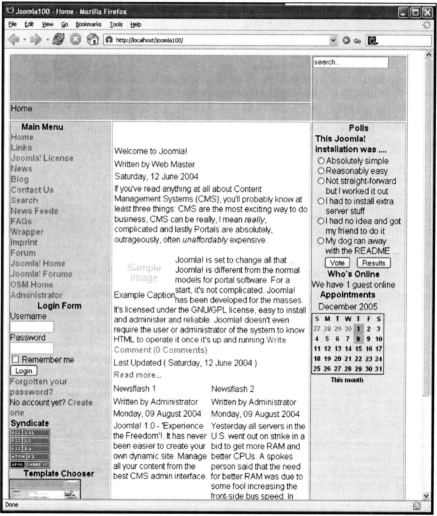

Figure 10.4: Template with Dynamic Data

To refine the visual aspect, we will take a small step into CSS formatting. Copy the following code into your `template_css.css` file (Listing 10.5). Here it is specified that the default font is Arial, the links are not to be underlined, and the script will be displayed in another color and bold font if you roll over a link with your mouse cursor (see `http://en.selfhtml.org/css/`).

Listing 10.5: template_css.css

```
body {
font-family: Arial, Helvetica, Sans Serif;
}
a:link, a:visited {
color: #ff6600;
text-decoration: none;
font-weight: bold;
}
a:hover {
color: #C43C03;
text-decoration: none;
font-weight: bold;
}
```

Now your template looks a little more attractive. Point the mouse at the Search link in the main menu. The link is displayed in bold and in another color:

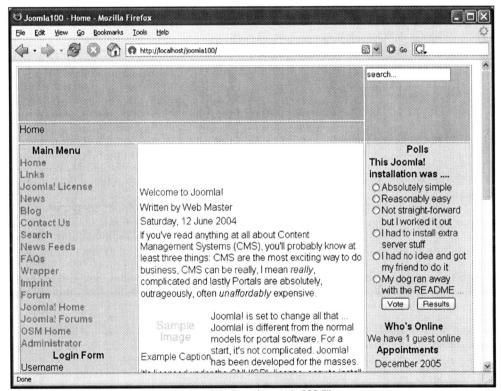

Figure 10.5: Template with CSS File

Creating a Template Package

To complete your template, create a current preview picture of your template (`template_thumbnail.png`) and pack all the files with subdirectories into a zip archive.

In addition, assign all files and folders to the folder `[pathtoJoomla!]/templates/joomla_book/` and pack all the contents into the `joomla_book.zip` file. Make a backup of this file and the zip file.

To test the installation, remove the template from the Template Manager. To accomplish this, specify another template as the default (select the template and click Default), delete the newly created template by selecting it, and clicking Delete.

Installation with the Joomla! Template Installer

After you have eliminated traces of development, go to the menu Installers | Template Site, select the `Joomla!book.zip` file, and click Upload File & Install. You will see the success screen of the template installer. A description from the XML file is displayed in the following figure:

Figure 10.6: Uploading the New Template

If you click Continue, the newly created template is displayed in the Template Manager with a preview picture:

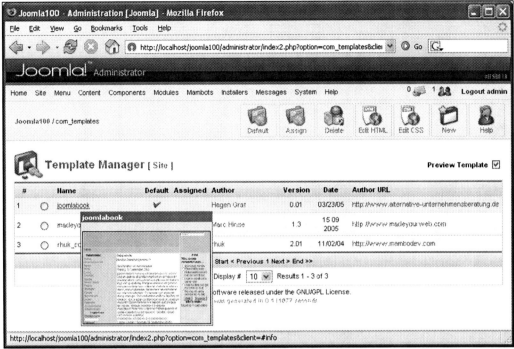

Figure 10.7: New Template in the Template Manager

Creating Templates with Dreamweaver Extension

There is an extension for the HTML editor Dreamweaver with which you can produce templates.
You need a current version of Dreamweaver (MX 2004 and higher) and you can install the
Template Builder Extension there. The program was originally written for Mambo 4.5.1, but it
works well with the Joomla! versions as well.

Installation

Download the `mambosolutionsDW_107.zip` file. Start Dreamweaver, click on Comands |
Administration Extensions. The Macromedia Extension manager opens. Select the file and click
on Install.

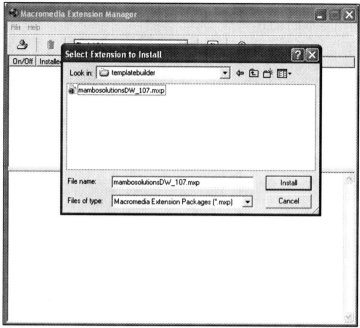

Figure 10.8: Install Dreamweaver Extension

Create New Template File

In order to activate the extension, you have to restart Dreamweaver. Open a new document of the type dynamic page. Click on File | New | Dynamic Page | PHP (Figure 10.9).

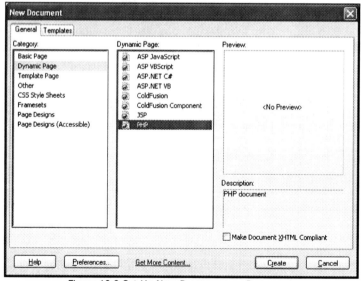

Figure 10.9 Set Up New Dreamweaver Document

After the file has been created, you will see a MamboOS palette in the top area. There are a number of buttons there with which you can insert the template elements (Figure 10.10).

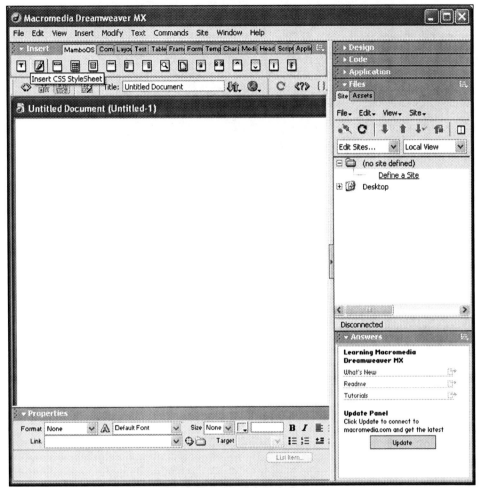

Figure 10.10: Template Palette in Dreamweaver

The first thing you have to do is to delete the header in the source code window that was produced by Dreamweaver (Figure 10.11) and replace it with the Joomla!-specific one.

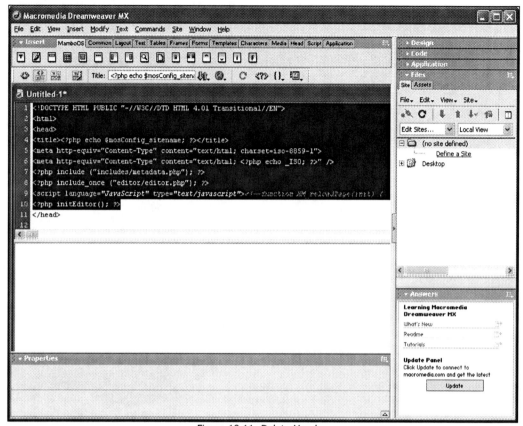

Figure 10.11: Delete Header

After that, in succession, click on the icons Insert Head Code, Insert Title, and Insert CSS StyleSheet (Figures 10.12, 10.13 and 10.14).

Figure 10.12: Add Joomla! Head Code

Figure 10.13: Add Joomla! Title

Figure 10.14: Add Joomla! CSS StyleSheet

Now you have exactly the source code in your header that a Joomla! template needs (Figure 10.15) and which, a while ago, we had to type manually.

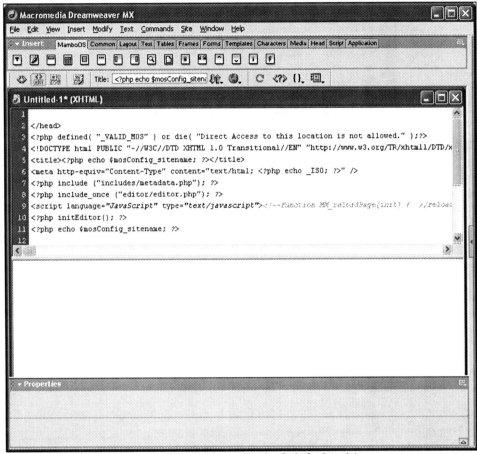

Figure 10.15: Necessary Header Code for Joomla!

Template Structure

Other than the special header, you now need the structure of your website. You can create this structure with the help of a `table` or with HTML `div` tags. I will describe the table version here.

If the layout mode is still activated in your Dreamweaver, please terminate it.

Produce a table structure as described in the previous example. By clicking on Insert | Table, you can create your desired structure. You have a lot of options of producing complex table structures and to nest the tables with Dreamweaver. I am consciously showing a simple version (Figure 10.16). Color the table according to your desires (Figure 10.17).

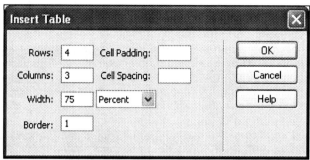

Figure 10.16: Setting Up a Simple Table

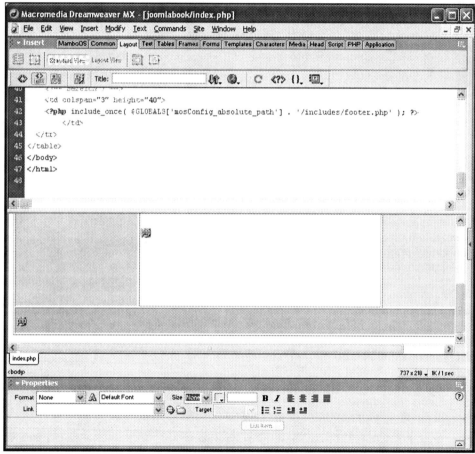

Figure 10.17: Table Structure

Now save the file. Set up a new subdirectory under [pathtojoomla!]/templates with the name mytemplate and save the file in it with the name index.php. In addition set up a css directory and an images directory (Figure 10.18).

In the images directory, please deposit all images and graphics that you will use in your template. You can create the graphics with a commercial graphics program such as Photoshop or an Open Source solution such as Gimp and by means of Dreamweaver place them in your template.

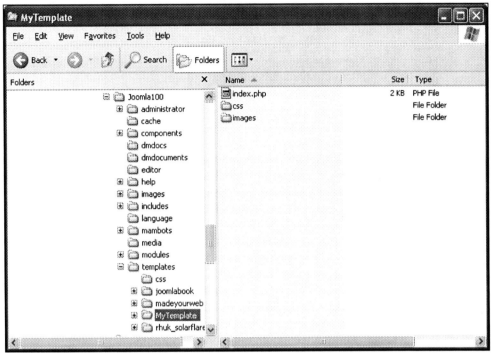

Figure 10.18: Directory Structure of Your Template

The CSS file that is valid for the entire template is in the css directory, as the name implies. It has to have the name template_css.css. You can create the file with Dreamweaver or copy an already existing CSS file from another Joomla! template. If you create the file with Dreamweaver, Dreamweaver changes the header of your template by inserting a link to the newly created CSS file there.

```
<link href="css/template_css.css" rel="stylesheet" type="text/css" />
```

You will need the absolute path and thus the version that we already inserted a while ago in your subsequent template within Joomla!. Dreamweaver does not evaluate the PHP tags in our situation. The PHP variables do not contain a value and therefore the CSS link that was set up by the extension leads to nowhere.

Thus use the link inserted by Dreamweaver at first and remove it again later.

I recommend to you to use an already existing CSS file since the Joomla!-specific classes are already defined in it. Therefore copy the CSS file or its contents from the rhuk_solarflare_ii template into your freshly created CSS file.

Insertion of the Joomla! Modules

Now you have the basis for inserting the Joomla! modules. Move the cursor to the spot in your table where you want to have, for example, a search field and click on the Insert Search icon in the option bar (10.19).

Figure 10.19: Insert Search Field

In the design window you can now see a search field and all kind of HTML and JavaScript code was added in the source code.

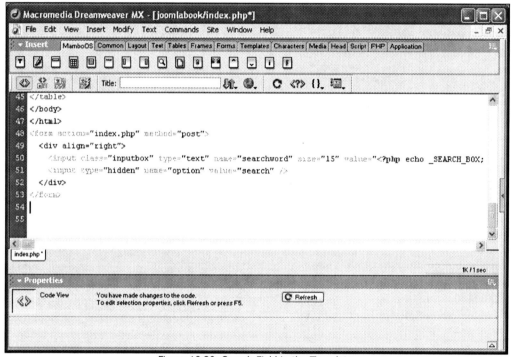

Figure 10.20: Search Field in the Template

Now you can gradually insert the dynamic elements into the appropriate table fields by clicking on the respective icons (Figure 10.21).

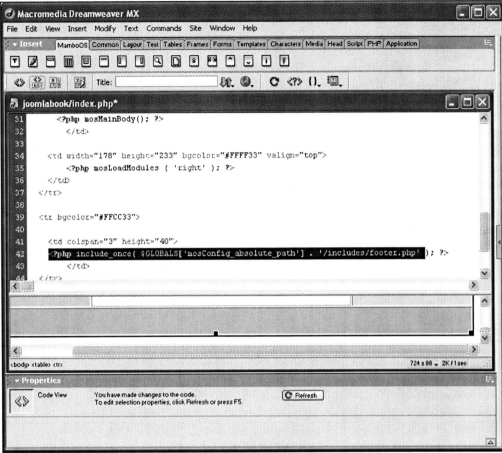

Figure 10.21: Template with Joomla! Modules

Live Site

To be able to view the template in your Joomla! installation, you have to create the XML file with the name templateDetails.xml. A basic version without pictures looks like this:

Listing 10.6: templateDetails.xml

```xml
<?xml version="1.0" encoding="iso-8859-1"?>
<mosinstall type="template" version="1.0.0">
    <name>mytemplate</name>
    <creationDate>09/21/05</creationDate>
    <author>Hagen Graf</author>
    <copyright>GNU/GPL</copyright>
    <authorEmail>hagen@aubkunden.de</authorEmail>
    <authorUrl>http://www.alternative-unternehmensberatung.de</authorUrl>
    <version>0.1</version>
    <description>... description</description>
    <files>
        <filename>index.php</filename>
```

```
            <filename>template_thumbnail.png</filename>
        </files>
        <images>
            <filename>...</filename>
        </images>
        <css>
            <filename>css/template_css.css</filename>
        </css>
    </mosinstall>
```

The descriptions from the *Creating a Template Package* section also apply here.

After the XML file has been created, you can select your new template in Joomla! Administration (Figure 10.22), specify it as the default, and view your Joomla! site live (Figure 10.23).

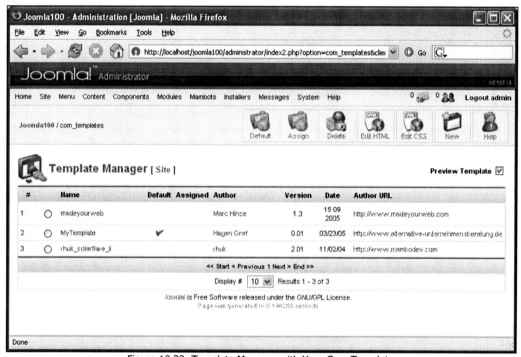

Figure 10.22: Template Manager with Your Own Template

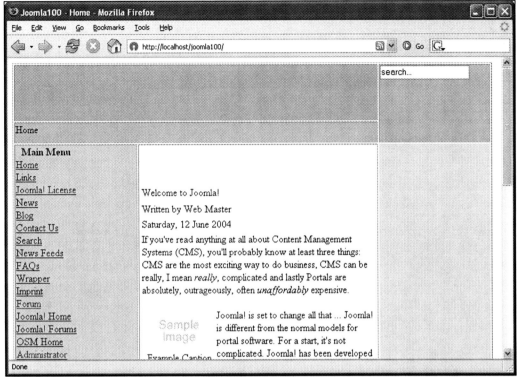

Figure 10.23: Your Website with Your Template

With this construct, you can now work in Dreamweaver, use the design mode and the many features of Dreamweaver and examine the live result on your website immediately after saving.

You can create a logo and graphic elements with a graphics program and insert them into the HTML code with Dreamweaver.

You can even configure Dreamweaver in such a way that your newly modified template file is automatically updated on the distant FTP or WebDAV server of your provider.

To take advantage of that, set up a Dreamweaver site with the root path to your Joomla! files and the appropriate access data to your live site (Figure 10.24).

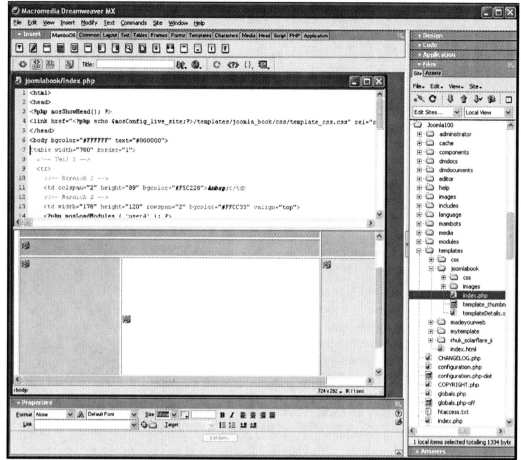

Figure 10.24: Dreamweaver with Site Utilization

Templates and <div> Tags

At the moment, Joomla! works with HTML table representations when it comes to content. In the next versions of Joomla!, this process will change in order to accommodate the requirements of barrier-freedom.

The <div> tag will replace and supplement the <table> tag in HTML.

Thus you can include several HTML elements such as text and graphics in a shared area. This area at first doesn't affect anything except that it starts in a new line of the text flow. The <div> tag does not have any other properties. The big advantage, however, results from the combination of <div> tags with CSS statements.

These properties of the <div> tags make it interesting to produce templates that are controlled by a CSS file.

Marc Hinse's template, which is included, uses this technology. It doesn't contain any `table` tags any more and instead builds the entire "tabular" structure by means of `<div>` tags. Take a look at the original source code of this template in order to get familiar with this technology. You can find more information about `<div>` tags online. Dreamweaver also supports this technology.

As an example, I have extracted all of the `<div>` tags from the template, in order to give you an overview of the structure (Listing 10.7). The `id` attributes refer in each case to a class in the corresponding CSS file.

Listing 10.7: Extract from the `/templates/madeyourweb/index.php` file

```
<div id="accessibility"></div>
<div id="pagewidth-800" >
    <div id="header" >
        <div id="top-top">
            <div id="search"></div>
            <div id="topmenu"></div>
        </div>
        <div class="clr"></div>
        <div id="top-bottom"></div>
        <div id="banner"></div>
    </div>
    <div id="outer-800" >
        <div id="pathway"></div>
        <div id="leftcol"></div>
        <div id="maincol-broad-800" >
            <div id="maincol-wide-800" >
                <div id="<?php echo $usera; ?>"></div>
                <div id="<?php echo $userb; ?>"> </div>
            <div class="clr"></div>
            <div class="content"></div>
        </div>
        <div id="rightcol-broad"> </div>
        <div class="clr"></div>
    </div>
    <div id="footer-800" ></div>
</div>
```

You can find the corresponding CSS classes in Listing 10.8

Listing 10.8: Extract from the `/templates/madeyourweb/css/template_css.css` file

```
...
#header {
height:   116px;
width:    100%;
}
#top-top {
height: 30px;
width: 100%;
background: transparent;
}
...
```

The height and the width of the area to be formatted are specified with the `height` and `width` attributes. The `background` attribute determines the color of the background. Thus the table structure can be emulated without `table` tags and even be extended by many functions (to fade in, fade out, shift...) by means of the pixel-exact formatting of areas.

Barrier Free Joomla!

Barrier freedom starts in the head! In many countries, it is a specific topic that has even been regulated. Complete barrier freedom and fundamental accessibility are difficult to achieve on the Internet, but, of course, not impossibly in principle. The term accessibility is often associated in this connection. When authorities offer their services for sale on the Internet, they must be accessible for as large a number of inhabitants as possible.

Barrier free access to a website is the same as a ramp for wheelchair users on a bus or a traffic light that beeps when the light changes to green, so that the blind will hear it.

Accessibility is a distinct advantage for a company and/or a public service offerer. Every visitor to a website is also a potential customer. This topic transcends far beyond people with handicaps or older people and will win worldwide importance.

Criteria for Accessible Websites

In order to give you a conception of the necessary changes to your website, here are a few criteria.

Clarity

Every website should be clear and fast to comprehend. Information should preferably be in those places in which the user expects it.

Browser Compatibility

There are different kinds of Internet browsers. From the text-based Lynx on the Linux console, through browsers on cell phones, PDAs and other mobile terminals to various browsers on various operating systems (OSX, Linux, Unix, Windows, OS2). All these terminals have different resolutions and can or cannot display graphics, can or cannot run JavaScript code, can or cannot play Flash movies, and so on.

Remember that there are also character recognition programs and, for example, Braille keyboards for blind people. These programs are also browsers!

Valid Source Code and Logically Structured Page Architecture

Navigation, layout, and contents are the important facets of a website. They must be developed logically content-wise and be semantically correct. XHTML is a standard. The source code that you use should be valid!

Contrasts

A high-contrast representation of website content must be ensured to accommodate visually impaired users.

Graphics and Pictures

A lot of output devices for handicapped people cannot represent graphics. Therefore it is absolutely necessary to have an alternative way of representing content.

Font Sizes

The writing must also be readable on older and alternative systems.

Additional Criteria and Information

In order to get a feeling for the genuine requirements, take a quick look at Section 508 (http://www.section508.gov/).

The Reality

At first, the reality is a little frightening. There is hardly a website that conforms to these simple and plausible rules. "Eye Candy", animations and complicated navigation rule most websites. A process of rethinking is, however, taking place with the increased popularity of content management systems and also because of the regulatory laws.

Companies that offer their goods on the Internet are slowly realizing that accessible websites are also good for the business. Customers simply find it easier to navigate! The websites of barrier-free sites are, by the way, extremely popular with customers compared with other online banking websites!

In real life you have to deal with different user groups, various user terminals, and different requirements. Thus, your website will always be a compromise! Don't set your requirements too high and start simply.

Is Joomla! Barrier-Free?

In order to make it short: no. In accordance with the Joomla! roadmap, the next versions of Joomla! will place a lot of value on this topic and accessibility of the website as mentioned above could be made possible.

Is it Possible to make Joomla! Barrier-Free?

In order to answer this question just as briefly: yes!

The Technology

Joomla uses! an XHTML table layout. Table tags are insurmountable for a barrier-free setup and should be avoided. Therefore the part in the Joomla! system in the program code that is responsible for the output has to be changed. Angie Radtke has a kludge for this purpose that can be installed as a component. Besides this kludge, you need a read-more Mambot, which changes the Read more link in Joomla! contents in such a way that that it can be read out.

If you now build the following into your structure, accessibility will look pretty good:

- A clear, table-free structure,
- Valid XHTML,
- Scalable fonts,
- Appropriate color choices,
- Sufficient contrast

From a purely technical perspective, you are now well prepared for the future.

You can test the functionality with various tools. You can find an overview of the usual tools, among other places, on Jan Eric Hellbusch's website.

The People

Now we come to the people that set up contents on the website, the editors. Here you have to wake up their sense of responsibility.

This, for example, is a valid and also semantically correct text input:

```
<h1>first order heading</h1>
<p>first paragraph</p>
<p>second paragraph</p>
```

What looks so simple is so difficult to get implemented. One could let the heading look like a heading even with the change of script attributes. The following command has a similar effect; however, it is no longer a heading:

```
<span class="heading">first order heading</span>
```

The following command would be the correct version:

```
<h1 class="heading">first order heading</h1>
```

How can you get an editor to learn this?

In the text-processing world there are two programs thatrepresent the standard in editing of texts, OpenOffice and Microsoft Word. It is absolutely necessary to have a similar tool with similar capabilities to make text input possible for web pages. The WYSIWYG editor used by Joomla! is only a small start.

Here is another example of the correct formulation of a graphic with the `title` and `longdesc` attributes.

```
<img src="companylogo.png" width="100" height="130" border="0"
alt="companylogo" title="This is our company logo" />
<img src="companylogo.png" width="100" height="130" border="0"
alt="companylogo" longdesc="companylogo.txt" />
```

In the `longdesc` attribute, the reference is to a separate description.

Many such "little things" must be considered. The WYSIWYG editor that comes with Joomla! is not really usable for these tasks. In order to nevertheless enable easy editing, you can deactivate functions of the editor in the source code. Detailed knowledge of the JavaScript language is, however, necessary for this.

The correct phrasing is also importantly when it comes to the people that write the text! A small summary about the subject matter of the article has to be in the opening text. The language must be easily understandable and proper for the target group. Everything you learned in your journalist courses suddenly is important again.

Barrier-Free Sites with Joomla!

Angie Radtke has already created several barrier-free projects with Joomla! and/or Mambo. Here is an example of a barrier-free website for 3tc (Figure 10.25).

Figure 10.25: Barrier free Website foundation-deutsche-welthungerhilfe.de

You can find additional examples of barrier-free sites on the website of the W3C site.

Summary

This chapter showed you how to create your own template packages. The Joomla! project tries to make Joomla! web pages usable by people with disabilities. We discussed different ways to make Joomla! barrier free. In the next chapter we will make our own components, modules, and Mambots.

11

Your Own Program Extensions

Let's say that you want to solve a problem for which there is still no finished Joomla! component. Maybe you are a used car dealer and you need a list of your used cars that you can maintain with Joomla! Administration, or a list of your branches. Simply extend the functional range with new components, modules, and Mambots. What looks very complicated at first sight is definitely feasible with beginner-level knowledge of PHP.

After your experience with the building of templates, you already know the rudiments of what is to come. You need:

- A new component consisting of the front end, the Joomla! administration, and a special table in the database
- An additional module to display the entries on your homepage
- A search Mambot, in order to be able to browse your new content

So that you get an idea of what we are talking about, here is an example of a simple list on the homepage (Figure 11.1).

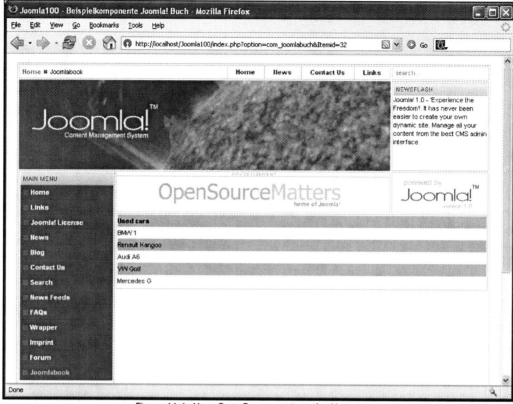

Figure 11.1: Your Own Component on the Homepage

Our list has auto types. You could, of course, fill the example with different data (branches, offers, etc.). For the customer, it is usually sufficient to see the list. He or she doesn't have to be able to edit the entries.

The administrator, however, has to administer the list. By *administer* one means:

- Make new entries
- Modify existing entries
- Delete existing entries

In order to avoid overly complicating the example, we are displaying and working on only one field. The principle will become clear that way and one can easily extend the example into multiple fields. You can see the basic administrative interface of the list here (Figure 11.2). It should be possible to implement the above-specified functions. In addition, you naturally need a special toolbar for the display of the list and one for the editing mode. You need the capability of publishing and of closing the entries, and you naturally want to have the publishing and deletion functions in a batch-processing mode, so that you can mark the checkboxes before the entries and subsequently publish, for example, several entries at one time.

Figure 11.2: Your Own Component in Joomla! Administration

Sample joomlabook Component

Let's start with the component. Since it can become the basis for many different lists, let us call it joomlabook. You can download the finished example (see Appendix) and install it just like all components; but you can also reproduce it manually. Reproduction has the advantage that you will gradually check out the structures and maybe get a taste for it.

The MySQL Table

Since you are starting completely from scratch, you need a new table in MySQL. There are many ways to create the desired table.

You can:

- Write a PHP program that creates the table
- Work from the MySQL console
- Control MySQL with a tool like phpMyAdmin

With XAMPP Lite and most web space providers, you receive the phpMyAdmin (http://www.phpmyadmin.net/) tool for database management. With this program, which is written in PHP just like Joomla!, you can easily manipulate your MySQL tables directly.

Call up phpMyAdmin in XAMPP Lite by inputting the `http://localhost/phpmyadmin` URL in your browser (Figure 11.3):

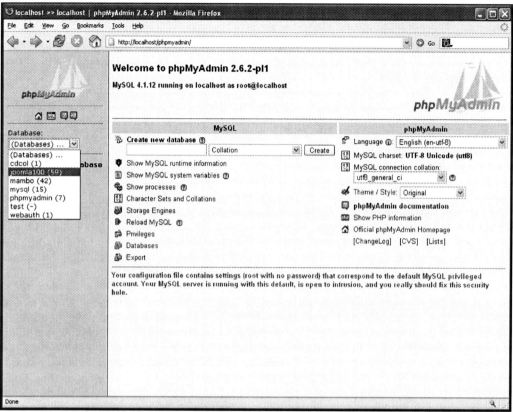

Figure 11.3 phpMyAdmin

In the left area, select the database that contains your Joomla! tables. In this case, it is the `joomla100` database. If you only have one database in your hosting packet, you end up directly in your Joomla! database with some providers by calling up phpMyAdmin. With XAMPP Lite you can set up as many databases as you want.

Databases like MySQL are controlled with SQL commands. The Structured Query Language is a data manipulation language that has similarities to set theory, which emerged in the seventies. The idea behind the language is to use just a few commands, like alter, delete, insert, and create with a precisely defined quantity of data.

With the CREATE TABLE command, you set up a new table. You have to describe the individual fields (name, size, type) and specify an index. By means of this index, each data record receives a unique number and later, when conducting a search, can be addressed with this number. With the AUTO_INCREMENT function, you guarantee that the number (the key) is incremented by 1 automatically when inserting a new data record.

With the INSERT command, you insert data records. Here you assign data to the individual fields of the table.

For the component example, you need SQL commands to create a table and insert data. To deliver these SQL commands to the database, select your database in phpMyAdmin and click on the SQL link. You will see an HTML form into which you can insert the SQL commands and send them directly to the database.

Listing 11.1: SQL Commands for the Example Table

```
-- Table structure for table `mos_joomla_book`
CREATE TABLE `mos_joomla_book` (
          `id` INT NOT NULL AUTO_INCREMENT,
          `text` TEXT NOT NULL,
          `published` TINYINT(1) NOT NULL,
          PRIMARY KEY (`id`) );
-- Data for table `mos_joomla_book`
INSERT INTO `mos_joomla_book` VALUES (11,'BMW 1', 1);
INSERT INTO `mos_joomla_book` VALUES (9,'Renault Kangoo', 1);
INSERT INTO `mos_joomla_book` VALUES (8,'Audi A6', 1);
INSERT INTO `mos_joomla_book` VALUES (7,'VW Golf', 1);
INSERT INTO `mos_joomla_book` VALUES (10,'Mercedes G', 1);
```

Enter the commands in the form and click Go (Figure 11.4).

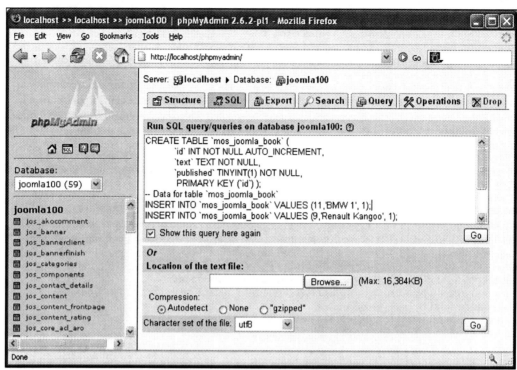

Figure 11.4: Importing the Table Structure

MySQL creates the new mos_joomla_book table and inserts five data records. Click mos_joomla_book and then Browse to see the following result:

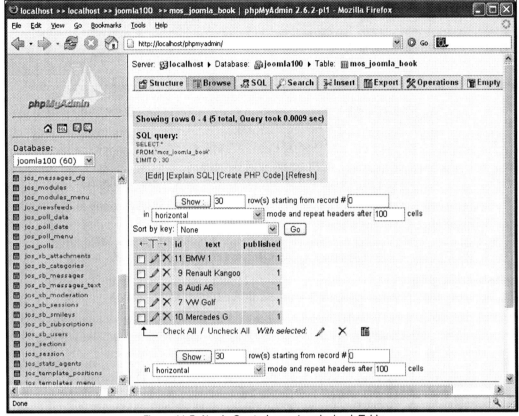

Figure 11.5: Newly Created mos_joomla_book Table

The description is located in the text field; the published field is used to administer a publication status. The value 1 means that the appropriate entry is published on the website. The value 0 prevents publication.

With this, we have created the table and can leave phpMyAdmin for now.

We created the table and inserted the values into the data base by hand, because our component is not yet finished and thus cannot be installed from the Component Installer. The Component Installer later assumes this job with the automatic installation of Joomla!. You have to specify the necessary SQL commands for the correct initialization of your components in a separate XML configuration file.

The Front End

Your homepage is the front end. To increase the anticipation a little bit, we will start with the display of the list in the front end.

If you take a quick look into your [pathtoJoomla!]/components directory, you will notice that all directories begin with com_ followed by a description (com_contact, com_content, and so on).

This is where your installed components are stored. To open a component in the browser, specify the name of this subdirectory as value in the option parameter in the URL:

```
http://localhost/joomla100/index.php?option=com_contact
```

For your components, create a new subdirectory with the name [pathtoJoomla!]/components/com_joomlabook. Create two files in this subdirectory:

- joomlabook.php: This file contains the logic in pure PHP code. For example, the database is queried here and the result is transmitted to an array.

- joomlabook.html.php: This file contains the presentation of the data in the array. PHP is also used here, but the emphasis lies on HTML and CSS code.

joomlabook.php

This file consists of four arrays and a few more lines (see Listing 11.2).

The first array ensures that it is not possible to open the file directly by the input of the file name.

```
defined('_VALID_MOS') or die('Direct access to this file is prohibited.');
```

The file can only be opened from another file. This is a security measure because the component is not executable without the Joomla! system. Moreover, the source code of the second (joomlabook.html.php) file is merged here. Since this merging is standard for the HTML interface, there is a getPath() procedure that looks in the same directory for an appropriate file to merge with. The name is created dynamically from the directory's name with an html.php ending.

```
require_once($mainframe->getPath('front_html'));
```

In the second array, parameters are transferred. Here the HTML title of the page appears in the upper blue bar of the browser. There is a methodology for that purpose—setPageTitle.

The third array contains a case differentiation. You can open the component with different parameters and interpret them here. For example, the differentiation here could be between an overview and an individual view. With the used car list, the name of the entry could be constructed as a link and by clicking it, a detailed description of the vehicle could be shown.

```
switch( $task ) {
  case 'free':
    // more display possibilities
    break;
  default:
    listJoomlabook();
    break;
}
```

The fourth array contains the actual logic. Here the database is queried, a result array is created, and the showtable() procedure in the HTML_joomlabook class is opened. This class is in the merged joomlabook.html.php file.

Here is the complete source code:

Listing 11.2: joomlabook.php

```php
<?php

//Array 1
/* ensure that this file is called up by another file */
defined( '_VALID_MOS' ) or die( 'Direct access of this file is prohibited.' );
// Loading of the HTML class
require_once( $mainframe->getPath( 'front_html' ) );

//Array 2
$mainframe->setPageTitle( "Example component Joomla! book" );

//Array 3
switch( $task ) {
....case 'free':
........// more display possibilities
........break;
....default:
........listJoomlabook();
........break;
}

//Array 4
function listJoomlabook( ) {
....global $database;
..../* SQL query of all published entries */
....$query = "SELECT * FROM #__joomla_book WHERE published='1'" ;
....$database->setQuery( $query );
....$rows = $database->loadObjectList();
....HTML_Joomlabook::showTable( &$rows );
}
?>
```

joomlabook.html.php

The joomlabook.html.php file (see Listing 11.3) contains the HTML_Joomlabook class. A class is like a structural plan with many procedures. A while ago already we had learned about two methods of a class, (getPath() and setPageTitle()). If these methods were not already pre-defined in Joomla!, then we must write the class and methods ourselves now. Our small class contains only the showTable() method.

An array is handed over to the showTable procedure (&$rows). The array is the result of the database query and contains the list of all entered data records. The list should be represented in a table. To achieve this, a foreach loop continues running until there are no more elements.

```php
...
foreach ($rows as $row) {
...
```

With each run a different value is generated for the variable $k. $k controls the CSS class of a table row (class="sectiontableentry<?php echo ($k+1); ?>"). Consequently, the rows are reproduced in two different colors as illustrated in Figure 11.1.

In principle, as many procedures as desired can be implemented in the class; beside the table view there could also be, for example, an individual view.

```
HTML_Joomlabook::showtable($rows);
```

This is a static class, (HTML_Joomlabook) whose method (showtable($rows)) can be called directly. Class name and method name are separated by two colons.

Listing 11.3: joomlabook.html.php

```php
<?php
/* ensuring that this file is called up from another file */
defined( '_VALID_MOS' ) or die( 'Direct access to this file is prohibited.' );
class HTML_Joomlabook {
// Procedure for building the table
 function showTable( &$rows  ) {
        ?>
        <table width="100%" border="0" cellspacing="0" cellpadding="0"
         align="center">
            <tr>
                <td height="20" class="sectiontableheader">
                <?php echo "Heading"; ?>
                </td>
            </tr>
        <?php
        $k = 0;
        // readout of the data sets in the array
        foreach ($rows as $row) {
            ?>
            <tr>
            <td height="20" class="sectiontableentry<?php echo ($k+1); ?>">
            <?php echo $row->text; ?>
            </td>
            <?php
            $k = 1 - $k;
        }
        ?>
        </table>
        <?php
    }
}
```

Integration into the Main Menu

Since we have not *properly* installed the component here yet, Joomla! doesn't even know that it is indeed present. However, you can open it via the URL http://localhost/joomla/index.php? option=com_joomlabook.

You can merge the components with the main menu at this stage of development via the Link-URL option. In Joomla! Administration, click Menu | mainmenu | New. At the bottom right, select Link-URL and click Next. Here you can enter a description and the above-mentioned link:

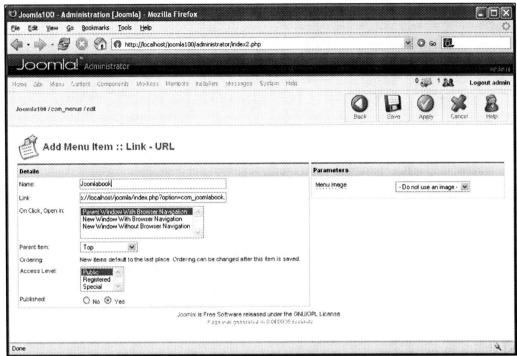

Figure 11.6: Menu Entry per URL

If you open your website, you should see the used cars menu link. Click on it to view the table shown in Figure 11.1.

You can see that the table is automatically adjusted to the template. That was surprisingly simple, wasn't it? You should seriously try to become familiar with object-oriented programming and the syntaxes of PHP, HTML, and CSS.

Joomla! Administration

Displaying data on the web page was relatively simple, but administering data, naturally, will be a little more complex. Here you have to display the data, modify it, reinsert it, and delete it. This implies substantially more functionality than on the web page.

The Component Table

Joomla! administers the menu entries of all components in the `jos_components` table. Since you are not using an installer and building everything by hand, you need two new menu entries. One menu entry ensures that your new component is shown in the component menu, and the second entry defines the Edit Entries suboption

Open phpMyAdmin, select the `jos_components` table, click SQL, insert the two SQL commands (see Listing 11.4), and click OK to confirm. We have provided the ID 80. The second entry refers to the first entry. Therefore it is important that the ID numbers agree. At this time there are at most 32 entries in the table, therefore this method should work.

Listing 11.4: SQL Commands Menu Entry

```
INSERT INTO `jos_components` (`id`, `name`, `link`, `menuid`, `parent`,
`admin_menu_link`, `admin_menu_alt`, `option`, `ordering`, `admin_menu_img`,
`iscore`, `params`) VALUES (80, 'Joomla! book', 'option=com_joomlabook', 0, 0,
'option=com_joomlabook', 'Joomla! book', 'com_joomlabook', 0,
'js/ThemeOffice/component.png', 0, '');
INSERT INTO `jos_components` (`id`, `name`, `link`, `menuid`, `parent`,
`admin_menu_link`, `admin_menu_alt`, `option`, `ordering`, `admin_menu_img`,
`iscore`, `params`) VALUES (50, 'Edit entries', '', 0, 80,
'option=com_joomlabook&act=all', 'Edit entries', 'com_joomlabook', 0,
'js/ThemeOffice/component.png', 0, '');
```

By inserting these two data sets, you extend the Components menu by a main joomla!book entry and an Edit Entries submenu entry:

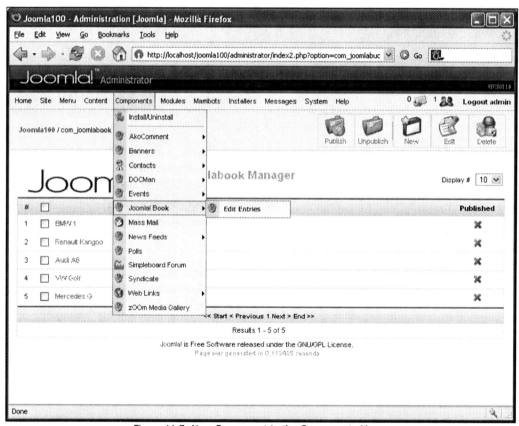

Figure 11.7: New Component in the Components Menu

In addition, you can specify what the respective menu entry calls up (option=com_ joomlabook&act=all') and the picture that is to appear on the left, next to the menu ('js/ThemeOffice/component.png'). You can find the pictures in the [pathtoJoomla!]/ includes/js/ThemeOffice folder.

This time you need, not two, but five files. Create a subdirectory called com_joomlabook under the [pathtoJoomla!]/administration/components/ directory. In this subdirectory, create the following five files:

- admin.joomlabook.php
- joomlabook.class.php
- admin.joomlabook.html.php
- toolbar.joomlabook.html.php
- toolbar.joomlabook.php

admin.joomlabook.php

This file contains the logic of your components. Here we go another step further and partially swap the database queries to joomlabook.class.php. In principle, the structure is specified like the front-end logic. The file is more extensive, since several cases are possible and each case must be implemented with a function. In addition, the access rights are examined at the beginning, since we are in Joomla! administration.

Listing 11.5: admin.joomlabook.php

```php
<?php
/* ensure that this file is not called from another file */
defined( '_VALID_MOS' ) or die( 'Direct access to this file is prohibited.' );

// Here a check is performed to see whether the logged in user has the rights
if (!($acl->acl_check( 'administration', 'edit', 'users', $my->usertype,
                                               'components', 'all' )
        | $acl->acl_check( 'administration', 'edit', 'users', $my->usertype,
                                               'components', 'com_contact' )))
{
    mosRedirect( 'index2.php', _NOT_AUTH );
}

// Loading of the database class and the HTML class
require_once( $mainframe->getPath( 'admin_html' ) );
require_once( $mainframe->getPath( 'class' ) );

$id     = mosGetParam( $_GET, 'id', 0 );
$cid    = mosGetParam( $_POST, 'cid', array(0) );
if (!is_array( $cid )) {
    $cid = array(0);
}

// case differentiation
switch ($task) {
    case "publish":
        publishJoomlabook( $cid, 1, $option );
        break;
    case "unpublish":
        publishJoomlabook( $cid, 0, $option );
        break;
    case "new":
```

```
                    editJoomlabook( 0, $option );
                    break;
              case "edit":
                    editJoomlabook( $cid[0], $option );
                    break;
              case "remove":
                    removeJoomlabook( $cid, $option );
                    break;
              case "save":
                    saveJoomlabook( $option );
                    break;
              case "cancel":
                    cancelJoomlabook( $option );
                    break;
              default:
                    showJoomlabook( $option );
                    break;
        }
        // Publishing of the entries
        function publishJoomlabook( $cid, $publish, $option ) {
              global $database;
              if (count( $cid ) < 1) {
                    $action = $publish ? 'publish' : 'unpublish';
                    echo "<script> alert('Select a item to ".$action."');
                                        window.history.go(-1);</script>\n";
                    exit;
              }
              $cids = implode( ',', $cid );
              //$database->setQuery( "UPDATE #__joomla_book SET published=($publish)
              //WHERE id IN ($cids)");
              $database->setQuery( "UPDATE #__joomla_book SET published=".$publish."
                                        WHERE id IN ($cids)");
              if (!$database->query()) {
                    echo "<script> alert('".$database->getErrorMsg()."');
                                        window.history.go(-1); </script>\n";
                    exit();
              }
              if (count( $cid ) == 1) {
                    $row = new mosJoomlabook( $database );
                    $row->checkin( $cid[0] );
              }
              mosRedirect( "index2.php?option=$option" );
        }
        // create a new entry (id = 0)
        // or change entry with id = n
        function editJoomlabook( $id, $option ) {
              global $database;
              $row = new mosJoomlabook( $database );
              $row->load( $id );

              HTML_Joomlabook::editJoomlabook( $row, $option );
        }
        // deletion of entries
        function removeJoomlabook( $cid, $option ) {
              global $database;
              if (!is_array( $cid ) || count( $cid ) < 1) {
                    echo "<script> alert(Please select an entry to delete ');
                                        window.history.go(-1);</script>\n";
                    exit;
              }
              $cids = implode( ',', $cid );
              $database->setQuery( "DELETE FROM #__joomla_book WHERE id IN ($cids)" );
              if (!$database->query()) {
                    echo "<script> alert('".$database->getErrorMsg()."');
                          window.history.go(-1); </script>\n";
```

```
        }
        mosRedirect( "index2.php?option=$option" );
    }
    // save entry
    function saveJoomlabook( $option ) {
        global $database;
        $row = new mosJoomlabook( $database );
        if (!$row->bind( $_POST )) {
            echo "<script> alert('".$row->getError()."'); window.history.go(-1);
                                                    </script>\n";
            exit();
        }
        if (!$row->store()) {
            echo "<script> alert('".$row->getError()."'); window.history.go(-1);
                                                    </script>\n";
            exit();
        }
        mosRedirect( "index2.php?option=$option" );
    }
    // abort the current action
    function cancelJoomlabook( $option ) {
        global $database;
        $row = new mosJoomlabook( $database );
        $row->bind( $_POST );
        $row->checkin();
        mosRedirect( "index2.php?option=$option" );
    }
    // list entries
    function showJoomlabook($option) {
        global $database, $mainframe;
        $limit = $mainframe->getUserStateFromRequest(
                                    "viewlistlimit", 'limit', 10 );
        $limitstart = $mainframe->getUserStateFromRequest(
                            "view{$option}limitstart", 'limitstart', 0 );
        // count entries
        $database->setQuery( "SELECT count(*) FROM #__joomla_book" );
        $total = $database->loadResult();
        echo $database->getErrorMsg();
        require_once("includes/pageNavigation.php");
        $pageNav = new mosPageNav( $total, $limitstart, $limit );
        # main database query
        $database->setQuery( "SELECT * FROM #__joomla_book ORDER BY id LIMIT
                                    $pageNav->limitstart,$pageNav->limit" );
        $rows = $database->loadObjectList();
        if ($database->getErrorNum()) {
            echo $database->stderr();
            return false;
        }
        HTML_Joomlabook::showJoomlabook( $rows, $pageNav, $option );
    }
```

joomlabook.class.php

Here the data set structure is swapped into its own class, derived from the mosDBTable class. mosDBTable is a class in the /includes/database.php file and makes fundamental procedures for database access available.

Listing 11.6: joomlabook.class.php

```
<?php
/* ensure that this file is called from another file */
defined( '_VALID_MOS' ) or die( 'Direct access to this file is prohibited.' );
class mosJoomlabook extends mosDBTable {
    // Declaration and initialization of the instantiation variable
    // INT(11) AUTO_INCREMENT
    var $id=null;
```

```
// TEXT
var $text=null;
// TINYINT(1)
var $published=null;

// The constructor is called by the instantiation
function mosJoomlabook( &$db ) {
  $this->mosDBTable( '#__joomla_book', 'id', $db );
}
}
?>
```

admin.joomlabook.html.php

As described in the front-end component, the HTML_joomlabook class refers to the presentation of
the data. The HTML and CSS structures are created on the basis of the data from
admin.joomlabook.php that was transferred by means of the $row array.

Listing 11.7: admin.joomlabook.html.php

```
<?php
/* ensure that this file is called from another file */
defined( '_VALID_MOS' ) or die( 'Direct access to this file is prohibited.' );
class HTML_joomlabook {
  function showJoomlabook( &$rows, &$pageNav, $option ) {
    // HTML starts here, combined with short PHP commands for table creation
    global $my;
    mosCommonHTML::loadOverlib();
    ?>
    <form action="index2.php" method="post" name="adminForm">
    <table class="adminheading">
    <tr>
      <th><img src="/joomla100/images/joomla_logo_black.png" align="middle"
        />Joomlabook Manager</th>
    </tr>
    </table>
    <table class="adminlist">
    <tr>
      <th width="20" class='title'>#</th>
      <th width="20" class='title'><input type="checkbox" name="toggle"
        value="" onclick="checkAll(<?php echo count($rows); ?>);" /></th>
      <th class='title'>Entries</th>
      <th class='title'>Published</th>
    </tr>
    <?php
    $k = 0;
    for ($i=0, $n=count($rows); $i < $n; $i++) {
      $row = $rows[$i];

      $link= 'index2.php?option=com_joomlabook&task=editA&hidemainmenu=1&id='.
        $row->id;
      $img  = $row->published ? 'tick.png' : 'publish_x.png';
      $task = $row->published ? 'unpublish' : 'publish';
      $alt = $row->published ? 'Published' : 'Unpublished';

      $checked      = mosCommonHTML::CheckedOutProcessing( $row, $i );

      ?>
      <tr class="<?php echo "row$k"; ?>">
        <td align="center"><?php echo $i+$pageNav->limitstart+1;?></td>
        <td><input type="checkbox" id="cb<?php echo $i;?>" name="cid[]" value=
          "<?php echo $row->id; ?>" onclick="isChecked(this.checked);" /></td>
        <td><a href="#edit" onclick="return listItemTask('cb<?php
          echo $i;?>','edit')"><?php echo $row->text; ?></a></td>
```

```php
        <td width="10%" align="center"><a href="javascript: void(0);" onclick=
            "return listItemTask('cb<?php echo $i;?>','<?php echo $task;?>')">
            <img src="images/<?php echo $img;?>" border="0" alt="" /></a></td>
    </tr>
    <?php
        $k = 1 - $k;
    }
?>
    <tr>
    <th align="center" colspan="10"> <?php
        echo $pageNav->writePagesLinks(); ?></th>
    </tr>
    <tr>
    <td align="center" colspan="10"> <?php
        echo $pageNav->writePagesCounter(); ?></td>
    </tr>
    </table>
    <input type="hidden" name="option" value="<?php echo $option; ?>" />
    <input type="hidden" name="task" value="" />
    <input type="hidden" name="boxchecked" value="0" />
    <input type="hidden" name="hidemainmenu" value="0">
    </form>
<?php
}

// this method represents the edit mask
function editJoomlabook( &$row, $option ) {
    mosMakeHtmlSafe( $row, ENT_QUOTES );
    // JavaScript Code for checking forms starts here
?>
    <script language="javascript" type="text/javascript">
        function submitbutton(pressbutton) {
            var form = document.adminForm;
            if (pressbutton == "cancel") {
                submitform( pressbutton );
                return;
            }
            // do field validation
            if (form.text.value == '') {
                alert( "Please enter a value into the field." );
            } else {
                submitform( pressbutton );
            }
        }
    </script>
    <form action="index2.php" method="post" name="adminForm" id="adminForm"
        class="adminForm">
    <table border="0" cellpadding="3" cellspacing="0">
    <tr>
        <td>Eintrag: </td>
        <td><input class="inputbox" type="text" size="50" maxlength="100"
                name="text" value="<?php echo $row->text; ?>" /></td>
    </tr>
    </table>
    <input type="hidden" name="id" value="<?php echo $row->id; ?>" />
    <input type="hidden" name="option" value="<?php echo $option; ?>" />
    <input type="hidden" name="task" value="" />
    </form>
<?php
}
}
?>
```

toolbar.joomlabook.php

This file controls the various functions that can be invoked by clicking the icons in the toolbar and thereby represents the logic of the toolbar. The `toolbar.joomlabook.html.php` file is merged with the presentation class.

Listing 11.8: toolbar.joomlabook.php

```php
<?php
/* ensure that this file is called from another file */
defined( '_VALID_MOS' ) or die( 'Direct access to this file is prohibited.' );
require_once( $mainframe->getPath( 'toolbar_html' ) );
switch($task) {
    case "new":
    case "edit":
        menuJoomlabook::MENU_Edit();
        break;
    default:
        menuJoomlabook::MENU_Default();
        break;
}
?>
```

toolbar.joomlabook.html.php

Here the toolbar is assembled as shown in Listing 11.9. Procedures of the `mosMenu` class are called up twice: once for the list view and once for the edit view:

Figure 11.8: Toolbar in List mode

Figure 11.9: Toolbar in
Edit Mode

Listing 11.9: toolbar.joomlabook.html.php

```php
<?php
/* ensure that this file is called from another file */
defined( '_VALID_MOS' ) or die( 'Direct access to this file is prohibited.' );
class menuJoomlabook {
    function MENU_Default() {
        mosMenuBar::startTable();
        mosMenuBar::publishList();
        mosMenuBar::unpublishList();
        mosMenuBar::divider();
        mosMenuBar::addNew();
        mosMenuBar::editList();
        mosMenuBar::deleteList();
        mosMenuBar::spacer();
        mosMenuBar::endTable();
    }
    function MENU_Edit() {
        mosMenuBar::startTable();
        mosMenuBar::save();
        mosMenuBar::cancel();
        mosMenuBar::spacer();
```

```
                mosMenuBar::endTable();
        }
    }
    ?>
```

Test

After creating these files, you can test the component and completely administer the data sets from Joomla! administration. You can set up new texts, delete, change, and publish existing ones. By previous marking of the entries, you can work on several entries at one time when publishing and deleting.

Create Installation Package

Besides the program files, you need two files with the installation text (see Listing 11.10) and the uninstallation text (see Listing 11.11). You also need an XML file as instruction file for the installer (see Listing 11.12).

install.joomlabook.php

Listing 11.10: install.joomlabook.php

```
<?php
function com_install() {
    echo "Thank you for the installation. If you are having problems, contact
                                                hagen@aubkunden.de.";
}
?>
```

uninstall.joomlabook.php

Listing 11.11: uninstall.joomlabook.php

```
<?
function com_uninstall() {
echo "Thank you for using this component. The component will now be
                uninstalled. If you have questions or comments,
                        please contact hagen@aubkunden.de.";
}
?>
```

joomlabook.xml

Here you describe your new component to the Component Installer. You have to include all information such as metadata, all file names, and the necessary SQL instructions (Query) in XML tags. The Component Installer picks this file out, creates, depending upon type (component, module, template, or Mambot), new subdirectories, copies the files that are described in the XML file to the correct place, and creates the necessary database tables. Thus, doing everything that you had to do manually before.

Listing 11.12: joomlabook.xml

```
<?xml version="1.0" ?>
<mosinstall type="component">
  <name>joomlabook</name>
  <creationDate>22.09.2005</creationDate>
  <author>Hagen Graf</author>
  <copyright>GNU/GPL</copyright>
  <authorEmail>hagen@aubkunden.de</authorEmail>
  <authorUrl>www.alternative.unternehmensberatung.de</authorUrl>
```

```
<version>1.0</version>
<files>
  <filename>joomlabook.php</filename>
  <filename>joomlabook.html.php</filename>
</files>
<install>
  <queries>
    <query>DROP TABLE IF EXISTS `jos_joomla_book`;</query>
    <query>CREATE TABLE `jos_joomla_book` (
        `id` INT NOT NULL AUTO_INCREMENT,
        `text` TEXT NOT NULL,
        `published` TINYINT(1) NOT NULL,
        PRIMARY KEY (`id`) )
    </query>
  </queries>
</install>
<uninstall>
  <queries>
    <query>DROP TABLE IF EXISTS `jos_joomla_book`;</query>
  </queries>
</uninstall>
<installfile>
  <filename>install.joomlabook.php</filename>
</installfile>
<uninstallfile>
  <filename>uninstall.joomlabook.php</filename>
</uninstallfile>
<administration>
  <menu>Joomla! book</menu>
  <submenu>
     <menu act="all">Edit entries</menu>
  </submenu>
  <files>
    <filename>admin.joomlabook.php</filename>
    <filename>admin.joomlabook.html.php</filename>
    <filename>joomlabook.class.php</filename>
    <filename>toolbar.joomlabook.php</filename>
    <filename>toolbar.joomlabook.html.php</filename>
  </files>
</administration>
</mosinstall>
```

To create the installation packet, you have to copy the created files into a directory and compress them all into a zip package named com_joomlabook.zip. You can install this zip file with the Component Installer and, if required, make it available for download. Before you do that, you should uninstall the version that you created manually from the Component Installer.

Name ▲	Size	Type
admin.joomlabook.html.php	4 KB	PHP File
admin.joomlabook.php	5 KB	PHP File
install.joomlabook.php	1 KB	PHP File
joomlabook.class.php	1 KB	PHP File
joomlabook.html.php	1 KB	PHP File
joomlabook.php	1 KB	PHP File
joomlabook.xml	2 KB	XML Document
toolbar.joomlabook.html.php	1 KB	PHP File
toolbar.joomlabook.php	1 KB	PHP File
uninstall.joomlabook.php	1 KB	PHP File

Figure 11.10: Files in the Joomla!book Component

Modules

A module is lot simpler. Modules do not have a real administration interface. Modules are always concerned with representation on your website and merging of your template. Modules usually attach themselves to existing components. Thus, you can assume that certain tables and your contents are already present and can be maintained. You need two files; one for the logic (in this case, the presentation is handled mainly by the template) and an XML file for the installer module. Both files start with the name mod_.

Source Code

In comparison to the component, this file is built quite simply. A database query and the representation of the results in a foreach loop is all there is to it. Save the following file at [pathtojoomla]/modules/

Listing 11.13: mod_joomlabook.php

```php
<?php
defined('_VALID_MOS') or die( 'Direct Access to this location is not allowed.'
);
global $mosConfig_offset;
// SQL command to retrieve the last 5 entries from the DB
$database->setQuery("SELECT * FROM #__joomla_book LIMIT 5");
$rows = $database->loadObjectList();
echo "<ul>\n";
if ($rows) {
    foreach ($rows as $row) {
    echo " <li>" . $row->text . "</li>\n";
    }
    echo "</ul>\n";
}
?>
```

mod_joomlabook.xml

Here as well, you have to enclose the relevant data for the Installer module in XML tags, just as with the component.

Listing 11.14: mod_joomlabook.xml

```xml
<?xml version="1.0" encoding="iso-8859-1"?>
<mosinstall type="module" version="4.5.2">
    <name>Joomlabook</name>
    <author>Hagen Graf</author>
    <creationDate>03/27/2005</creationDate>
    <license>GNU/GPL</license>
    <authorEmail>hagen@aubkunden.de</authorEmail>
    <authorUrl>www.alternative-unternehmensberatung.de</authorUrl>
    <version>1.0</version>
    <description>
<![CDATA[<p>With this module, 5 entries of the Joomlabook test component are
displayed .</p><p> created by <a href = mailto:hagen@aubkunden.de >
hagen@aubkunden.de </a></p><p>Have fun with this module!</p><p><i><a href
="http://www.alternative-unternehmensberatung.de" target = "_blank" >
alternativeunternehmensberatung.de </a></i></p><p>27/03/2005</p>]]>
    </description>
    <files>
       <filename module="mod_joomlabook">mod_joomlabook.php</filename>
    </files>
</mosinstall>
```

Installation

Pack the two files in a zip package with the name mod_joomlabook.zip and install it with the installer module:

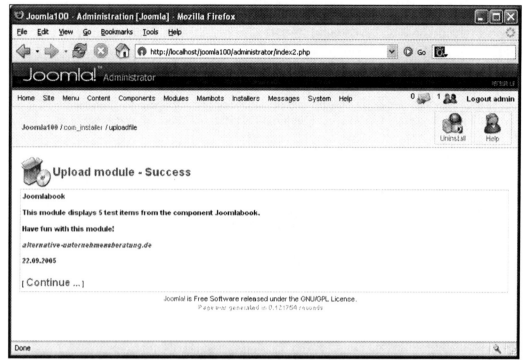

Figure 11.11: Installation Notice of the Joomlabook Module

Activate the module from Site Module Manager.

View of the Website

You will see the entries on the website in the left module space:

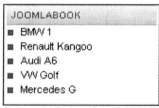

Figure 11.12: Joomlabook Module

Mambots

You need a Mambot to browse the list. Just like modules, create the PHP file with the logic (see Listing 11.15) and the XML file with the description (see Listing 11.16). Pack both files in a zip package, `bot_joomlabook.zip`, and install it with the Mambot Installer:

Figure 11.13: Installation Notice of the joomlabook Mambot

Listing 11.15: joomlabook.searchbot.php

```php
<?php
defined( '_VALID_MOS' ) or die( 'Direct Access to this location is not
allowed.' );
$_MAMBOTS->registerFunction('onSearch', 'botSearchSections');
/**
* Sections Search method
* The sql must return the following fields that are used in a common display
* routine: href, title, section, created, text, browsernav
* @param string Target search string
* @param string mathcing option, exact|any|all
* @param string ordering option, newest|oldest|popular|alpha|category
*/
function botSearchSections($text, $phrase='', $ordering=''){
  global $database, $my;
  $text = trim( $text );
  if ($text == '') {
    return array();
  }
  switch ( $ordering ) {
    case 'alpha':
      $order = 'a.name ASC';
      break;
    case 'category':
    case 'popular':
```

```
        case 'newest':
        case 'oldest':
        default:
          $order = 'a.name DESC';
    }
    $query = "SELECT * FROM #__joomla_book"
          . "\n WHERE ( text LIKE '%$text%' )"
          . "\n AND published = '1'"
          . "\n ORDER BY $text";
    $database->setQuery( $query );
    $rows = $database->loadObjectList();
    $count = count( $rows );
    for ($i = 0; $i < $count; $i++){
        $rows[$i]->href = 'index.php?option=com_joomlabook&task=free&id='.
                          $rows[$i]->secid .'&Itemid='. $rows[$i]->menuid;
        $rows[$i]->section     = 'Joomlabook list';
    }
    return $rows;
}?>
```

Listing 11.16: joomlabook.searchbot.xml

```xml
<?xml version="1.0" encoding="iso-8859-1"?>
<mosinstall version="1.0" type="Mambot" group="search">
    <name>Joomlabook searchbot</name>
    <author>Hagen Graf</author>
    <creationDate>22.09.2005</creationDate>
    <license>GNU/GPL</license>
    <authorEmail>hagen@aubkunden.de</authorEmail>
    <authorUrl>www.alternative-unternehmensberatung.de</authorUrl>
    <version>1.0.0</version>
    <description>This Mambot searches the entries of the Joomlabook component
    </description>
    <files>
        <filename Mambot="joomlabook.searchbot" > joomlabook.searchbot.php
        </filename>
    </files>
    <params/>
</mosinstall>
```

If you activate the Mambot from the Mambots | Site Mambots menu, your list is searched via the search field on the website. After entering a search word, the text field in the database is scanned and the results are displayed in the common search mask as shown in Figure 11.14.

The searchbot is kept simple on purpose. The individual view of each list element should be linked to the place of discovery within the search results, so that the searcher can go there. Since we did not plan an individual view in our component, we cannot display a link here.

Figure 11.14: The joomlabook Searchbot in Action

Summary

This chapter gives an overview on producing components, modules, and Mambots.

You can use components from similar applications and develop them further. For example, our Joomlabook component has one table view. Look for a component with an individual view (com_contact) and extend your Joomlabook with this functionality. The same is true for specified parameters in modules. You can look for a model and create your own module.

What looks complicated at first sight is quite transparent on closer inspection.

Have fun experimenting!

Online Resources

Joomla! is an Open Source project that collects ideas and experiences of hundreds of thousands of people, bundles them together, continues to develop them and makes them available online.

You will always find the most current information online. Your primary source for information is the Joomla.org website at `http://www.joomla.org/`.

It is sub-divided into these areas:

- `http://help.joomla.org`
- `http://forum.joomla.org`
- `http://developer.joomla.org`

You can really find everything you need to successfully implement Joomla!.

Downloads

The software packages you need can be downloaded from the respective project pages.

Keep in mind, however, that it is almost certain that more current versions will be available on the appropriate websites.

Windows

- Development environment: XAMPP Lite (`xampplite-win32-1.4.15.zip`)
- Pack program: Filzip (`filzip.exe`)

Linux

An Apache, PHP, and MySQL environment is contained in every current Linux package and is often preinstalled.

Operating-System Independent

The following table is a list of Joomla! downloads you would require while you implement the steps discussed in the book:

Chapter	File	Description
2	Joomla_Stable_1.0.0.tar.gz	Joomla source code version 1.0.0
7	Simpleboard-1.1.0-Stable.zip	Forum component
7	Mod_simpleboard5.zip	Forum module
7	Com_events-1.2.zip	Calendar component
7	Mod_events_cal-1.1-beta.zip	Calendar module
7	bot_events_search-1.1.zip	Calendar Mambot
8	Com_zoom_25b3.zip	Picture gallery component
8	Com_akocomment20.zip	Comment component
8	cb_akocommentbot.zip	Mambot for Comment component
8	docmanV13_RC_1.zip	Document management component
8	Mod_mostdownV10_RC_1.zip	Module for DOCMan
8	bot_searchV10_RC_2.zip	Mambot for DOCMan
9	VirtueMart_1.0.1-COMPLETE_PACKAGE	Shop component: complete package with modules
9	jos100germani.zip jos100germanf.zip	German language files (Sie and Du forms of address)
9	MambelFish_1.5.zip	MambelFish component
9	Mbf_module.zip	MambelFish module
9	Mbf_searchbot.zip	MambelFish Search mambot
11	Joomlabook.zip	Your own template
11	com_joomlabook.zip	Your own component
11	mod_joomlabook.zip	Your own module
11	bot_joomlabook.zip	Your own Mambot
A	Joomla!V4.5.2-API-Html.zip	Joomla! API

Table A.1: Downloads

Template Structures

Templates consist of a number of elements. The most important ones are the CSS arrays and the embedded PHP commands.

CSS

In Joomla! Templates, certain names for certain arrays have become common. These arrays are also called classes in CSS. I would like to show you four examples. If a class is called that does not exist in the CSS file, nothing changes in the display. Because of the multiplicity of versions and extensions, it is always prudent to check the HTML code and to try to get an overview of the classes used.

Header

Here you can see the CSS commands (Listing A.1) in the header and the respective places on the website (Figure A.1). The CSS code is to serve as example. Not all places are provided with CSS examples. Take a look at CSS files of the predefined templates in order to find further examples.

Listing A.1: CSS Commands in the Header

```
.title {
  font-family: sans-serif;
  font-size: 20px;
  font-weight: bold;
  color : #000000;
  margin-left: 10px;
}
.button {
  font-family       : Verdana, Arial, Helvetica, sans-serif;
  font-style        : normal;
  font-size         : 10px;
  font-weight       : bold;
  background-color  : #F0F0F0;
  color             : #000000;
  border            : 1px solid #CCCCCC;
}
```

Figure A.1: Header

Menu Array

Here you can see the CSS commands in the menu array (Listing A.2) and the corresponding places on the website (Figure A.2).

Listing A.2: CSS Commands in the Menu Array

```
table.moduletable td {
  font-size         : 11px;
  font-weight       : bold;
  color             : #000000;
  text-align        : left;
  width             : 100%;
  letter-spacing: 2px;
  text-indent: 5px;
  padding-bottom: 3px;
}
a.sublevel:link, a.sublevel:visited {
  padding-left: 1px;
  vertical-align: middle;
  font-size: 11px;
  color: #ff6600;
  text-align: left;
}
a.sublevel:hover {
  color: #ff9e31; text-decoration: none;
}
a.mainlevel:link, a.mainlevel:visited {
  display: block;
  color: #ffffff;
```

```
      font-weight: bold;
      background-image: url(../images/menu_bgr.png);
      background-repeat: no-repeat;
      width: 95%;
      text-indent: 15px;
      text-decoration: none;
      font-family: Verdana, Helvetica, Arial, sans-serif;
      line-height: 20px;
      margin-bottom: 1px;
}
a.mainlevel:hover {
   color: #333333;
}
.inputbox {
   font-family     : Verdana, Arial, Helvetica, sans-serif;
   font-size       : 10px;
   color           : #000000;
   background-color : #F0F0F0;
   border          : 1px solid #CCCCCC;
}
a:link, a:visited {
   color: #ff6600;
text-decoration: none;
}
a:hover {
   color: #ff3300;
   text-decoration: underline;
}
```

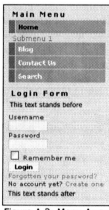

Figure A.2: Menu Array

Content Elements

Here you can see the CSS commands (Listing A.3) in the content array and the corresponding places on the website (Figure A.3).

Listing A.3: CSS Commands Content Elements

```
.createdate {
   font-family     : Arial, Helvetica, sans-serif;
   font-size       : 10px;
   color           : #999999;
   text-align      : left;
}
```

```
.contentheading {
  font-family      : Verdana, Arial, Helvetica, sans-serif;
  font-size        : 12px;
  font-weight      : bold;
  color            : #ff9900;
  text-align       : left;
}
.small {
  font-family      : Verdana, Arial, Helvetica, sans-serif;
  font-size        : 10px;
  color            : #999999;
  text-decoration  : none;
  font-weight      : bold;
}
.contentpane {
  background       : #dedede;
}
tr, td, p, div {
  font-family      : Verdana, Arial, Helvetica, sans-serif;
  font-size        : 11px;
  color            : #333333;
}
```

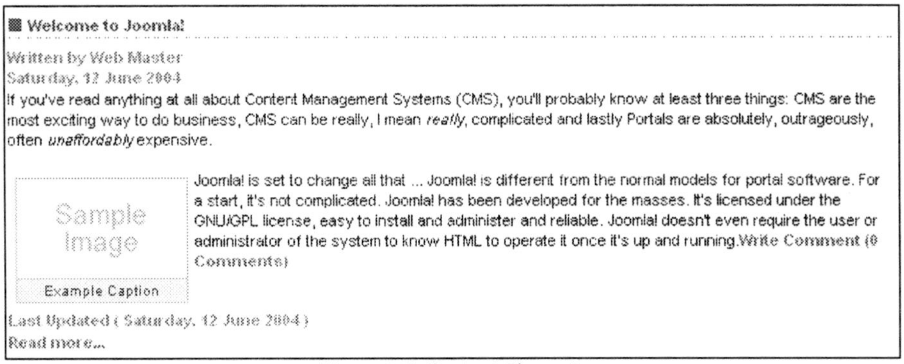

Figure A.3: Content Elements

News Overview

Here you can see the CSS commands in the News overview and the corresponding places on the website (Figure A.4):

Listing A.4: CSS Commands News Overview

```
.sectiontableheader {
  background-color : #CCCCCC;
  color            : #333333;
  font-weight      : bold;
}
.sectiontableentry1 {
  background-color : #F0F0F0;
}
```

Figure A.4: News overview

PHP and Other Insertions into the Index.php File of your Template

PHP-Code	Effect
`<?php`	first line

`defined( '_VALID_MOS' ) or die( 'Direct Access to this location is not allowed.' );`
`$iso = explode( '=', _ISO );`
`echo '<?xml version="1.0" encoding="'. $iso[1] .'"?' .'>';`
`?>`
`<!DOCTYPE html PUBLIC "-//W3C//DTD XHTML 1.0 Transitional//EN"`
`"http://www.w3.org/TR/xhtml1/DTD/xhtml1-transitional.dtd">`
`<html xmlns="http://www.w3.org/1999/xhtml">`
	direct access to the file is prevented with this and the proper XHTML header is specified.

HEAD	
`<?php mosShowHead(); ?>`	The creation of the meta tag is defined in Global Configuration

`if ( $my->id ) {`
`  initEditor();`
`}`
	Initialization of the WYSIWYG-editor

`<meta http-equiv="Content-Type" content="text/html; <?php echo _ISO; ?>" />`	Declaration of the correct content type
`<link href = "<?php echo $mosConfig_live_site; ?>/templates/rhuk_solarflare_ii/css/template_css.css" rel="stylesheet" type="text/css"/>`	Composition of the CSS file

PHP-Code	Effect
BODY	
`<?php mosPathway(); ?>`	path to the page
`mosLoadModules ( '[place]', [, $style])`	Loading of the module to the position [place]. `$style` is:
	0 module is represented in a table of columns (`<td> ... </td>`)
	1 module is represented horizontally in a cell
	−1 module is represented without a surrounding table
	−2 module is represented in Joomla!'s barrier-free format (`<div> ... </div>`)
`mosCountModules( '[ort]' )`	counting of the modules at position [place]
`<?php mosMainBody(); ?>`	content array
`<?php include_once( $GLOBALS[ 'mosConfig_absolute_path' ] . '/includes/footer.php' ); ?>`	footer

Table A.2: PHP Insertions into the index.php File of aTemplate

Switching Images (Logos) in the Template

In order to exchange a logo, you first have to check the source code of the appropriate template. Graphics and pictures can be defined in the HTML and in the CSS structure. Graphics usually have a size that is coordinated with the template.

If you now want to switch pictures, you can do this in a number of ways.

Version 1

1. Create a graphic that fits in regards to resolution and file size.
2. Load the graphic into Joomla!'s Media Manager.
3. Click on the graphic to get the link to the graphic.
4. Change the corresponding `<img src= >` tag in the source code of your template to the new picture.

Version 2

1. Create the new graphic with the same name as the graphic in your template.
2. Simply overwrite the old graphic with the new one.

Joomla! API

The **Application Program Interface (API)** describes in which place which function/method in the source code is present and what it does. It consists of descriptions that are automatically extracted from the source code with the help of a documentation program. In addition to these descriptions, an example of use is described in each case. The Joomla! team members make this information available on the Help server at `http://help.joomla.org/content/section/12/125/`.

Here is an example for the `mosHTML::integerSelectList` method (Figure A.5):

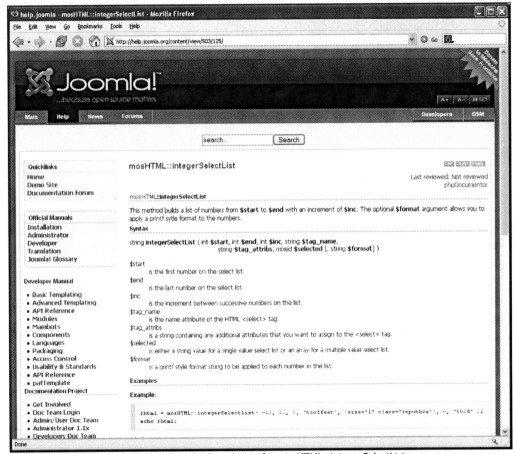

Figure A.5: Joomla! Description for mosHTML::integerSelectList

Forgot your Admin-Password

If you have forgotten your Admin password, you can change it directly in the database. To do that you need a tool like phpMyAdmin. In the XAMPP Lite environment you can launch it in your browser from the `http://localhost/phpmyadmin` URL.

There you select the database you are using. There is a jos_users table in this database. In this table, look for the user admin. The password is encrypted with the MD5 procedure. You can change it by selecting the MD5 entry in the option list, left beside the field, and entering the password in plain language (Figure A.6).

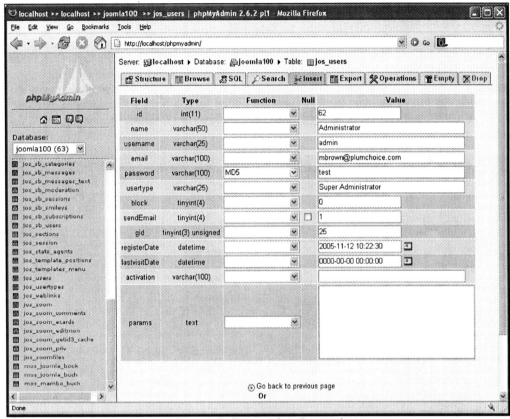

Figure A.6: Change Admin Password

Many providers also offer phpMyAdmin for the maintenance of your database.

Migration from Mambo to Joomla!

It is possible that many of you already have a Mambo website and now want to switch to Joomla!. In principle you now have to deal with several problems:

1. The entire website has to be backed up.
2. The common source code files have to be updated.
3. Additional components, modules, and Mambots have to be updated.
4. Your own program changes have to be updated.
5. Tour contents must survive the update without damage.

On the basis of this list, you can see that the more standard components that you use, the simpler the update is, and the more individualized your website is, the more difficult this is. There are, at the moment, no generally accepted rules for the updates, so that you have to first collect information and create an individual update plan for your site.

Back Up Data

Use the appropriate tool from your provider to do a MySQL dump. In most cases, this will be phpMyAdmin, which is also used in the XAMPP Lite environment. Click on the Export tab, mark all tables and mark all fields in the Structure checkbox. Select all of the Inserts in the Data checkbox. In the bottom area you have to mark the Sending checkbox and the desired format. If the provider has this option, you should choose the zipped version here; the compressed database can be up to 95% smaller than the normal database! Confirm your selection by clicking on the Go button. (Figure A.7).

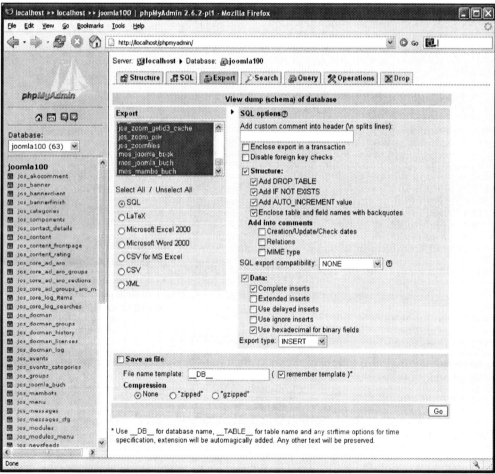

Figure A.7: Back up Database with phpMyAdmin

The contents of the database are now extracted and prepared for download. The file contains all of the SQL commands that you need to create the tables with your content in another database. It thus represents an optimal method of backing up your files (Figure A.8).

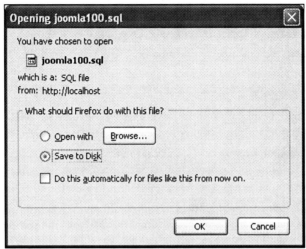

Figure A.8: Downloading the DB Backup

From phpMyAdmin you can import the data again. Click on the SQL link, select the file with the backed up data and click on the OK button. All of the SQL commands that are located in the file are now executed and your data is reconstructed (Figure A.9).

Figure A.9: Importing the Backed-up Data

Back Up Files

In addition to the data in the database, you should also back up the source code files. Use the FTP program of your choice and copy the entire Joomla! folder.

The Source Code Files have to be Updated

This is where the actual update is done. You can probably get the best instruction for that in the Joomla.org website.

Create a new folder and copy all of the new Joomla! files into it.

Do NOT attempt to install Joomla! from the web installer with an update! The installer would create new, empty tables and the worst-case scenario is that it would overwrite your database tables.

There must not be an installation directory in order to organize the update. In the long run, you should delete it. For now just rename it (install_old), since we will still need a file from that directory.

Copy your Mambo configuration.php file into the new Joomla! directory. Change the $mosConfig_absolute_path and $mosConfig_live_site variables in the code of the file to correspond to the new Joomla! folder.

Copy all additional templates, components, modules, Mambots, and language files from your old Mambo directory to your new Joomla! directory.

Here is a list of the standard folders that you are NOT allowed to COPY. These folders represent the Joomla! kernel. Do NOT copy any folders that are outside of these mentioned folders. Only copy those additional folders that you have installed from the installer and that are in the mentioned folders and not in the following list!

Templates:

1. /administrator/templates/mambo_admin
2. /administrator/templates/mambo_admin_blue
3. /templates/rhuk_solarflare_ii

Components:

1. /administrator/components/com_admin
2. /administrator/components/com_categories
3. /administrator/components/com_checkin
4. /administrator/components/com_config
5. /administrator/components/com_installer
6. /administrator/components/com_languages
7. /administrator/components/com_mambots
8. /administrator/components/com_massmail
9. /administrator/components/com_media

10. `/administrator/components/com_menumanager`

11. `/administrator/components/com_menus`

12. `/administrator/components/com_modules`

13. `/administrator/components/com_sections`

14. `/administrator/components/com_statistics`

15. `/administrator/components/com_syndicate`

16. `/administrator/components/com_templates`

17. `/administrator/components/com_trash`

18. `/administrator/components/com_typedcontent`

19. `/administrator/components/com_users`

20. `/components/com_banners`

21. `/components/com_contact`

22. `/components/com_content`

23. `/components/com_frontpage`

24. `/components/com_login`

25. `/components/com_messages`

26. `/components/com_newsfeeds`

27. `/components/com_poll`

28. `/components/com_registration`

29. `/components/com_rss`

30. `/components/com_search`

31. `/components/com_user`

32. `/components/com_weblinks`

33. `/components/com_wrapper`

Module:

1. `/administrator/modules/mod_components`

2. `/administrator/modules/mod_fullmenu`

3. `/administrator/modules/mod_latest`

4. `/administrator/modules/mod_logged`

5. `/administrator/modules/mod_mosmsg`

6. `/administrator/modules/mod_popular`

7. `/administrator/modules/mod_quickicon`

8. `/administrator/modules/mod_toolbar`

9. `/administrator/modules/mod_unread`

10. `/modules/mod_archive`

11. `/modules/mod_banners`

12. `/modules/mod_latestnews`

13. `/modules/mod_login`

14. `/modules/mod_mainmenu`

15. `/modules/mod_mostread`

16. `/modules/mod_newsflash`

17. `/modules/mod_online`

18. `/modules/mod_pathway`

19. `/modules/mod_poll`

20. `/modules/mod_random_image`

21. `/modules/mod_related_items`

22. `/modules/mod_rssfeed`

23. `/modules/mod_search`

24. `/modules/mod_sections`

25. `/modules/mod_stats`

26. `/modules/mod_templatechooser`

27. `/modules/mod_whosonline`

28. `/modules/mod_wrapper`

Mambots:

1. `/mambots/content/geshi`

2. `/mambots/content/legacybots`

3. `/mambots/content/moscode`

4. `/mambots/content/mosemailcloak`

5. `/mambots/content/mosimage`

6. `/mambots/content/mosloadposition`

7. `/mambots/content/mospaging`

8. `/mambots/content/mossef`

9. `/mambots/content/mosvote`

10. `/mambots/editors/none`

11. `/mambots/editors/tinymce`

12. `/mambots/editors-xtd/mosimage.btn`

13. `/mambots/editors-xtd/mospage.btn`

14. `/mambots/search/categories.searchbot`

15. `/mambots/search/contacts.searchbot`

16. `/mambots/search/content.searchbot`

17. `/mambots/search/newsfeeds.searchbot`

18. `/mambots/search/sections.searchbot`

19. `/mambots/search/weblinks.searchbot`

Languages:

1. `/language/english`

If you now call up your website from the new directory, it should work.

Database Update

In the `/installation/sql/migrate_Mambo4523_to_Joomla_100.sql` file that comes with your Joomla! package, you get a file with SQL commands for a database update. Load this file into your old Mambo database with phpMyAdmin as described above. You can follow the modifications that are executed by the update by looking at the content of the file. In our case, modifications are made in the administrator template and in the modules.

You can delete the installation directory after this action!

In future versions of Joomla! (1.0.x), appropriate SQL files will be included.

Updating Additional Components, Modules, and Mambots

After you have completed the above actions, you have to update all of he additional components, modules, and Mambots that you have installed!

Updating Program Modifications

Only you know what changes you have made! Try to reconstruct these changes.

Your Contents

If everything has worked so far, your contents should now be visible in Joomla!.

Backup without Global Variables

Mambo and Joomla! require a PHP attribute by the name `register_globals = on`. This switch controls the visibility of global variables, which, among other ways, can wind up in your programs from the outside via a form or `Get` string.

This attribute is responsible for fundamental security problems and it is better if you use the attribute `register_globals = off`. Even thought his switch doesn't protect you from all problems, it is a tremendous help in increasing your security.

In order to prepare Joomla! accordingly, rename the `[pathtoJoomla!]/globals.php` file to `[pathtoJoomla!]/globals.php-on` and the `[pathtoJoomla!]/globals.php-off` file to `[pathtoJoomla!]/globals.php`.

The Joomla! kernel will certainly work. Check to see if all of your components are working as well. If you have problems, change the attributes back to `globals off` and pay attention to the update of the respective components.

Index

A

access rights, 9
accessibility. *See* barrier freedom
AkoComment component
  comment, editing, 174
  installing, 173, 174
  settings, 174, 175
apt command, 24
archive manager, 112
avatar, 158

B

backend, 9, 49
banner, 45
barrier freedom
  criteria, 272, 273
  Joomla!, 273, 274
  text editor, 274
  website, example, 274, 275
board, 153

C

calender. *See* Events component, 176
Cascading Style Sheets
  about, 248
  commands, defining, 248, 249
  template, 304-306, 308
category manager, 111
category, creating, 98-102
CMS. *See* Content Management System
component, 10
  about, 115
  AkoComment. See AkoComment component
  creating, 279
  DOCMan. See DOCMan component
  Events. See Events component
  Joomla!. See Joomla! component
  Mambelfish. See Mambelfish component
  Simpleboard. See Simpleboard component
  Virtuemart. See Virtuemart component

components menu

banner, creating, 117-119
contact, creating, 120-123
installation, 115-117
mass mailing, 124, 125
news feeds, creating, 126, 127
news feeds, working, 131-134
polls, working, 128-130
weblink, working, 135, 136
compressed tarball, 28
configuration setting, 9
content, 9, 42
  structure in Joomla!, 97, 98
content management, 5
Content Management System, structure, 9
content menu
  archive content, 112, 113
  category, 111
  category, creating, 98-102
  content items manager, 103, 104
  frontpage, 112
  image, inserting, 107, 108
  publishing parameters, 105-107
  sections, 110
  static content manager, 104
Corporate Identity (CI), 247
CSS. *See* Cascading Style Sheets
customizing Joomla!
  menu name, modifying, 51, 52
  template, changing, 52, 54

D

database, creating, 279, 281, 283
Debian, 24
div tag, 270, 271
DOCMan component
  about, 198
  category, creating, 200, 201
  component, merging into a website, 214-216
  document, managing, 207-211
  file, uploading, 203, 204
  installing, 199

license, 212
user group, creating, 201-203
Dreamweaver extension
    installing, 259, 260
    Joomla! modules, inserting, 266, 267
    table, creating, 263, 264
    temolate file, creating, 260-263
    template, viewing, 267, 268

E

e-commerce. *See* **Virtuemart component**
Events component
    appointment, settings, 182
    category, managing, 178, 179
    configuring, 176, 178
    Event mambot, 186
    Event module, 185
    event, managing, 179-182
    installing, 176
Extensible Markup Language, 249
extension. *See also* **component**
    Dreamweaver. *See* Dreamweaver extension
    types, 153

F

favicon, 64
feed, 47
forum
    creating, 159-162
    definition, 153
    deleting, 165
    sample data, loading, 166
    Simpleboard, creating, 159-162
frontend, 9, 39
frontpage manager, 112
functions, 45

G

gallery. *See* **Zoom media gallery**
global configuration
    cache, settings, 73
    content, settings, 66-69
    database, settings, 69
    locale, settings, 65
    mail, settings, 72
    metadata, settings, 71, 72
    SEO, settings, 73, 74

    server, settings, 70, 71
    statistics, settings, 73
    website, settings, 61, 63-65

H

help menu, 57-59
Hinse, Marc, 53
HTML, 6, 247, 248
Hyper Text Markup Language, 6, 247, 248

I

index.php file, 308, 309
installers menu, 94

J

JavaScript, 55
Joomla!
    accessibility. *See* barrier freedom
    administration, 50
    API, 310
    backend, 49
    component, creating, 279
    configuring, online store, 228
    customizing. *See* customizing Joomla!
    downloads, 304
    features, 13
    frontend, 39
    history, 8, 9
    installing. *See* Joomla! installation
    Mambo, migrating from, 311-317
    module. *See* module
    multilingualism, 239
    structure, 9
    template, creating, 249
    versions, 11, 12
    web page, examples, 13-18
Joomla! administration
    components menu. *See* components menu
    configuration, 55-57
    content menu. *See* content menu
    CSS file, 164
    data, administering, 287
    help menu, 57-59
    language file, installing, 235
    module menu. *See* module menu
    site menu, 60
    template installer, 258, 259

Z

Zlib, 19
Zoom media gallery
    gallery, creating, 189, 190
    gallery, integrating into website, 197
    installing, 188
    media, managing, 191, 192
    media, settings, 193, 194
    thumb codes, creating, 192

Special offer on the Joomla! 1.5 Beta 1 book

Since you have bought version 1.0 of the Joomla! book, you are eligible for a discount on the new Joomla! book "*Building Websites with Joomla! 1.5 Beta 1*".

The highlights of this book are:

- ➤ Install and configure Joomla! 1.5 beta 1
- ➤ Customize and extend your Joomla! site
- ➤ Create your own template and extensions
- ➤ Three bonus templates
- ➤ *Free eBook upgrades up to 1.5 Final Release*

For more information on this book, please visit *http://www.packtpub.com/joomla/book*

[30% Discount] on Print Book

You can get *30% discount* on the cover price of the new Joomla! print book. To get the discount, enter *tnirp.almooj.001* in the 'Promotional Code' field in your shopping cart and click 'Update'.

[50% Discount] on eBook

You can get *50% discount* on the list price of the new Joomla! eBook. To get the discount, enter *kooBe.almooj.002* in the 'Promotional Code' field in your shopping cart and click 'Update'.

[30%+80% Discount] on Print and eBook

This is special bundle offer that includes the print book and eBook. In this offer, you can get *30% discount* on the print book and *80% discount* on the eBook. To get the discount, enter *eldnub.almooj.003* in the 'Promotional Code' field in your shopping cart and click 'Update'.

[Free Final Version] Upgrade Offer

If you buy the Joomla! 1.5 Beta 1 book (print or eBook) now from PacktPub.com, we will send you free eBook versions of all future versions of this title up to and including the final 1.5 release. We currently expect to update the book for either the final release or another beta in mid 2007.

Please contact us at *service@packtpub.com* if you need more information on this offer.

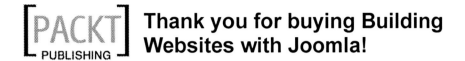

Thank you for buying Building Websites with Joomla!

Packt Open Source Project Royalties

When we sell a book written on an Open Source project, we pay a royalty directly to that project. Therefore by purchasing *Building Websites with Joomla!*, Packt will have given some of the money received to the Joomla! project.

In the long term, we see ourselves and you—customers and readers of our books—as part of the Open Source ecosystem, providing sustainable revenue for the projects we publish on. Our aim at Packt is to establish publishing royalties as an essential part of the service and support a business model that sustains Open Source.

If you're working with an Open Source project that you would like us to publish on, and subsequently pay royalties to, please get in touch with us.

Writing for Packt

We welcome all inquiries from people who are interested in authoring. Book proposals should be sent to authors@packtpub.com. If your book idea is still at an early stage and you would like to discuss it first before writing a formal book proposal, contact us; one of our commissioning editors will get in touch with you.

We're not just looking for published authors; if you have strong technical skills but no writing experience, our experienced editors can help you develop a writing career, or simply get some additional reward for your expertise.

About Packt Publishing

Packt, pronounced 'packed', published its first book "*Mastering phpMyAdmin for Effective MySQL Management*" in April 2004 and subsequently continued to specialize in publishing highly focused books on specific technologies and solutions.

Our books and publications share the experiences of your fellow IT professionals in adapting and customizing today's systems, applications, and frameworks. Our solution-based books give you the knowledge and power to customize the software and technologies you're using to get the job done. Packt books are more specific and less general than the IT books you have seen in the past. Our unique business model allows us to bring you more focused information, giving you more of what you need to know, and less of what you don't.

Packt is a modern, yet unique publishing company, which focuses on producing quality, cutting-edge books for communities of developers, administrators, and newbies alike. For more information, please visit our website: www.PacktPub.com.

Printed in the United Kingdom
by Lightning Source UK Ltd.
124364UK00001B/199-218/A